Nils Klimanis

Generic Programming and Algebraic Multigrid

# Nils Klimanis

# Generic Programming and Algebraic Multigrid

## Building Blocks for Scientific Computing

VDM Verlag Dr. Müller

## Imprint

Bibliographic information by the German National Library: The German National Library lists this publication at the German National Bibliography; detailed bibliographic information is available on the Internet at http://dnb.d-nb.de.

Cover image: www.purestockx.com

Publisher:
VDM Verlag Dr. Müller Aktiengesellschaft & Co. KG , Dudweiler Landstr. 125 a, 66123 Saarbrücken, Germany,
Phone +49 681 9100-698, Fax +49 681 9100-988,
Email: info@vdm-verlag.de

Zugl.: Göttingen, Georg-August-Universität, Diss., 2006

Produced in USA and UK by:
Lightning Source Inc., La Vergne, Tennessee, USA
Lightning Source UK Ltd., Milton Keynes, UK
BookSurge LLC, 5341 Dorchester Road, Suite 16, North Charleston, SC 29418, USA

ISBN: 978-3-8364-3301-3

# Contents

# Chapter 1

# Introduction

Nowadays, many fields in natural sciences, engineering, and economics are hardly imaginable without the computer aided numerical simulation of scientific phenomena. The area of *scientific computing*, that adresses the computational solution of these problems, has become a subject of its own. Its approach is to gain understanding, mainly through the analysis of mathematical models, implemented on computers. Among these models, partial differential equations play an important role in modelling physical, chemical, biological or even financial processes.

Giving an explicit solution of these equations is however not always possible in many cases of interest. For example the central problem in computational fluid dynamics, the Navier-Stokes equations, that describe the movement of liquids and gases, are more than 160 years old, and it is still not known, if global solutions exist in the general, three-dimensional case. It is one of seven open mathematical problems, for which the *Clay Mathematics Institute* in the year 2000 announced a prize of 1 million dollars (the *Millenium Prize problems*, [Fef00]). Dropping the requirements for solutions in the classical sense, Jean Leray ([Ler34]) in 1934 showed, that weak solutions exists for reasonable small time intervals and small inital conditions.

Weak solutions in general lead to approximation methods, like finite elements or finite volumes, that calculate the solution on discrete grid points. These discretizations produce large and sparse linear systems, that can be solved with numerical linear algebra methods. For this purpose, however, exact methods like Gaussian elimination or LU decomposition are only viable if the dimension number $n$ of the matrix is not too large, since their run-time complexity is about $O(n^3)$. Although there have been several efforts to devise exact algorithms, that e.g. exploit the special sparsity structure of the matrix (like SuperLU, [DEG$^+$99], or UMFPACK [DD99]), the usage of these methods on current workstations and personal computers, nevertheless is limited to dimensions $n$ lying between 10000 and 100000, depending on the sparse matrix structure. This is the reason for applying iterative methods instead.

The order of magnitude of typical matrix sizes can be illustrated by looking at a characteristic number of the Navier-Stokes equations. In this context, the *Reynolds number*[1] $Re$ is usually defined as

$$Re_\Omega := \frac{\|\mathbf{u}\|_\Omega L}{\nu}.$$

and gives a measure for the relation of the amount of viscosity $\nu$ to the velocity $u$ of the flow. The variable $L$ is the characteristic length of the considered domain $\Omega$, thus $L = \text{diam}\,\Omega$ gives an average over the whole domain.

For the *direct numerical simulation* (DNS), the accuracy of the solution mainly depends on the number of unknowns, the degrees of freedom of the mesh. Thus, the problem size increases with the degree of the required accuracy – it is known that the number of mesh points needed to resolve all flow structures is of order $O(Re^{9/4})$ in 3D, due to Kolmogorov's theory of turbulence, which predicts

---

[1]Osborne Reynolds (1842 - 1912), was a British physicist and engineer, who pioneered the study of conditions in which the flow of fluids transitions from laminar to turbulent.

small scale flow structures down to the size of $O(Re^{-3/4})$. Many industrial applications however (e.g. the flow around an aircraft), exhibit Reynolds numbers greater than $10^7$, resulting in turbulent flows.

Over the years, several ways out of this dilemma have been explored. Turbulence models, like *large eddy simulation* or the *Reynolds-averaged Navier Stokes model* simulate the smaller structures in the flow, and thus reduce the number of unknowns. *Domain decomposition methods* split the problem area into several smaller parts, offering a way of parallelization for distributed computing. *Adaptive mesh refinement* techniques are intended to increase the number of unknowns in the grid only in those areas, where the solution changes rapidly.

But in the end, the inversion of sparse (and in most cases unsymmetric and extremely ill-conditioned) matrices in the core of the numerical software, is the most time consuming part of the computation. While Krylov subspace methods tend to reduce the run-time complexity to an order of $O(n^2)$, the class of *multigrid methods* often exhibits a nearly optimal $O(n)$ behaviour. However, multigrid is anything but a black-box solver – if it shall contribute a substantial acceleration of the solution process, all components have to be chosen with great care and must be adapted to the concrete mathematical problem. And especially, in complex geometrical situations and unsmooth data, one observes also convergence problems. Therefore, in the 1980's, several *algebraic multigrid methods* (AMG) have been devised to overcome these problems and the adaption of algebraic multigrid to flow problems is a central topic in this thesis.

The conventional approach of applying AMG to the linearized Navier-Stokes equations, namely the Oseen equations

$$-\nu\Delta\mathbf{u} + (\mathbf{b}\cdot\nabla)\mathbf{u} + \nabla p + c\mathbf{u} = \mathbf{f},$$
$$\nabla\cdot\mathbf{u} = g,$$

was based on decoupling schemes, that used Schur-complement methods to decouple the equations for the velocity $\mathbf{u}$ and the pressure $p$. An AMG solver was then simply used to invert the Schur complement or the part of the equation that corresponds to a convection-diffusion problem.

Our approach will be to develop an algebraic multigrid variant, that is applied to the whole coupled linear system. Earlier work in this area was contributed e.g. by [Raw95] and [Web01] for the finite volume approach. One of the few fully coupled AMG variants for the Oseen equation using finite element discretizations was presented in [Wab03] for the so-called *unknown* approach. There, the variables, that belong to one physical quantity, are grouped together, equation by equation:

$$\begin{pmatrix} A & B_1^T \\ B_2 & C \end{pmatrix} \begin{pmatrix} u \\ p \end{pmatrix} = \begin{pmatrix} f \\ g \end{pmatrix}.$$

In contrast to that, we propose a method which is based on the *point-wise* approach. Here, the variables belonging to one grid point are grouped together, leading to a sparse matrix that has small dense block matrices as entries:

$$\begin{pmatrix} F_{11} & \cdots & F_{1M} \\ \vdots & \ddots & \vdots \\ F_{M1} & \cdots & F_{MM} \end{pmatrix} \begin{pmatrix} x_1 \\ \vdots \\ x_M \end{pmatrix} = \begin{pmatrix} b_1 \\ \vdots \\ b_M \end{pmatrix}.$$

We construct a way of defining a strong coupling between these small blocks $F_{ij}$, as an analogon to the scalar case, based on the convection-diffusion part. According interpolation weights are suggested, in order to define prolongation and restriction operators for the coarse grid correction.

Another issue in scientific computing is the optimal utilization of the computer hardware architecture. A naive implementation with inefficient data structures is capable of spoiling the run-time behaviour of the fastest algorithm. Modern programming methods can help to implement highly sophisticated numerical algorithms and efficiently integrate them into a software system. It was during the 1990's that the scientific community discovered C++ for the purpose of scientific computing. Intrinsic language features such as templates, inlining, overloading, specialization and new developments, like *expression templates*, *static polymorphism*, and *compile time algorithms* contributed to reaching the performance of Fortran and C libraries, in some cases even outperforming them. Todd Veldhuizen's Blitz++ library is a good example in this context ([Vel98]).

Today, we have the situation, that the increasing complexity of numerical algorithms, like e.g. algebraic multigrid, also have an increasing requirement for equally complex (and efficient) data structures, like e.g. various efficient matrix types. Therefore, a heavy focus in this thesis will lie on the software design aspects, the programming methods and benefits, C++ can offer in order to build efficient (in terms of run-time and memory consumption), highly flexible, and reusable software components for the application in numerical linear algebra.

The two central topics in this thesis, generic type construction in C++ from computer science, and algebraic multigrid from numerical mathematics, are organized into three parts. The aim of the first part is to optimize existing and explore and apply new data structures for linear systems under the employment of modern programming techniques. We try to transfer some of the ideas of (object-oriented) software design into the area of scientific computing, hence the title *scientific programming*. An abstract representation of matrix types, as a generalization of sparse and dense matrices is developed in the first chapter. In the second chapter, we extend the *mixin layer* programming approach and suggest a solution for the according object construction problem for a generic matrix type library. A performance comparison with a C library finally shows the competitiveness of the chosen approach.

The second part introduces algebraic multigrid for scalar convection-diffusion-reaction equations. Here we analyze the classical AMG, following the ideas of John Ruge and Klaus Stüben, and leveraging some of the requirements needed for the convergence theory with respect to unsymmetric problems. Afterwards, we exemplarily study the effects of coarsening and relaxation on two examples, one in 2D and one in 3D.

In the third part, the ideas of the middle part are transferred and adapted to the linearized Navier-Stokes equations. We were able to successfully apply a fully coupled AMG method to the 2D Stokes and Oseen equations. Here, the problem was discretized using stabilized equal-order ($P_1$-$P_1$-stab) elements, and the a point-wise ordering of the unknowns. As the numerical experiments suggest, this point-wise coupled AMG method turns out to be a nearly optimal ($O(N)$) solver for the Stokes problem. The Oseen problems, especially for decreasing viscosity parameter $\nu$, need longer iteration times, but the observed $h$-dependency is by far less dramatic than for the considered Krylov solvers that are used for comparison.

# Part I

# Scientific Programming

# Chapter 2

# Generic programming for scientific computing

In the area of numerical mathematics a wide range of algorithms uses linear algebra methods in one way or the other, be it to solve rather large stiffness matrices stemming from finite element methods, be it to compute the mapping of a geometric transformation in a CAD program. The field of applications is so immense that each problem domain has a need for special matrix types and algorithms operating on them.

Although the mathematical parts (II and III) of this thesis are concerned with problems and algorithms for scientific computing – numerical linear algebra methods and finite element methods – the matrix types and components introduced in this first part are intended to be applied in a much wider range of mathematical problems.

Furthermore, the methods of software construction that are presented in Chapter 3 are certainly applicable to the area of software design in general.

In this chapter, in Sections 2.1 and 2.2, we first analyze what a modern numerical linear algebra software has to provide. Then, in Section 2.4, we give a short introduction of some programming methods that are special to C++ and that will be important for the library design. They are further deepened in Chapter 3.

Section 2.4 gives an (admittedly not complete) overview of existing libraries. Afterwards, in the last Section, we develop a classification of matrix types and a basic storage concept as a foundation of the matrix library design presented in the next chapter.

## 2.1 Aspects of scientific computing

A finite element code for problems like the convection-diffusion equation (Section 4.1 in Part II) or the Navier-Stokes equation (Section 7.1 in Part III) consists of a great number of components: the mesh-generator, the discretizer, maybe an error-estimator for adaptivity, a time-stepping-procedure for time-dependent problems, and a linear-algebra-solver just to mention a few.

There are of course several strategies to generate an approximate solution to the problem. A successful solver strategy must face many different aspects of the problem, including mathematical, numerical and programming issues. In order to achieve a satisfying runtime behaviour, one should keep in mind the following aspects:

- Reducing the number of unknowns. Always try to avoid unnecessary mesh points where possible, for example by using adaptive mesh refinement. Where the solution promises to change quickly, more points/elements are needed, whereas in areas where the solution exhibits small gradients, less points are needed. This is especially important in a 3-dimensional problem setting.

- Using the appropriate solver for the problem. There is no solver that is optimal for all problems, so taking the right solver, that exploits the mathematical properties of the problem can reduce the computing time further.

- Parallelizing the code. Many tasks can be executed in parallel, many approaches have been devised (e.g. domain decomposition methods) for massive-parallel machines as well as for workstation clusters in a local area network.

- Optimizing the implementation. Taking advantage of cache architectures and vectorization. Modern computer languages such as C++ can help generate code that may not only be faster but also better to maintain and to reuse than Fortran or C code. The best numerical algorithm may be unacceptably slow in a naive implementation.

Besides the mathematical difficulties of the underlying problem (and the mathematical methods used to overcome this problem) the complexity of the software components and their interaction should not be underestimated.

## 2.2   Requirements for a modern matrix library

From a computer scientists point of view, we have the following requirements for numerical software.

1. *Efficiency.* The code should be fast and use the hardware resources (memory, CPU) as efficiently as possible. This means that modern hardware concepts like cache and pipelining should be taken care of.

2. *Reusability.* The software should be designed such that the methods can be applied to other problems and data structures as well without rewriting great amounts of code.

3. *Easy maintenance.* The complexity of the code should be easy to handle, even by users and programmers which are not identical to the original author.

Early numerical codes were written in Fortran [BHZ54], which was the first high-level programming language that offered convenient language features to describe mathematical algorithms as well as high execution speed of the compiled programs. With the success of UNIX since the 1970's, many libraries have been ported to, or newly created for the C [Rit75] programming language.

These codes mostly satisfied the first requirement but hardly the other two. However for the next generation of numerical software, we are dealing with an increasing number of mathematical methods to be integrated into the solution process. This increasing mathematical complexity can be overcome by modern programming methods that a programming language like C++ ([Str97]) provides.

One might object that the first requirement is incommensurate with the other two, i.e. that efficiency can only be achieved by messy, hand-optimized Fortran or C code. However, our aim is to show that modern C++ code can not only compete with these libraries, but also offers greater flexibility.

In the following subsections, we would like to discuss in detail the requirements of a modern numerical linear algebra library (with respect to algebraic multigrid).

### 2.2.1   General linear algebra

Our intention is to create an open and easily extendable library for numerical linear algebra that can deal with a wide range of different matrix types and supplies the user with an efficient interface to the data structures. A matrix library has to offer at least

- data structures that can represent different types of matrices (e.g. dense, sparse, diagonal, etc.) in arbitrary dimensions without unnecessary memory overhead,

- vector types in arbitrary dimensions and appropriate functions/methods to add, subtract and scale vectors.

Furthermore, numerical algebra methods rely on speed efficient data structures for the matrices. Traditionally, they require

- a quick random access on the matrix entries for manipulating the matrix itself (mainly for dense matrix computations, like LU or QR decomposition) or

- a fast interface to apply the effect of a matrix on a vector (matrix-vector multiplication, applied widely in e.g. Krylov methods)

### 2.2.2 Algebraic multigrid

Matrix types for algebraic multigrid (AMG) need a few further properties. But also other methods (e.g. Jacobi iteration) can benefit from feature like:

- random access on the *rows* of the matrix,

- a direct access to the diagonal entries,

- the ability to create subsets of matrix rows (or subsets of the matrix in general).

A very important AMG-specific algorithm that is hardly found in any matrix library is

- the ability to perform a multiplication of two sparse matrices.

### 2.2.3 Block matrix types for discretized PDEs

Various mathematical problems lead to matrices that can be organized into blocks. For example, the special structure of linear systems arising from the discretization of partial differential equations in computational fluid dynamics (e.g. Navier-Stokes, Oseen), demand for special matrix types, that can store the additional structural information.

A library should be able to provide us with certain block matrix types, meaning that the matrix is or can be separated in several rectangular blocks. Especially, the library should be able to handle these cases:

- Dense block matrices, that have in turn sparse matrices as entries. Typically this type is used if we discretize a PDE that consists of several equations. Each equation is discretized separately and the number of equations equals the dense (vertical) dimension of the matrix. For example, a two-dimensional Oseen problem, discretized with $P_2$-$P_1$ Taylor-Hood finite elements without pressure stabilization would result in a matrix

$$A = \begin{pmatrix} A_{11} & A_{12} & A_{13} \\ A_{21} & A_{22} & A_{23} \\ A_{31} & A_{32} & 0 \end{pmatrix}$$

  because of two equations for the velocity and one for the pressure. The matrices $A_{11}, A_{22} \in \mathbb{R}^{n \times n}$, $A_{13}, A_{23}, A_{31}^T, A_{32}^T \in \mathbb{R}^{n \times m}$, with $n > m$ in turn have a sparse structure, that directly corresponds to the underlying discretization mesh.

- Sparse block matrices, that have small dense matrices as entries. This type is required when discretizing the above problem with equal-order elements, for example $P_1$-$P_1$-stab, but this time reordering the entries such that values for different components of the equation that belong to one mesh-point are grouped together. This time $A$ has the structure

$$A = \begin{pmatrix} A_{11} & \cdots & A_{1n} \\ \vdots & \ddots & \vdots \\ A_{n1} & \cdots & A_{nn} \end{pmatrix}. \tag{2.1}$$

Now $A$ has a sparse structure representing the mesh information and $A_{ij}$ are small, dense $3 \times 3$ matrices, most of which are zero (cf. Section 8.2). That this type of structure has major advantages concerning the memory requirements as well as the execution speed of iterative solvers was e.g. demonstrated in [DLH00].

- Sparse block matrices, that have sparse matrices as entries. In bio-chemical problems describing a reaction between particles (e.g. coupled Poisson-Boltzmann equations) we obtain a sparse matrix like in (2.1) whose sparsity structure represents the geometry/mesh information as supplied before. However the matrix entries $A_{ij}$ are now also sparse – they embody the structure of the reaction graph.

The cases mentioned above refer to problems where the block matrix structure is a direct consequence of the geometrical/physical nature of the underlying problem. Special mathematical algorithms can exploit this structure, e.g. Schur complement methods, incomplete block factorizations, block SOR methods, etc., thus it seems reasonable to store theses blocks separately. But also from a software engineering standpoint, it is advantageous to let these blocks be own matrix types/classes again, since then the according algorithms access the data structures via a uniform matrix interface. Generic programming and polymorphism ensure that the correct algorithms are called recursively.

### 2.2.4   General block matrix types

In general, it should be possible to construct arbitrary block matrices, meaning matrices, that have other matrices as entries, regardless of the type of the entries. There exist at least two good reasons – that have their origin in computer hardware issues – for subdividing matrices in blocks:

- The memory architecture of modern computers is a hierarchical design, it consists of the main RAM and several cache levels[1]. Calculations that can run fully in a cache without adressing the slower main memory (because of the locality and the small size of the participating data structures) are carried out comparatively fast. The sparse matrix-vecor vector product, widely used in iterative solution schemes like Krylov subspace methods, however is a computation where the indirection of the sparse matrix storage (and the irregularity of the access pattern) subsequently causes *cache misses* for large data structures, slowing down the overall performance. Studies have shown, that appropriate blocking (see e.g. [IY01] and [NVDY04]) can speed up the performance significantly.

- Another way of reducing the computation time is to distribute the workload on several processors and/or computers. For numerical linear algebra methods, the parallelization of the matrix-vector or matrix-matrix product, e.g., requires the matrix to be partitioned into as many stripes as there are processing units. If we consider a shared memory multiprocessing system, the easiest way is to define these stripes as rectangular block matrices that are assigned to the according threads. Especially since multicore CPUs become more and more popular, even for desktop computers, the software developers should take this possibility into account.

These two aspects can be combined with the block matrix types mentioned in the previous section. Furthermore they are not restricted to matrices stemming from discretized PDE's or other physical problems. For example, sparse matrices also arise in the data mining or web search engine context. There, one also would like to be able to use the above acceleration techniques.

## 2.3   C++ Techniques and Scientific Programming

In the early years of C++, it seemed that this language wasn't well suited for high performance numerical computing. Even if the main framework of the software was written in C++ to take

---

[1]For example the DEC/Compaq Alpha CPU family and the Intel Xeon and Itanium CPU series support up to three cache levels.

advantage of the possibilities of object-oriented design, the time critical parts were still written in Fortran.

However, in the past years many efforts were made to overcome the problems with performance issues that appeared when C++ was used in scientific computing (see e.g. [VJ97]).

In this section we would like to present an overview of some of the classic performance (and design) problems and recent techniques that seem to be promising to solve these problems.

### 2.3.1 Expression templates

The lack of performance of C++ was evident when evaluating e.g. vector expressions like z=w+x+y because of the pairwise evaluation of the overloaded + operator and because of the needed temporary variables. This problem was overcome through the expression templates technique (see also the description of Blitz++ in Subsection 2.4).

In our library, we use a special expression template technique for the evaluation of sparse matrix expressions (see Section 3.7).

### 2.3.2 Static polymorphism

Another obstacle is the excessive use of virtual functions . *Run time polymorphism* may be advantageous for a small number of relatively large objects. However, if one applies virtual functions to a large number of objects of a relatively small size (e.g. in a long loop), then we observe a significant performance breakdown. Because the compiler does not know in advance which function to call for such an object – the one in the base class or the one in a derived class – it cannot optimize the according function calls. Therefore, virtual functions should be avoided for these cases and *compile time polymorphism* (also called *static polymorphism*) be applied instead.

The idea behind this method is to exploit the template facilities of C++ for generic programming. For writing a generic algorithm (i.e., an algorithm that doesn't work on a special data type, but rather on a type T that is given to the algorithm as a parameter) we need to impose certain properties on the parameter type T. In EIFFEL, e.g., this can be done by requiring the class T to be *conform* to a certain base class B, meaning that T derives from B. Since we don't have this mechanism in C++[2], we regard every type T that offers the required interface (a superset of the interface of B) to be valid as a parameter type for our algorithm, dropping the requirement of T being a subclass of B. As long as the parameter type is known at compile time, the compiler can do all optimizations for the specified type, and can even use specialized/overloaded versions of the algorithm.

### 2.3.3 Callback inlining

Callback functions are used widely (not only) in numerical software. A classical field of application is the numerical integration or the assemblation of a stiffness matrix. In general, a certain method has to be applied to a large number of elements (objects) in a container.

The typical solution in C is to provide a pointer to a function. However this often leads to a poor performance, since these function calls mostly cannot be inlined and optimized by the compiler.

In C++ one should use *function objects* (*functors*) (see 3.1.1) instead. The function object is passed as a template argument and thus can be inlined by the compiler. Another approach would be to pass function pointers as template arguments.

Since the functor approach is the more general one, we use it throughout our library.

## 2.4 An overview of existing numerical linear algebra libraries

A great number of libraries for linear algebra have been developed during the last decades. One of the first ones were the *Basic Linear Algebra Subprograms* (*BLAS*), [LRKK79], for dense matrices and

---

[2]although there are efforts to emulate this conformity relationship in C++, see [MS00]

vectors in Fortran (and later on in C). BLAS is optimized for *saxpy* (scalar alpha x plus y) operations like

$$z := \alpha x + y, \quad \alpha \in \mathbb{R}, x, y, z \in \mathbb{R}^n, \tag{2.2}$$

or *gaxpy* (generalized A x plus y) where $\alpha$ is replaced by a $n \times n$ matrix $A$. Sparse matrix libraries like the NIST *Sparse BLAS*, [RP] for C and *SPARSKIT* [Saa90] for Fortran were the next step of evolution. They offer compressed storage formats for sparse matrices and several numerical methods based upon these data structures. The Fortran package *SMMP* [BD93] e.g. even offers sparse matrix-matrix multiplication for the compressed row storage format.

These libraries were built for special purposes, and their performance can hardly be beat by other approaches. However, they are not suitable for all applications, because of their rather monolithic design, and their algorithms being restricted to a single type of data structure only. Extensions and modifications were difficult and hardly possible without rewriting large parts of the code.

For example, the CBLAS library, which is an implementation of BLAS for C, comes with nearly every source file in four variants: one for single precision real values, one for double precision real values, one for single precision complex values and one for double precision complex values. This replication of source text bloats up the code and is prone to errors. Mind also that changes to just *one* algorithm that is equivalent for all these types (whether it be single or double, real or complex) must be made in *each* of those files. This is of course due to the lack of native generic programming in C, which in C++ simply can be realized by templates.

In the 1990's, with the appearance of C++ and its great success, also new numerical libraries have been devised. Packages like *LAPACK++* (*Linear Algebra PACKage in C++*, [DPW93]), *SparseLib++* [DLN$^+$94] and *MV++* [Poz97] were the first towards object-oriented numerics. However, they mostly were mere translations from their C predecessors, only encapsulating the functionality in C++ classes. Hardly any of these made use of the new C++ features like templates, operator overloading or iterators.

It was only the next generation of numerical linear algebra libraries that incorporated these techniques. Some of them shall be presented in the following.

**Blitz++**

The *Blitz++* library [Vel98], [Vel01] offers multidimensional arrays, including vectors, matrices and tensors. It is restricted to dense arrays, so sparse matrices are not supported. Nevertheless it implements a very interesting approach to handle arbitrary expressions of arrays, such as

$$z := -\alpha v + w - x + \beta y, \quad \alpha, \beta \in \mathbb{R}, v, w, x, y, z \in \mathbb{R}^n. \tag{2.3}$$

Carrying out this operation with normal BLAS operations would consume three consecutive calls to a saxpy function like in (2.2) or a specialized function. In C++ with overloading the operators *, + and - we were able to write without any further circumstances

```
z = -alpha * v + w - x + beta * y;
```

However, this would result in the need for five temporary vectors, and five loops being generated. This is the reason why conventional approaches in C++ are so slow compared to Fortran. The classical solution to this problem (in Fortran and C) would need specialized functions for each possible expression. This is the reason, why in Blitz++ the *expression template* technique is used.

The idea is that the result of an operation like x+y is not a **vector**, but an instance of a new type, a class template that models a vector expression. This type just stores the expression tree and provides a member function like `operator[](int i)`, which evaluates the expression at entry i. No assignment and no computation is done until the program execution reaches the assignment operator =. Then only one loop is generated, which iterates over all entries i of the expression calling the operator [] each time. Obviously, no temporary vectors need to be introduced.

Expression templates were pioneered by Todd Veldhuizen [Vel95] and have proved to be nearly as fast as Fortran codes, sometimes (for small vector sizes) even faster. In any case, this programming technique offers a greater flexibility.

The lack of sparse matrix formats forbids the use of Blitz++ for our intention of implementing algebraic multigrid. However, it provides an easy interface and powerful data structures for finite differences and structured grids *(stencils)*. This is due to the simplifications that can be applied in these cases. Several other libraries and packages like *EXPDE* (see [Pfl01]) or *POOMA* go in the same direction.

## POOMA

*POOMA* [Old02] is a toolkit that was developed at the Los Alamos National Library, and which, like Blitz++ targets dense vector, matrix and tensor computations. It also offers data structures that contain grids for finite difference methods. Sparse matrix formats and linear algebra methods are not directly supported.

Its main benefit however is the easy and automatic parallelization. Containers (for vectors, etc.) can be split into patches and then be distributed over several processors.

POOMA also uses intensively techniques like *template metaprogramming* to supply the compiler with as much information as possible already at compile time. The included *Portable Expression Template Engine* framework (*PETE*, [CCH+]) implements expression templates for POOMA's data structures. PETE can also be used to add expression template functionality to other array/vector classes.

## TNT

The *Template Numerical Toolkit* (*TNT*, [Poz02]) is intended to be the successor of LAPACK++ and SparseLib++. It offers some dense matrix and vector formats, whereas the support for sparse matrices is only rudimentary yet. Until now, templates were used only for specifying the entry type, and since no iterators were used for abstraction, algorithms have to be written for every container type separately. Moreover, sparse matrix-matrix multiplication is not supported.

## MTL

The *Matrix Template Library* (*MTL*, [Sie99]) by Jeremy Siek surely is one of the most modern matrix libraries available. It offers several types of matrices, including dense, banded and sparse. The user can choose the type of matrix by specifying four template parameters: element type, shape, storage and orientation. For example, the line

```
typedef matrix<double,rectangle<>,compressed<>,row_major>::type SparseMatrix;
```

defines `SparseMatrix` to be a type that stores a rectangular sparse matrix with double precision real entries which are stored in the classical compressed row storage format.

Since the element type can be chosen via template parameter, and the data structure does not have any requirements concerning the element type, one is not restricted to simple scalar types like `double` or `complex<double>`, one may also use a matrix type here, which would lead to a matrix of matrices.

As Blitz++, the MTL makes intensive use of *template metaprogramming* which can be seen as an own language on template level, and which allows the user to specify every option that is known at compile time, and then in turn allows the compiler to optimize the according data structures and algorithms, see also Section 3.5

Furthermore, the MTL consequently separates data structures and algorithms, using iterators as an intermediate abstraction layer.

With the MTL comes the *Iterative Template Library* (ITL) that supplies the user with several numerical linear algebra methods like Conjugate Gradient, GMRES, BiCGStab, etc.

Having all these advantages in mind, there are a few things to criticize. The construction of the matrix classes with generators and the choice of several parameters shadows that, for example the compressed row/column format is mainly implemented by the `generic_comp2D<>` class which in turn is quite large and monolithic and seems to be built only for this single purpose, and is therefore hardly reusable.

Another issue is the lack of possibilities to add additional functionality to existing data structures. For example, we would like to add a view of the matrix that in row $i$ only gives us the strong neighbours $S_i$ (see Definition 5.2.22).

Furthermore, the sparse matrix-matrix multiplication that the MTL provides is not suited for our purposes, since it requires the size of the resulting matrix to be known in advance. Otherwise it returns an error, at least in the current implementation.

### Boost uBLAS

The *Boost* [Boo] project was started by members of the C++ Standards Committee Library Working Group as an extension of the Standard Template Library (STL). Nowadays, according to their web site, thousands of programmers contribute to it. It is a collection of several libraries that are built for a wide range of purposes, among which are e.g. graph data structures and algorithms, quarternions, regular expressions, etc. The focus of Boost is however the generic programming paradigm – most libraries intensively use the template facilities of C++.

The Boost library for numerical linear algebra is the *uBLAS* [uBL] library. It was mainly designed to implement the BLAS functionality on C++ level, with extensions such as several matrix types (such as sparse, symmetric, banded, triangular matrices, etc.). Expression templates are used to efficiently evaluate vector and matrix expressions.

However, its algorithms only allow matrices and vectors to be filled with scalar values. The according traits only cooperate with the C/C++ builtin types and refuse to work when matrices or vectors are in turn used as entry types.

Looking at uBLAS from a software design standpoint, one still observes very little code reusage. For example, iterator classes are defined for each matrix class separately. Moreover, every matrix type is an own class repeating standard member functions.

## 2.5 A classification of matrix types

A great amount of different storage formats has been devised in the past in order to represent the mathematical properties of the matrices. The main reason was of course, to save space by leaving out the zero elements. But also storing and accessing the matrix entries in a certain order, e.g. row-wise, column-wise or diagonal-wise was useful for some algorithms. A good overview is presented e.g. in [Saa90].

As we want to lay out the design for a new matrix library, we intend to investigate what these storage formats have in common in order to identify orthogonal, independent and reusable components which can be used to build matrix data structures.

### 2.5.1 Basic assumptions

We would like to formulate certain properties and interrelations of matrices in terms of the language normally used for *weighted and directed graphs*.

First of all, we define graphs and mappings between graphs and matrices. Normally, a graph $g$ is defined as a tupel $(V, E)$ of a set of *vertices* (or *nodes*) $V$ and a set of *edges* $E$ bewteen these vertices. Here we use an only slightly different approach:

**Definition 2.5.1** (Graphs). *Let* $\mathbb{K}$ *be a set of weight/entry values (usually, but not necessarily, a field). Furthermore, let* $V_n$ *be a set of* vertices *(or* nodes*) with cardinality* $\#\left[V_n\right] = n \in \mathbb{N}$.

1. A graph $g$ is defined as a tupel $(V_n, E)$ of a set of vertices $V_n$ and a set of edges $E$ bewteen these vertices. An edge $e \in E$ from a vertex $x \in V_n$ to a vertex $y \in V_n$ is denoted as $(x, y) = e$.

2. A directed graph or digraph is a graph where the edges have a direction, i.e. $(x, y) \neq (y, x)$ for $x, y \in V_n$, $x \neq y$.

3. A weighted graph/digraph consists of edges $E$ that also have a weight $\alpha \in \mathbb{K}$. Its edges will be denoted as $e = (x, y, \alpha)$.

4. Then we define $G_n := G(V_n, \mathbb{K})$ as the set of possible weighted digraphs with $n$ vertices and where each vertex $x \in V_n$ has at most one edge to another vertex.

5. The set $E_n := E(V_n, \mathbb{K})$ is the set of possible weighted edges $(x, y, \alpha)$ with vertices $x, y \in V_n$ and weight $\alpha \in \mathbb{K}$.

A graph $g \in G(V_n, \mathbb{K})$ is thus fully characterized by its set of edges $E = E(g) \subset E(V_n, \mathbb{K})$. A set of edges $E \subset E(V_n, \mathbb{K})$ on the other hand fully describes a graph $g \in G(V_n, \mathbb{K})$, which is why there is an isomorphic mapping between the sets $G(V_n, \mathbb{K})$ and $E(V_n, \mathbb{K})$. Thus, for our purposes, we will identify a graph with its set of edges.

**Remark 2.5.2.** In the previous definition, the case $x = y$ is explicitly allowed, i.e. there may be edges $(x, x)$ that point from one vertex $x$ to itself. Thus for $g \in G_n$ we have for the cardinality of $E(g)$ :

$$0 \leq \#\big[E(g)\big] \leq n^2.$$

For $n \in \mathbb{N}$ let the index set $I_n = \{1, \ldots, n\}$ denote the set of rows (columns) of (any) matrix $A \in \mathbb{K}^{n \times n}$. We now use $I_n$ also as an index set for $V_n : \{v_1, \ldots, v_n\}$ and define the isomorhism

$$v : V_n \longrightarrow I_n$$
$$v_i \mapsto v(i) := i, \quad \text{for} \quad v_i \in V_n.$$

We then introduce the mapping

$$\Phi : G(V_n, \mathbb{K}) \longrightarrow \mathbb{K}^{n \times n},$$
$$g \mapsto A, \quad g \in G(V_n, \mathbb{K}), \quad A = (a_{ij})_{i,j=1}^n \in \mathbb{K}^{n \times n},$$

which maps $g$, or equivalently – because of the isomorphism between the sets $G(V_n, \mathbb{K})$ and $E(V_n, \mathbb{K})$ – the edges of $g$, onto the matrix entries of $A$. It consists of the components $\Phi_k$, $k = 1, \ldots, \#\big[E(g)\big]$ with:

$$\Phi_k\big((x, y, \alpha)\big) = \alpha =: a_{v(x), v(y)}, \quad \text{for} \quad (x, y, \alpha) \in E(g).$$

This mapping is only well-defined if restricted to the subset

$$D(V_n, \mathbb{K}) := \{g \in G(V_n, \mathbb{K}) \mid \#\big[E(g)\big] = n^2\},$$

(also known as complete graphs), resulting in $\Phi|_{D(V_n, \mathbb{K})}$ being an isomorphism. The mapping between the remaining set

$$G(V_n, \mathbb{K}) \setminus D(V_n, \mathbb{K}) = \{g \in G(V_n, \mathbb{K}) \mid \#\big[E(g)\big] < n^2\} =: S(V_n, \mathbb{K})$$

and $\mathbb{K}^{n \times n}$ has to be extended to be well-defined, using now the components

$$\Phi(x, y) := a_{v(x), v(y)}$$

with

$$a_{v(x), v(y)} := \begin{cases} \alpha & (x, y, \alpha) \in E(g), \\ 0 & else. \end{cases}$$

**Remark 2.5.3.** *The sets $D(V_n, \mathbb{K})$ and $S(V_n, \mathbb{K})$ form the bridge between mathematics and computer science. $D(V_n, \mathbb{K})$ corresponds to* dense *matrices i.e. matrix data structures, that store each matrix entry, whether it be zero or not. The set $S(V_n, \mathbb{K})$ corresponds to* sparse *matrices, i.e. matrix data structures, that avoid to store entries that are zero (assuming all entries that are not stored to be zero).*

**Definition 2.5.4** (Initial and terminal vertex). *If $e \in E$ is an edge with $e = (x, y)$, (or $e = (x, y, \alpha)$ for weighted graphs) we define*

$$\text{source}(e) := x,$$
$$\text{target}(e) := y.$$

*we say that $x$ is the* initial vertex *or* source node *of $e$, and $j$ is its* terminal vertex *or* target node.

With $\text{nnz}_A = \#[E]$ we will denote the number of edges (*nonzero entries*). For reasons of simplicity we will often identify a node $x_i \in V_n$ with its index $i$, and the set of nodes $V_n$ with the set of indices $I_n \subset \mathbb{N}$.

**Remark 2.5.5.** *We can extend this view to arbitrary rectangular matrices $A \in \mathbb{R}^{n \times m}$ by considering two sets, the set of source nodes $V_S := \{s_1, \ldots, s_n\}$ and the set of target nodes $V_T := \{t_1, \ldots, t_m\}$. For $n < m$ we have $V_S \subsetneq V_T$, for $n > m$ we have $V_T \subsetneq V_T$. For square matrices, the sets are equal.*

**Assumption 2.5.6.** *Furthermore we demand $E(g)$ to have some ordering, such that the edge information can be stored in one sequence. This implies an ordering of the matrix entries of the associated matrix $\Phi(g)$.*

We haven't specified an order of the sequence of edges yet, since *any* reasonable order is possible, as long as we *interpret* it in the correct way. This means, as long as we are able to identify the position $(i, j)$ of an edge $e$ while iterating through the sequence of edges, the ordering is considered to be valid. However, for the moment, we will restrict ourselves to the following ordering:

**Assumption 2.5.7** (Row major ordering). [3] *The edges in $E$ are ordered ascendingly by their source nodes such that edges with the same source node are ordered ascendingly by their target node. This means, for elements $e_i$, $e_j$ from the sequence of edges with $i \neq j$ and*

$$e_i = (x, y) \quad resp. \ (x, y, \alpha)$$
$$e_j = (v, w) \quad resp. \ (u, w, \beta)$$

*we have:*

$$i < j \quad \Longleftrightarrow \quad (x < u) \quad or \quad (x = u \quad and \quad y < w).$$

Of course, other orderings may be possible, for example the *column major ordering* of $A$ which is equivalent to row major ordering of the matrix $A^T$. Another common way is the ordering by diagonals, which is suitable e.g. for band matrices.

An example for the row major ordering is illustrated by the graph in Figure 2.1 and its adjacency matrix in Figure 2.2. Once the nodes are numbered, the edges have an unequivocal ordering, shown in Table 2.1

---

[3]This determination is arbitrary, and only to illustrate the idea in what follows. A column major ordering would be just as fine. Later on we will relax this restriction to include other orderings.

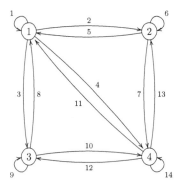

Figure 2.1: Graph

$$\begin{pmatrix} 1 & 1 & 1 & 1 \\ 1 & 1 & 0 & 1 \\ 1 & 0 & 1 & 1 \\ 1 & 1 & 1 & 1 \end{pmatrix}$$

Figure 2.2: Adjacency matrix

| edge number | 1 | 2 | 3 | 4 | 5 | 6 | 7 | 8 | 9 | 10 | 11 | 12 | 13 | 14 |
|---|---|---|---|---|---|---|---|---|---|---|---|---|---|---|
| source | 1 | 1 | 1 | 1 | 2 | 2 | 2 | 3 | 3 | 3 | 4 | 4 | 4 | 4 |
| target | 1 | 2 | 3 | 4 | 1 | 2 | 4 | 1 | 3 | 4 | 1 | 2 | 3 | 4 |

Table 2.1: Edge sequence

We can now define the neighbourhood of a node in the graph context.

**Definition 2.5.8** (Neighbourhood). *The* full neighbourhood *of a node* $i \in V_S$ *consists of all nodes* $j \in V_T$ *to which there is an edge that has $i$ as a source node:*

$$\bar{\mathcal{N}}_i = \{j \in V_T | \ \exists e \in E : \text{target}(e) = j \ \wedge \ \text{source}(e) = i\},$$

*whereas the* pure neighbourhood $\mathcal{N}_i$ *of $i$ will be defined without the node $i$ itself:*

$$\mathcal{N}_i := \bar{\mathcal{N}}_i \setminus \{i\}. \tag{2.4}$$

**Remark 2.5.9.** *The reason for the definitions of the two different neighbourhood sets $\bar{\mathcal{N}}_i$ and $\mathcal{N}_i$ is that in Section 5.2, in the AMG context, we will use merely (2.4), which is equivalent to Definition 5.2.16. However, for many considerations, it is more reasonable to work with the full neighbourhood, therefore the term $\bar{\mathcal{N}}_i$ is introduced here, to achieve a consistent notation.*

From these assumptions and observations, we now want to abstract a storage format for general matrix types.

### 2.5.2 Basic storage concept

Looking at what storage formats (for a summary see [Saa90]) like the *Compressed Row Storage* (*CRS*, also referred to as *Compressed Sparse Row*, *CRS* or the Yale sparse matrix format), the *Modified Compressed Row Storage* or the *Block Compressed Row Storage* have in common with (row major) dense matrices, we observe that the entries are ordered row-wise, eventually leaving out all (or most of) the zero entries. Again the entries might be stored in only one sequence, row by row.

The *Symmetric Sparse Skyline Storage* is equivalent to storing either only the lower or only the upper part of a symmetric matrix in the *Compressed Row Storage*.

The *Symmetric Skyline Storage* is similar to the last format, except, that it stores the dense rows with varying lengths. For every row, from the first nonzero entry to the diagonal (respectively from the diagonal to the last entry) everything is stored. This of course might lead to storing some zero entries, however it makes indexing easier since the according column indices don't need to be stored, except for the first one.

A scheme like the *Coordinate Storage*, although usually not ordered in the sense of Assumption 2.5.7, might be reordered and then interpreted in the above way.

The *Nonsymmetric Skyline Storage* and the *Unsymmetric Sparse Skyline Storage* differ from the symmetric versions by storing the (strict) lower part in the Symmetric (Sparse) Skyline Storage and the upper part in a column oriented Symmetric (Sparse) Skyline Format (i.e. storing the transpose of the upper part in the Symmetric (Sparse) Skyline Storage).

### Orthogonal properties

From the differences and common properties of the above storage formats we deduce now an abstract formulation of matrix formats. Basically, it is a generalization of the CRS (and similar) formats. It is characterized by the following properties:

1. The type of the matrix entries. This is typically a type for simple scalar values like `double` or `float`. But we might want to store a matrix which again has matrices as entries e.g. in applications where the whole matrix has a block substructure like mentioned in Sections 2.2.3 and 2.2.4, and as introduced in Chapter 9.

2. The type of the indices. This is usually some common signed or unsigned integer type like `short`, `int`, `long int`, etc.

3. The vertical dimension and whether it is *fixed* at compile time (and thus equal for all objects of this class), *constant* at run time (different objects of this class can have different dimensions) or *variable* (the dimension of a matrix object can be changed during run time).

4. The horizontal dimension with the same three options as for the vertical dimension.

5. The type of sequence of the index $j_i \in V_T$ of the *first* target node of a source node $i \in V_S$. The $j_i$'s may vary with $i$ (sparse formats) or be *constant* (dense format) independently of $i$. If it is constant we may want to distinguish a constant already known at compile time (we will call this *fixed*) from one not known before run time. If it varies, we may want to distinguish between the type of variation: it might be *computable* out of $i$, or it might be completely random (we will call this *arbitrary*).

6. The number of target nodes $\in V_T$ of a source node $i \in V_S$, i.e. the cardinality of $\bar{\mathcal{N}}_i$. Again we have the choice of *constant, fixed, computable* and *arbitrary*.

7. The type of numbering of the target nodes. This may be *consecutive*, meaning an integer interval (in a dense matrix or the Skyline Storage format) or *arbitrary* (in a usual sparse matrix).

8. The values of the weights. These are of course usually *arbitrary*, but we might think of cases when they are *constant* (e.g. Hadamard matrices) or *fixed* (e.g. permutation matrices, adjacency or incidence matrices). One may also consider matrices that have entries that are computable out of $i \in V_S$ and $j \in V_T$ (e.g. Hilbert matrices).

**Remark 2.5.10.** *As one can easily see, the above properties do not influence each other, in the sense that the choice of one concrete property doesn't restrict the choice of the other properties. Thus we will call these properties* orthogonal.

These 8 properties form the basis of our *domain specific language* (DSL). A DSL is the language that provides a set of terms to describe a certain field of interest under the aspect of software engineering (see e.g. [Ben86] or [CE00]). We will use the DSL as an input to a *type generator* (see Section 3.6) to construct a desired type – in our case a specific matrix type.

### 2.5.3 Resulting matrix types

Let $A \in \mathbb{R}^{m \times n}$ and the number of a source node ($\cong$ row index) be denoted with $i \in V_S$. Then $\#[\bar{\mathcal{N}}_i]$ denotes the number of target nodes of $i$. $f$ is some simple function with

$$f : V_S \to V_T, \quad f(i) \mapsto \#[\bar{\mathcal{N}}_i].$$

| target node size | arbitrary numbering of target nodes | consecutive numbering of target nodes |
|---|---|---|
| *arbitrary* number of target nodes: $\#[\bar{\mathcal{N}}_i] \neq const$ | • general sparse matrix (compressed row storage) | • variable band matrix (skyline storage) |
| *computable* out of $i$: $\#[\bar{\mathcal{N}}_i] = f(i) \neq const$ | | • Hessenberg matrix,<br><br>• dense lower triangular matrix ($f(i) = i$),<br><br>• dense strict upper triangular matrix ($f(i) = n - i$) |
| *constant* number of target nodes: $\#[\bar{\mathcal{N}}_i] \equiv k \in \mathbb{N}, \forall i \in I$ (only known at run time) | • matrices arising from finite difference methods with periodic boundary conditions | • dense matrix ($k = n$),<br><br>• band matrix ($k < n$),<br><br>• diagonal matrix ($k = 1$) |
| *fixed* number of target nodes: $\#[\bar{\mathcal{N}}_i] \equiv k \in \mathbb{N}, \forall i \in I$ (known at compile time) | • permutation matrix ($k = 1$),<br><br>• incidence matrix ($k = 2$) | • small dense matrices like local point stiffness matrices as in (2.1) |

Table 2.2: Resulting matrix types

Table 2.2 now shows some examples of the matrix types that can be constructed when combining different types of target node numbering and different target node sizes. Note that, the matrix types in the right column of the table are not fully characterized by simply stating that they have a consecutive target node numbering – they need a first target index for each node $i$ (cf. property 5 above).

As one can see in this table, many different formats which are suitable for specially structured matrices already arise from the storage concept presented in the last section. But the table shows only one slice of the combinatorial possibilities. Looking only at the orthogonal properties 3 to 8 in Section 2.5.2 we get the theoretically number of $3 \cdot 3 \cdot 4 \cdot 4 \cdot 2 \cdot 4 = 1152$ possible matrix types. However, it is not claimed that all of them might be sensible or useful, which is why not all fields in Table 2.2 can filled with an according matrix type.

### 2.5.4   Additional properties

Afar from the resulting types described above, this should not be the end of the possibilities. For example we would possibly like to have a feature like in the Modified Row Storage, that allows us to directly access the diagonal entries of the matrix.

For some types, we might want to have a random access on matrix entries, or we might want to distinguish different ways to traverse with an iterator through the elements of the matrix.

Maybe, we would like to have a view on the matrix that gives us access to a submatrix only, or to an arbitrary subset of the matrix entries (for example only the strong negative neighbourhood $\mathcal{S}_i$ for every row index $i$).

To be exact we would like to have the following features:

9. Random Access. Choices: *true* or *false*.

10. One dimensional iterator access. Conceives the matrix as a linear sequence of data, providing one iterator to access all (physically) nonzero elements in a specific order defined by a basic definition like Assumption 2.5.7. Choices: *true* or *false*.

11. Two dimensional iterator access. Provides a two dimensional view on the matrix by interpreting it as a sequence of sequences ($n$ rows with nonzero entries). Choices: *true* or *false*.

12. Diagonal access. Provides an iterator that traverses only through the diagonal entries. Choices: *true* or *false*.

13. Orientation. Choices: *row-wise* or *column-wise*.

# Chapter 3

# Software components for numerical linear algebra

In this chapter, the library *Matrix Layers and Templates for Object-oriented Numerics* (MiLTON) is introduced, as well as the components it is made of (see Figure 3.1). MiLTON is designed to supply diverse matrix data types. They are assembled out of various smaller components, which we refer to as layers (cf. Sections 3.2 and 3.3). These in turn use several simpler data structures (sequences, functors and iterators), which are outlined in Section 3.1.

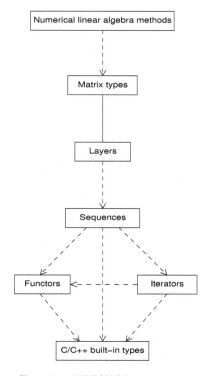

Figure 3.1: MiLTON Library structure

In Section 3.4 we describe the object construction mechanism. The metaprogramming constructs and traits are depicted in Section 3.5. Afterwards in Section 3.6 we show how to assemble the types and give type generation rules. Section 3.5 deals with the expression templates concept for matrix expressions (products and sums). The last section takes a look on the matrix-vector operations and its performance behaviour in comparison with another matrix library.

## 3.1   Simple data structures

The layers from which the actual matrix types are assembled, are built on top of simple data structures like *sequences*, *functors*, and *iterators*. Many of these classes seem to be trivial – and some of them are indeed. However, they are indispensible for our software construction purposes. Another reason for building these small classes, is that the smaller or simpler a class is, the easier it is also to adhere to the *programming by contract* paradigm. In contrast the syntax of a large class is often hard to maintain (and to understand).

Since many of these simple types didn't exist (at least not in that combination and with the desired properties) in a standard library, we had to provide them. These classes constitute the atoms of our library. They may however be replaced easily with standard components or classes from other libraries – as long as they provide the according interface – if these promise a better performance, for example.

The UML diagram in 3.1 already gives a short overview of the library structure. Roughly speaking, the more to the top a type is plotted, the higher is its level of complexity. The description of the library will follow the diagram roughly from the bottom to the top.

### 3.1.1   Functors

*Functors* or *function objects* were already described e.g. in [Str97], Section 18.4, and are an essential part of the STL. Functors are usually simple (small) objects, that provide

```
result_type operator()(argument_type_1 a1,..., argument_type_n an)
```

as a member function. They are used for specifying a method for other functions (e.g. modifying sequence functions like `for_each()` from the STL). In C, this was usually done with function pointers. The advantage of a function object however is that its class can even be passed as an argument for a template class, since it is known at compile time.

The STL provides some predefined functors like `plus`, `multiplies`, `negate`, etc. in the `functional` header file. However these are not sufficient for our purposes. For our library we supply the following functor classes:

| | |
|---|---|
| Name: | `template <class A>` |
| | `class identity;` |
| derived from: | `unary_function<A,A>` |
| supplies: | `const A operator()(const A& i) const` |
| purpose: | `operator()(i)` delivers i for every i of type `A` |

| | |
|---|---|
| Name: | `template <class A, class R>` |
| | `class linear;` |
| derived from: | `unary_function<A,R>` |
| supplies: | `const R operator()(const A& i) const` |
| purpose: | `operator()(i)` delivers `factor` * i for every i of type `A`. |
| | The value of `factor` is supplied with the contructor. |

| | |
|---|---|
| Name: | `template <class A, class R, A factor>` |
| | `class fixed_linear;` |
| derived from: | `unary_function<A,R>` |
| supplies: | `const R operator()(const A& i) const` |
| purpose: | `operator()(i)` delivers `factor * i` for every `i` of type `A`. |
| | The value of `factor` is supplied as a template argument. |

| | |
|---|---|
| Name: | `template <class A>` |
| | `class constant;` |
| derived from: | `unary_function<A,A>`, `binary_function<A,A,A>` |
| supplies: | `const R operator()(const A& i) const` |
| | `const R operator()(const A& i, const A& j) const` |
| purpose: | `operator()(i)` and `operator()(i,j)` deliver `value` for every `i,j` |
| | of type `A`. The value of `value` is supplied with the contructor. |

| | |
|---|---|
| Name: | `template <class A, A value>` |
| | `class fixed_constant;` |
| derived from: | `unary_function<A,A>`, `binary_function<A,A,A>` |
| supplies: | `const R operator()(const A& i) const` |
| | `const R operator()(const A& i, const A& j) const` |
| purpose: | `operator()(i)` and `operator()(i,j)` deliver `value` for every `i,j` |
| | of type `A`. The value of `value` is supplied as a template argument. |

| | |
|---|---|
| Name: | `template <class A1, class A2, class A3, class R>` |
| | `class addmul;` |
| derived from: | `trinary_function<A1,A2,A3,R>` |
| supplies: | `const R& operator()(const A1& a, const A2& x, A3& y) const` |
| purpose: | `operator()(a,x,y)` computes `y = y + (a * x)`. |

| | |
|---|---|
| Name: | `template <class A1, class A2, class A3, class R>` |
| | `class submul;` |
| derived from: | `trinary_function<A1,A2,A3,R>` |
| supplies: | `const R& operator()(const A1& a, const A2& x, A3& y) const` |
| purpose: | `operator()(a,x,y)` computes `y = y - (a * x)`. |

Functors can be conceived as be a generalization of functions and objects. They have a type that can be passed as a template argument to other classes or template functions. They can be instantiated as an object. And the () operator can be called on them like a function call.

This is the reason for the existance of such simple functors like `identity` and `linear`.

## 3.1.2 Sequences

We use the term *sequence* for data structures, that offer a linear access to their data, i.e. that can be traversed linearly (with an *iterator*). Thus, vectors (arrays), lists, stacks and queues are sequences. But with this term, we explicitly would like to include *mathematical* sequences as well. This leads to a unified approach because mathematical sequences then can be also supplied as a genuine C++ type. The idea of sequences can be seen as a *design pattern*.

**Sequence information types**

In Section 2.5.2, we have distinguished between different types of information that is stored in a sequence. This is due to the fact, that we have abstracted from the view of a sequence as a mere array of data. Besides being *traversable* (with, e.g. an iterator), we define sequences to be data structures that have

- an index type (for the size and random access by an index)

- a value type for the entries,

- a length/size,

- and an information type.

While the first three are self-explanatory, we mean by the fourth property the way, the information is stored (or gained). It can have the following values:

- *constant*: the value at a certain position $i$ is a constant value $c$, independently of $i$. The value of $c$ is *not* known at compile time.

- *fixed*: the value at position $i$ is a constant value $c$ independently of $i$. The value of $c$ is already known at compile time.

- *computable*: the value at position $i$ can be computed by a function $f$ out of $i$.

- *arbitrary*: the value at position $i$ cannot be computed by a function, and thus must be stored explicitly (e.g. in an array).

One might argue, that at least *constant* values are a special case of *computable* values (with the special function $f(i) := c, \forall i$. This is indeed correct, but the *constant* property type is provided for convenience in this library.

Note that sequences of the first three types are of course read-only, whereas the *arbitrary* type is the only sequence where information can be overwritten.

The sequences implented in this library are further described in the Appendix A.2.

### 3.1.3 Iterators

The concept of iterators is a powerful abstraction, a *design pattern*, that was created as a medium layer between a container/data structure and an algorithm operating on this container. An iterator itself is a data type that allows (indirect) access to the containers' data.

In the STL, some of the iterators are implemented as classes (e.g. the `std::list` and `std::map` iterators) some are only pointers (the one from `std::vector`). A main philosophy in designing C++ was to give iterators the same interface as pointers, in order to use them exchangeably in generic algorithms.

Within our library, every iterator that is exported in the interface, is implemented as a class, except for iterators that originate from the arbitrary data sequences. Moreover, for the small helper data structures that are used internally we need appropriate iterators.

In order to do so, we need to extend the classical iterator concept and introduce a further abstraction. An iterator is not anymore a simple pointer to an existing block of data somewhere in the computers' memory. It may not point to any position in the heap (or stack) at all. If we have an iterator for a constant value sequence, the constant value is, of course, stored only once and not in an array with the same value in every position. Incrementing the iterator now only means to increment an internal index, but no real position in the memory.

All these iterators are constructed with a starting index (which defaults to zero in the default constructor) in order to implement the indexed iterator pattern.

Furthermore, as we want to give searching algorithms a hint, what kind of sequence they are treating, we extended the iterator categories.

## 3.2 Mixin Programming

The method of our choice to implement the functionality indicated by the orthogonal properties described in Section 2.5.2 is influenced by a technique called *mixin layers*. Mixins are a programming style that was originally introduced by *Flavors* [Dav86], an extension of the *Lisp* programming language. Later on it was adapted to the C++ programming language (cf. [SB98], [SB00]).

In this section we would like to introduce the concept of layer based programming in contrast to the classical object-oriented software construction.

### 3.2.1 Multiple inheritance

In the traditional object-oriented software design, the subject of interest is modelled with classes. Relationships between theses classes are modelled by inheritance or aggregation. This leads to a strict hierarchy in a software model.

For example, we construct data structures by writing classes which are subclasses of one or more other classes. If we want to accumulate functionality in a class, we need to specify all base classes (directly or indirectly) when we write this class. Thus, the inheritane tree is fixed and cannot be changed without rewriting the classes as we see in the example UML diagram in Figure 3.2.

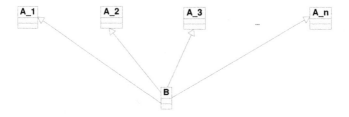

Figure 3.2: Classical multiple inheritance

Multiple inheritance is supported for example by C++ and EIFFEL. However, not all object-oriented programming languages support the inheritance from multiple base classes. The designers of Java, for example, decided to restrict the language to only single inheritance, meaning that a class can inherit from only one base class. The reason for this restriction lies in two main problems which can arise when using multiple inheritance:

- Ambiguous methods in two or more base classes. A subclass intends to call a method, that is defined in more than one base class, cf. Figure 3.3. This type of error however, can be reported by the compiler. In EIFFEL, this problem is solved by redefining the according methods in the subclass. In C++, name conflicts are resolved by calling a member explicitly with the `classname::membername` convention (*qualified call*).

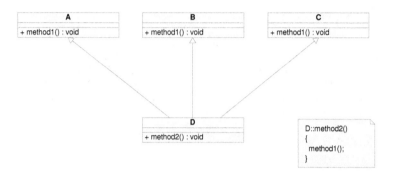

Figure 3.3: Ambiguous methods

- Diamond inheritance, cf. Figure 3.4. If A is a virtual base class of B and C (that means, there is only one copy of A included in D), we have the situation that A::method() is called twice when we invoke D::method(). There may be cases where this is not the desired behaviour (cf. [PSM97]).

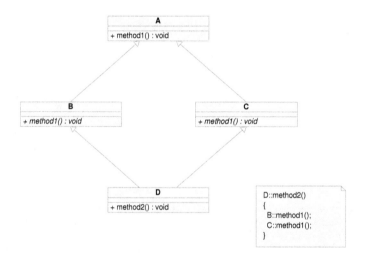

Figure 3.4: Diamond inheritance

Although there are individual solutions to the above described problems, multiple inheritance stays a source of programming flaws, and every programmer has to use it with great care in his design. Thus, efforts were being made to linearize the inheritance, e.g. the *phunctor* approach in [PSM97]. Another approach are mixins.

## 3.2.2 Mixins

The problems with multiple inheritance are not the only drawbacks of classical inheritance in object-oriented programming languages. Another one is that a subclass cannot be defined without specifying its base class. This is overcome by the *mixin* programming construct (also referred to as *abstract subclasses* in [BC90]). The class a mixin inherits from, is specified at the place of instantiation, rather than at the place of definition of the mixin class.

Mixins classes are most commonly implemented using *parameterized inheritance*. The idea is now to specify the base class as a (template) parameter. This concept is indicated in the UML diagram in Figure 3.5. The classes A_1, A_2, ..., A_n are now designed as mixin layers. They are not a part of a larger class hierarchy and thus can be written independently of other classes. The user/programmer now can linearly combine the components to bigger data structures that unite their functionality. In order to terminate the inheritance tree at the top, we need some normal base class at the end.

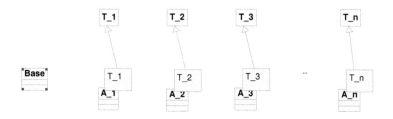

Figure 3.5: Mixin components

**Remark 3.2.1.** *We would like to point out on this occasion, that UML class diagrams are not able to describe the mixin layer paradigm to the full extent. For example, UML doesn't have a feature to clearly indicate that a class inherits from its template parameter. And especially for the possibilities of C++ concerning the implementation of mixin layers, it has no graphical analogon. Nevertheless, we try to illustrate the idea of mixins with example diagrams wherever it seems possible.*

In C++ a mixin can be defined using template classes:

```
──────────────────── Mixin in C++ ────────────────────
template <class T_1>
class A_1 : public T_1
{
    ... \\ class A_1 definition
};
```

Mixins basically are intended to combine two solutions of modern object oriented software construction problems. On the one hand, the linearization of inheritance supersedes multiple inheritance, and on the other hand they allow the reuse of single software components without changing the class hierachy.

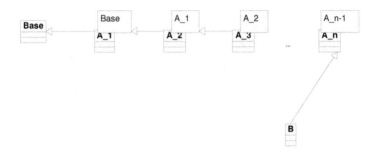

Figure 3.6: Example mixin composition

### 3.2.3  Mixin layers

Mixins layers are a variant of the mixin technique, intended for constructing arbitrary complex data structures out of small components. These components might be assembled in (nearly) any combination and order. Mixin layers were proposed in [SB98] as an implementation technique for *collaboration based designs*. Collaborations are a method to describe interdependencies of objects in an object-oriented design. A set of objects and protocol of interaction form a collaboration. The part of an object that satisfies a protocol of a certain collaboration is called the object's role in the collaboration.

An object can now participate in different collaborations as well as different objects can participate in the same collaboration. A whole software product is then defined as the composition of different (ideally) independent collaborations.

In [SB02] it was suggested to implement mixin layers in C++ using nested classes to represent the different roles:

```
                              —— Mixin layer ——
template <class BaseLayer>
class Layer : public BaseLayer
{
public:
  class FirstClass : public BaseLayer::FirstClass
  {
    ...
  };
  class SecondClass : public BaseLayer::SecondClass
  {
    ...
  };
  ...
};
```

## 3.3  Functional layers

In our library we extend the approach that was described in the previous section. Here the nested class is parameterized with the type from the bottom of the inheritance tree (which is reduced to a mere inheritance list). The whole functionality of the layer is implemented in the nested class `Type`.

```
───────────────── Functional layer ─────────────────
template <class BaseLayer>
class Layer
{
public:
  template <class Final>
  class Type : public BaseLayer::template Type<Final>
  {
    ...
  };
};
```

The idea is to (nearly) arbitrarily combine and accumulate data and functionality. If we need our matrix type to fulfill a certain interface, we simply add the according layer(s) to the type.

In order to construct a complete class, it is necessary to have a (rather simple) base class at the top to start with, and a class at the bottom to finalize the whole type. These classes are referred to as the `Base` layer and the `Final` layer.

This ensures that the complete type is known at each layer of the composition and e.g. a function that wants to return a reference to the current object (`*this`) can do this by calling the according function from the `Base` layer.

### 3.3.1 The base layer

The `Base` layer resides at the top of the inheritance list. Each nested class in each layer inherits from the according class in the `Base` layer.

```
───────────────── Base layer ─────────────────
struct Base
{
  template <class Final_>
  class Type
  {
  public:
    Type()
    {}
    template <typename Arg_>
    Type(Arg_& arg)
    {}
    typedef Final_ Final;
    Final & final()
    {
      return *static_cast<Final*>(this);
    }
    Final const & final() const
    {
      return *static_cast<Final const*>(this);
    }
  };
};
```

The empty templatized constructor is embodied in this class since it is part of the main constructor mechanism. Each layer has got such a constructor (besides the default constructor), it is a part of the solution to the constructor problem in mixin-based programming.

The constructor mechanism for our matrix types and the associated parameter aggregates are described in more detail in section 3.4.

Using the default constructor is always possible for our matrix types. All data members are then initialized to their default values. Depending on the used layers and their configuration we then might have an empty $0 \times 0$ matrix (usually for sparse matrix types) or a $n \times m$ matrix with $nnz$ entries (if $n, m, nnz$ are known at compile time).

### 3.3.2   The final layer

The Final layer resides at the bottom of each inheritance list. It is needed to finalize the type and to pass this finalized type through the complete hierarchy to the Base layer at the top. In addition to that, it encompasses functions that are essential for the expression templates (see Section 3.7) construct (the functions compute() and deleteTmp() as well as the operators += and =).

```
──────────────── Final layer ────────────────
template <class Base_>
struct Final
{
  class Type : public Base_::template Type<Type>
  {
  private:
    typedef typename Base_::template Type<Type> BaseType_;
  public:
    Type() : BaseType_()
    {}
    template <typename Arg_>
    Type(Arg_& arg) : BaseType_(arg)
    {}
  };
};
```

### 3.3.3   Layer configuration

The following classes are the layers that actually implement the orthogonal properties mentioned in Remark 2.5.10. There is no real one-to-one mapping of properties to layers, since e.g. is not possible (and not sensible) to separate the *value* of the vertical dimension of a matrix (say, 100) from its *type* (say, int) in the implementation. However it is possible, through the template mechanisms of C++, to specify them *independently*. The type, of course, has to be specified at compile time already, whereas for the value we have the choice of definition at compile *or* run time.

These options are passed to the layer class by using the matrix layer configuration construct. This can be any class that contains at least the subtypes ContainerType and MemoryClass. Our library offers two types of configuration classes, FixedConfig for compile-time constants and LayerConfig for any other storage type (mainly run-time automatic variables, pointers, and classes with static interfaces).

```
──────────────── Layer configuration ────────────────
template <class ContainerType_,
          class MemoryClass_=Value,
```

```
          class WeightMemoryType_=Value>
struct LayerConfig
{
  typedef ContainerType_    ContainerType;
  typedef MemoryClass_      MemoryClass;
  typedef WeightMemoryType_ WeightMemoryType;
};
```

───────────────── Fixed value configuration ─────────────────

```
template <class T, T i>
struct FixedConfig
{
  typedef T ContainerType;
  typedef Fixed MemoryClass;
  static const T member = i;
};
```

`ContainerType` specifies in which kind of data structure the data of the layer is stored. For a dimension this would be e.g. `unsigned int`. For the matrix entries this could be e.g. `std::vector<double>` or an array of a fixed length (however it can't be a C-type array like `double a[100]` since this is not an own type). The `MemoryClass` subtype determines how the type is stored in the layer. Here we have the choices of `Value`, `Pointer`, `Reference`, `Static` or `Fixed`. However the last choice only makes sense in combination with the `FixedConfig` struct, which is simply an implementation of a singleton design pattern. There, we have a compile time constant, stored in the configuration class. This concept enables the `Member` layer to access the data by

- a normal automatic variable,

- a pointer,

- a reference,

- static functions ,

- or as a compile time constant

(see Section 3.4). More about the `WeightMemoryType` subtype can be found at the description of the `WeightValuesLayer`.

### 3.3.4  Layer data storage concept

The goal of this concept is to separate the storage of the data from the functionality and the algorithms.

We can achieve this by using an additional class that stores the data member in one of the five ways mentioned above. It is realized by the `Member` template class.

There are basically two ways to make use of the stored data in the `Member` class. They are based on the prerequisites the according data type complies with. If it is just a variable of a type not further specified, we may simply want to encapsulate it. If it is a sequence (container) we may want to encapsulate its functionality.

**Layer name tags**

In order to store and to retrieve data with this standardized `Member` layer, we need to attach a tag to it. This is just an empty struct with an appropriate name. If we intend to store some data with the name *VariableName* we need to define the tag

```
────────────────── Layer name tag ──────────────────
struct VariableName {};
```

for the layer *VariableName*`Layer`. Adressing classes or functions via such name tags is a simple but indispensable metaprogramming technique, since the value of a tag is evaluated during compile time.

**The `Member` layer**

Whenever a layer needs to store data to implement its functionality, it needs an accompanying `Member` layer. In this case, the `Member` layer is made the direct base class of the funtionality layer.

```
────────────────── Standard Member layer ──────────────────
template <class BaseType_,
         class Config,
         class MemberName,
         class SizeType,
         class MemoryClass=Value>
class Member : public BaseType_
{
private:
    typedef typename Config::ContainerType MemberType;
public:
    typedef BaseType_  BaseType;
private:
    mutable MemberType member;
public:
    Member() : BaseType(), member()
    {}
    template <typename Arg_>
    Member(const MemberType& member_, Arg_& arg) : BaseType(arg)
    {
      SizeType size = arg.getSize(MemberName());
      if (size == 0)
          member = member_;
      else
          member = MemberType(size);
    }
    const MemberType& getMember() const
    {
      return member;
    }
    void setMember(const MemberType& member_)
    {
      member = member_;
    }
```

```
    template <class OtherType>
    void setMember(OtherType& othermember)
    {
      member = othermember;
    }
};
```

This template class is specialized for the several memory types mentioned in Section 3.3.3. Here we just show some excerpts from the specializations for Static and Fixed.

```
                        ____ Member layer for static functions ____
template <class BaseType, class Config, class MemberName, class SizeType>
class Member<BaseType,Config,MemberName,SizeType,Static> : public BaseType
{
private:
    typedef typename Config::ContainerType MemberType;
public:
    Member() : BaseType()
    {}
    template <typename Arg_>
    Member(const MemberType& member_, Arg_& arg) : BaseType(arg)
    {}
    static const MemberType getMember()
    {
      return typename Config::member();
    }
    static const SizeType getMemberSize()
    {
      return Config::member::size();
    }
    static typename Config::member::iterator begin()
    {
      return Config::member::begin();
    }
    static typename Config::member::iterator end()
    {
      return Config::member::begin();
    }
};
```

```
                        ____ Member layer for fixed values ____
template <class BaseType, class Config, class MemberName, class SizeType>
class Member<BaseType,Config,MemberName,SizeType,Fixed> : public BaseType
{
private:
    typedef typename Config::ContainerType MemberType;
public:
    Member() : BaseType()
    {}
```

```
   template <typename Arg_>
   Member(const MemberType& member_, Arg_& arg) : BaseType(arg)
   {}
   static const MemberType getMember()
   {
     return Config::member;
   }
};
```

### 3.3.5   Variable encapsulation

By *encapsulation of a variable* we mean that only the variable itself is of interest, rather than its member functions. This variable is referred to directly. If e.g. the variable to be stored has the name *VariableName*, it can be accessed via the function get*VariableName*(). This type of storage merely makes sense for small, simple types such as built-in types or small-sized containers.

The template parameter `Base_` specifies the preceding layer and is passed as a parameter to the `Member` layer whereas the `Config` parameter defines which specialization is going to be used.

──────────────── Variable encapsulation ────────────────

```
template <class Base_, class Config>
struct VariableNameLayer
{
  template <class Final_>
  class Type : public Member<typename Base_::template Type<Final_>,
                             Config,
                             VariableName,
                             typename Config::ContainerType,
                             typename Config::MemoryClass>
  {
  public:
    typedef typename Config::ContainerType VariableNameType;
    typedef VariableNameType size_type;
  private:
    typedef typename Base_::template Type<Final_> BaseLayer;
    typedef Member<BaseLayer,
                   Config,
                   VariableName,
                   size_type,
                   typename Config::MemoryClass> BaseType_;
    typedef Data<typename BaseLayer::DataType,
                 VerticalDimension,
                 VerticalDimensionType,
                 size_type,
                 Value> ParameterType;
    typedef Type<Final_> Type_;
  public:
    Type() : BaseType_()
    {}
    template <typename Arg_>
    Type(Arg_& arg) : BaseType_(arg.getValue(VariableName()),arg)
    {}
```

```
    void setVariableName(VariableNameType d)
    {
      BaseType_::setMember(d);
    }
    VariableNameType getVariableName()
    {
      return BaseType_::getMember();
    }
  };
};
```

Examples for variable encapsulation in our library are:

- `VerticalDimensionLayer`: This layer is responsible for storing the vertical dimension, i.e. the number of rows of the matrix. It has `getVerticalDimension()` as the only accessor function delivering of course what its name suggests.

- `HorizontalDimensionLayer`: It obviously does the same as the previous one, just for the horizontal dimension, i.e. the number of columns.

- `EncapsulationLayer`: The encapsulation layer is a special variant of variable encapsulation. Where all other layers are intended to be built on top of another layer (which is yet an incomplete type), the encapsulation layer is used to add functionality to an existing, complete (matrix) type. If e.g. an algorithm has certain requirements for a data structure (concerning the functionality) that the current one doesn't fulfill, then the type can be encapsulated in this layer and extended with other layers that implement the desired interface.

Note that the set*VariableName*() member function is only accessible (and sensible), if `MemoryClass` is not `Fixed`. Trying to instantiate that member function would result in a compile time error, since the specialization of `Member` for fixed values doesn't have an according member function.

### 3.3.6 Sequence encapsulation

If the stored data is known to be a sequence, then we are interested in encapsulating its functionality, meaning its member functions. For that purpose, we revert to a small set of member functions that are also widely used by the STL containers.

─────────────── Sequence encapsulation ───────────────
```
template <class Base_, class Config>
struct SequenceNameLayer
{
  template <class Final_>
  class Type : public Member<typename Base_::template Type<Final_>,
                             Config,
                             SequenceNameSequenceName,
                             typename Config::ContainerType::size_type,
                             typename Config::MemoryClass>
  {
  public:
    typedef typename Base_::template Type<Final_> BaseLayer;
    typedef typename Config::ContainerType SequenceNameContainerType;
    typedef typename SequenceNameContainerType::iterator
                  SequenceNameIterator;
```

```
      typedef typename SequenceNameContainerType::const_iterator
                   ConstSequenceNameIterator;
      typedef typename SequenceNameContainerType::value_type value_type;
      typedef typename SequenceNameContainerType::size_type size_type;
      typedef SequenceName LayerName;
      typedef Config LayerConfig;
    private:
      typedef Member<BaseLayer,
                   Config,
                   SequenceName,
                   size_type,
                   typename Config::MemoryClass> BaseType_;
      typedef Type<Final_> Type_;
    public:
      typedef Data<typename BaseLayer::DataType,
                   SequenceName,
                   SequenceNameContainerType,
                   size_type,
                   typename Config::MemoryClass> ParameterType;
    public:
      Type() : BaseType_()
      {}
      template <typename Arg_>
      Type(Arg_& arg) : BaseType_(arg.getValue(SequenceName()),arg)
      {}
      SequenceNameIterator SequenceName_begin()
      {
        return BaseType_::begin();
      }
      SequenceNameIterator SequenceName_end()
      {
        return BaseType_::end();
      }
      ConstSequenceNameIterator SequenceName_begin() const
      {
        return BaseType_::begin();
      }
      ConstSequenceNameIterator SequenceName_end() const
      {
        return BaseType_::end();
      }
    };
};
```

In addition to the iterator delivering ...begin() and ...end() functions, each layer may define other member functions that offer valuable information about the sequence, like e.g. the length. Examples for sequence encapsulation in our library include:

- **EdgeTargetsLayer**: The layer of edge targets is responsible for storing the numbers/indices of the targets of the edges (very much like the bottom row in Table 2.1) consecutively. The order of theses edge targets is not fixed - it depends on how the surrounding layers *interprete* them. But normally we have row-by-row or column-by-column ordering.

The additional accessor function `numberOfEdges()` delivers the total number of edges (i.e. the number of nonzero entries in the matrix) that can be stored. The `EdgeTargets_begin()` and `EdgeTargets_end()` member functions deliver STL-like iterators that iterate through the sequence of edge targets.

This layer is only of importance for sparse matrix types, i.e. matrix types where the numbering of the neighbouring targets is arbitrary (not consecutive and not even computable). Thus for dense matrices we need a different approach with the `FirstTargetsLayer`.

- `NeighbourhoodStartsLayer`: The neighbourhood starts layer is devised to give a sequence that stores information about where in the ordered sequence of edges a new neighbourhood begins. For sparse matrices, `NeighbourhoodStarts_begin()[i]` gives the index where the neighbourhood of node (variable) $i$ starts in edge target sequence (and in the weight value sequence).

  In order to make use of this information, the sequence of edge targets from the `EdgeTargetsLayer` doesn't even need to exist. For every matrix `NeighbourhoodStarts_begin()[i]` states the number of edges (nonzero entries) that are stored before $\mathcal{N}_i$. Thus

$$\texttt{NeighbourhoodStarts\_begin()[i+1]} - \texttt{NeighbourhoodStarts\_begin()[i]}$$

  gives the cardinality of $\mathcal{N}_i$ (i.e. the length of the $i$-th row/column).

- `WeightValuesLayer`: This layer stores the weights of the edges (i.e. the values of the matrix entries) in one long sequence of type `Config::ContainerType`, which must provide an STL type iterator. Thus, in the `Member` layer, a variable of type `Config::ContainerType` stores all nonzero elements of the matrix.

  The only accessor functions that this layer adds to the matrix type are `WeightValues_begin()` and `WeightValues_end()`, which yield an iterator that point to the start, respectively behind the end of the weight sequence.

- `FirstTargetsLayer`: The layer for the first targets sequence is needed for dense matrix types. Dense matrices differ from sparse matrices in the type of sequence they store their index information. The numbering of their neighbourhood is consecutive and not arbitrary, thus, we could use a *function value sequence*, see Section A.2, for that purpose.

  However, it would be cumbersome to construct one long sequence containing all targets of all nodes like it is provided in the edge targets layer, since in this case we somehow had to combine multiple sequences into one.

  Instead, we provide a layer, that stores the first target index for each node. For full dense matrices, this sequence would be a constant (or even fixed) value sequence with the value 0 (since we have zero based indices). Banded matrices may use a function value sequence at this point.

  The information in the first target sequence is used by other layers later in the hierarchy in order e.g. to construct appropriate row-wise iterators.

- `SliceLayer`: The slice layer can be used to indicate a subset of the matrix. More precisely, it defines one target node for each source node. It may be used e.g. to store the indices of the diagonal entries of a matrix.

- `StrongNeighbourhoodLayer`: The strong neighbourhood layer is capable of computing and storing the strong neighbourhood of a variable (cf. Sections 5.2.5 and 9.2.3 resp. 9.2.4).

  The member function `computeStrongNeighbours()` triggers the computation. Afterwards, the sequence of strong neighbourhoods can be accessed via the `StrongNeighbourhood_begin()` and `StrongNeighbourhood_end()` member functions.

- **SplittingLayer:** This layer offers to generate a splitting based on the previously computed strong neighbourhoods of the nodes/variables. After a call to `computeSplitting()`, the splitting sequence can be traversed by using the `Splitting_begin()` and `Splitting_end()` functions.

  If $i$ is a $C$-variable, then the according entry in the splitting sequence is 1, and 0 otherwise. In other words

  $$\texttt{Splitting\_begin()[i] == 1} \quad \Longleftrightarrow \quad i \in C$$

  and

  $$\texttt{Splitting\_begin()[i] == 0} \quad \Longleftrightarrow \quad i \in F.$$

  With `getCoarseDimension()` the cardinality of $C$ (i.e. the dimension of the coarse system) can be queried.

- **CoarseLevelMappingLayer:** Functionality for computing the mapping beween the fine level and the coarse level varibles is provided in this layer. With `computeCoarseLevelMapping()` the mapping is computed, and `CoarseLevelMapping_begin()` and `CoarseLevelMapping_end()` allow accessing it.

  If $i$ is a $C$-variable, then `CoarseLevelMapping_begin()[i]` gives its index in the next, the coarser level. If else $i$ is an $F$-variable, the value at the $i$-th position is undefined (these variable are to be interpolated through the surrounding $C$-variables).

- **NeighbourhoodStartsPartitionLayer:** Imposes a view on the matrix that restricts the access on a certain interval of rows (or columns, depending on how the matrix is interpreted via the `RowWiseLayer` or the `ColumnWiseLayer`). More precisely, an iterator over a section of the original edge target starts sequence is provided. An existing `NeighbourhoodStartsLayer` with its types is shadowed, its functions overwritten. Thus, using this layer merely makes sense when encapsulating a given matrix with the `EncapsulationLayer`.

- **PartitionLayer:** This layer provides an iterator to a sequence of partitions of a matrix. The `value_type` of this iterator is in turn a full matrix type, providing a row wise / column wise view on a certain part of the matrix. The `NeighbourhoodStartsPartitionLayer` is used to construct this entry type of the sequence.

  The `PartitionLayer` is mainly intended for parallelization in symmetric multiprocessing (SMP) environments with shared memory. On such machines, matrix-vector or matrix-matrix multiplications can be executed in parallel, thereby distributing the tasks associated with multiplying a partition, to an according number of threads.

### 3.3.7   Layers without data storage

Some layers don't need to store any data themself, they are able to offer their functionlity by simply using the appropriate information out of other (previous) layers and combining it in a new way.

#### Layers that purely offer functionality

Since there is no requirement for any data storage, these layers can do without an additional `Member` layer. Therefore, their basic declaration is much easier:

```
──────────────────────── Functionality layer ────────────────────────
template <class Base_>
struct FunctionalityNameLayer
{
  template <class Final_>
  class Type : public Base_::template Type<Final_>
```

```
 {
 public:
   typedef typename Base_::template Type<Final_> BaseType_;
   typedef Type<Final_> Type_;
   typedef FunctionalityName LayerName;
 public:
   Type() : BaseType_() {}
   template <typename Arg_>
   Type(Arg_& arg) : BaseType_(arg) {}
 };
};
```

The majority of layers without own data storage are more or less designed to increase the useability of the type, to offer a more comfortable interface. Included are the following layers:

- EdgeLayer: This layer offers iterators that point to a sequence representing the edges (without weights) of the graph associated with the matrix. The iterator type EdgeIterator has member functions node() and neighbour(), that provide the according neighbourhood information.

- WeightedEdgeLayer: This layer behaves exactly like the EdgeLayer, with additional access to the weights of the edges, available through the operator*() member function of the WeightedEdgeIterator type.

- RowWiseLayer: The row wise layer gives the matrix an orientation. By using this layer, it is defined that the entries are ordered increasingly row by row. A member type Orientation is publicly defined as RowWise and serves as a tag for algorithms that need this information (see e.g. the matrix-matrix multiplication in Section 3.7.2).

  The functions RowWise_begin() and RowWise_end() return iterators of type RowIterator that traverse through the rows of the matrix, and each such iterator in turn has begin() and end() functions that iterate through the current row. We refer to this concept as a two-dimensional iterator.

  Both iterator types, RowIterator and RowIterator::iterator are indexed iterators, i.e. they supply the function index() wich delivers the row number for the first type, respectively the column index for the second type.

  Additionally a type named MajorIterator is defined as RowIterator to ensure that an orientation associated iterator type is defined.

- ColumnWiseLayer: The column wise layer does the same as the row wise layer but with a column wise interpretation of the matrix data. Note that of course in each layer hierarchy only one orientation layer should be used. The MajorIterator type is defined as ColumnIterator

- SourceNodesLayer: The source nodes layer offers nearly the same information as the EdgeLayer, however this time the edges are grouped together by their source node. A two-dimensional iterator is offered like in the RowWiseLayer or ColumnWiseLayer, that provides the edge information without the weight.

- ConsecutiveSourceNodesLayer: This layer does for dense matrices what SourceNodesLayer does for sparse matrices.

- ConsecutiveRowWiseLayer: The row wise orientation layer for dense matrices.

- ConsecutiveColumnWiseLayer: The column wise orientation layer for dense matrices.

- `DiagonalLayer`: The diagonal layer makes use of the slice layer. The `Diagonal_begin()` and `Diagonal_end()` functions return indexed iterators that point to the diagonal entries of the matrix.

- `RandomAccessLayer`: This layer adds a random access function to the matrix type. It is built on top of an orientation layer. The

$$\text{operator()(const size\_type i, const size\_type j)}$$

  function returns a `MajorIterator::iterator` that points to the desired entry if it exists, or to the end of the row/column if it doesn't.

  The reason for the `operator()` function to deliver an iterator is that we would like to have only one common random access interface for each type of matrix, especially for sparse and dense. Since dereferencing the iterator is available at no additional cost, there is no time or space overhead.

  If one is unsure whether the entry exists, one can check if the returned iterator is equal to `RowWise_begin()[i].end()` or `ColumnWise_begin()[j].end()` respectively.

- `AssignmentLayer`: The assignment layer is intended as a pool for gathering functions that allow assignment from various types. Especially the assignment from the matrix expression classes (cf. Section 3.7) is handled here.

  Whenever we want to be able to assign values using the `=` operator, we have to include this layer in our type.

## 3.4   Aggregates

In this section, we would like to lay out our approach to the solution of the constructor problem in mixin based programming.

That there lies a problem, was first mentioned in [SB00]: If a type is constructed with various mixins, it is not a priori clear, how many and which parameters the constructor in a specific mixin class has to take in its definition. Writing constructors for each possible combination of mixins e.g. would increase the code basis more than exponentially.

A solution technique was proposed in [EBC00], using generic parameter classes (implemented as *type lists*), *configuration repositories* and *parameter adapters*. However it still needs a specific order of the parameters in the constructor, which is not evident from the DSL that the generator is provided with. Furthermore it needs configuration structures for every combination of mixins.

We use a different approach with aggregated parameter data structures that are used internally. Parameters for a constructor are then specified in a special call convention, see Sections 3.4.3 and 3.4.4.

### 3.4.1   The parameter aggregate

The purpose for the `Data` aggregate is to store the parameters for the construction of a layered type. The aggregate itself is assembled out of small and simple layers that have accessor functions to get and set variables.

A specific data of type `T`, associated with the tag `DataName`, is stored in the aggregate using the

$$\text{setValue(DataName m, const T\& t\_)}$$

function. The according data is retrieved using the

$$\text{getValue(DataName m)}$$

member function. Function calls concerning data that is not associated with the `DataName` tag are dispatched to the aggregated object b of type `Base`.

```
——————————————————— Data aggregate ———————————————————
template <class Base,
         class DataName,
         class T,
         class SizeType,
         class MemoryClass=Value>
class Data
{
public:
  typedef Base        BaseType;
  typedef T           StoredType;
  typedef DataName    NameType;
  typedef StoredType  MemoryType;
  typedef SizeType    size_type;
  typedef MemoryClass StorageType;
private:
  BaseType b;
  size_type size;
  NameDataTupel<NameType,T> t;
public:
  Data() : size(0) {}
  Data(const Data& d) : b(d.b), size(d.size), t(d.t) {}
  Data(const T& t_, const Base& b_) : b(b_), size(0), t(t_) {}

  void setSize(NameType m, size_type size_) { size = size_; }

  template <class OtherName, class MemberSizeType>
  void setSize(OtherName m, MemberSizeType size_) { b.setSize(m,size_); }

  size_type getSize(NameType m) const { return size; }

  const T& getValue(NameType m) { return t; }

  void setValue(NameType m, const StoredType& t_) { t = t_; }

  template <class MemberNameT, class MemberStoredT>
  void setValue(MemberNameT m, const MemberStoredT& t_) { b.setValue(m, t_); }
};
```

The dispatch for the retrieval of data is a bit more tricky than the setting of the data, since in this case the return type for this function is not known apriori in the current layer. In order to get the correct return type, we have to make use of a template metaprogramming mechanism which we call *stored type lookup*, cf. Section 3.5. The according member functions to retrieve data that is stored in another layer are described there.

This data aggregate can now be arbitrarily assembled to any size and with any type. We need an emtpy type at the top to terminate the structure and to enable `StoredTypeLookup` to determine whether a type is contained in the structure or not.

─────────────────────── Empty type ───────────────────────
```
struct EmptyType {};
```

We also have a specialization for storing pointers, which is especially useful when used as a parameter structure for the construction of objects, since it is cheaper in most cases to copy a pointer than to copy a whole data structure.

At last, we also have `getSequence` and `setSequence` member functions. These can be used instead of `getValue`, if the according layer needs to store a sequence.

### 3.4.2   A simple construction mechanism

As we have seen in Section 3.3.4, every layer that stores data has a definition of a `ParameterType`. An object of a concrete matrix type, e.g. named `MatrixType`, can now be constructed like in the following example.

─────────────── Object construction example 1 ───────────────
```
MatrixType::ParameterType parameter;
parameter.setValue(HorizontalDimension(),5000);
parameter.setValue(VerticalDimension(),10000);
parameter.setSize(NeighbourhoodStarts(),10001);
parameter.setSize(EdgeTargets(),100000);
parameter.setSize(WeightValues(),100000);
MatrixType A(parameter);
```

The above example constructs a rectangular $10000 \times 5000$ sparse matrix with free space for $100000$ nonzero entries, by setting the values of the dimensions and the sizes of the according sequences.

In the next example, we can see, that it is possible through the `setSequence` member functions of Data, to import data out of existing sequences.

─────────────── Object construction example 2 ───────────────
```
DataSequence<size_t,size_t> weights(1000);
DataSequence<size_t,size_t> targets(1000);
DataSequence<double,size_t> starts(101);
MatrixType::ParameterType parameter;
parameter.setValue(HorizontalDimension(),100);
parameter.setValue(VerticalDimension(),100);
parameter.setSequence(NeighbourhoodStarts(),starts);
parameter.setSequence(EdgeTargets(),targets);
parameter.setSequence(WeightValues(),weights);
MatrixType B(parameter);
```

However this way of constructing an object is clumsy and cumbersome for the user of the library. Instantiating a parameter object, initializing it and then creating the actual object is not what we are used in object-oriented programming. In the following, we present an advanced solution which combines aspects from [EBC00] with the above data aggregate.

### 3.4.3   Parameter constructor and adapter classes

Our intention is to supply a construction interface for objects of arbitrary type that allows to specify the initial data in different ways and in any order.

We prescribe the following format for constructor arguments. Every parameter in a constructor call has to be specified as follows:

- a name tag indicating the layer,
- a construction tag specifying the way the data is constructed in the end,
- the parameter itself.

More precisely, the name tag (e.g. `HorizontalDimension()`) acts as an instruction, where to insert the data in the layer hierarchy, and therefore declares the role the parameter plays in the whole data structure. The construction tag, which can be one of the types `Size`, `Value`, `Sequence` indicates the way the object in the `MemberLayer` is constructed. Using `Value` simply copies the parameter object. For sequences, we have the choice of constructing the member by using the size constructor, or, if we have an already constructed sequence, than we indicate with the tag `Sequence`, that we would like to use this extern source of data. The sequence is then either copied or a handle (pointer) to this sequence is stored, depending on how the type was assembled.

This concept is realized with a parameter constructor class and a parameter adapter class, that have generic constructors for up to $n$ parameters ($t1,\ldots,tn$) given by a total of $3n$ arguments.

```
—————————————— Parameter constructor class ——————————————
template <class MatrixType>
class ParameterConstructor
{
public:
  typename MatrixType::DataType p;
  ParameterConstructor() {}
  template <class Name1, class C1, class T1>
  ParameterConstructor(const Name1& n1, const C1& c1, const T1& t1) {
    p.setMember(n1,c1,t1);
  }
  template <class Name1, class C1, class T1,
            class Name2, class C2, class T2>
  ParameterConstructor(const Name1& n1, const C1& c1, const T1& t1,
                       const Name2& n2, const C2& c2, const T2& t2) {
    p.setMember(n1,c1,t1);
    p.setMember(n2,c2,t2);
  }
  template <class Name1, class C1, class T1,
            class Name2, class C2, class T2,
            class Name3, class C3, class T3>
  ParameterConstructor(const Name1& n1, const C1& c1, const T1& t1,
                       const Name2& n2, const C2& c2, const T2& t2,
                       const Name3& n3, const C3& c3, const T3& t3) {
    p.setMember(n1,c1,t1);
    p.setMember(n2,c2,t2);
    p.setMember(n3,c3,t3);
  }
  //...
};
```

A drawback of this approach is that we have to supply $n$ templatized constructors. However these constructors only vary in the number of arguments and can therefore be implemented using macros or other automatic code generation tools. An existing type `Type` can now be decorated with these constructors by defining e.g. `MatrixType` as `ParameterAdapter<MatrixType>`.

```
─────────────────── Parameter adapter class ───────────────────
template <class MatrixType>
class ParameterAdapter : public MatrixType
{
  typedef ParameterConstructor<MatrixType> Parameter;
public:
  template <class Name1, class C1, class T1>
  ParameterAdapter(const Name1& n1, const C1& c1, const T1& t1)
  : MatrixType(Parameter(n1,c1,t1)) {}
  template <class Name1, class C1, class T1,
            class Name2, class C2, class T2>
  ParameterAdapter(const Name1& n1, const C1& c1, const T1& t1,
                   const Name2& n2, const C2& c2, const T2& t2)
  : MatrixType(Parameter(n1,c1,t1,n2,c2,t2)) {}
  template <class Name1, class C1, class T1,
            class Name2, class C2, class T2,
            class Name3, class C3, class T3>
  ParameterAdapter(const Name1& n1, const C1& c1, const T1& t1,
                   const Name2& n2, const C2& c2, const T2& t2,
                   const Name3& n3, const C3& c3, const T3& t3)
  : MatrixType(Parameter(n1,c1,t1,n2,c2,t2,n3,c3,t3)) {}
  //...
};
```

### 3.4.4   Advanced construction mechanism

Now we are able to construct the objects from Section 3.4.2 in the following way:

```
─────────────────── Object construction example 3 ───────────────────
MatrixType A(HorizontalDimension(),Value(),5000,
             VerticalDimension(),Value(),10000,
             NeighbourhoodStarts(),Size(),10001,
             EdgeTargets(),Size(),100000,
             WeightValues(),Size(),100000);
```

Existing data can be used like this:

```
─────────────────── Object construction example 4 ───────────────────
DataSequence<size_t,size_t> weights(1000);
DataSequence<size_t,size_t> targets(1000);
DataSequence<double,size_t> starts(101);
MatrixType B(HorizontalDimension(),Value(),100,
             VerticalDimension(),Value(),100,
             NeighbourhoodStarts(),Sequence(),starts,
             EdgeTargets(),Sequence(),targets,
             WeightValues(),Sequence(),weights);
```

## 3.5 Template Metaprogramming

Metaprogramming with C++ templates (see e.g. [AG04] for an overview) is a powerful method to express and generate types with respect to certain dependencies. It allows certain computations to be carried out already at compile time and even complete instruction flow control structures can be incorporated. That template metaprogramming is possible was first discovered in 1994 by Erwin Unruh with his prime number compile time computation program (see [Unr94] or [VJ03]) during the San Diego Meeting of C++ Standardization.

The possibilities of C++ templates lead to the conclusion that they form a language of its own, and indeed, it was proven, that they are Turing complete ([Vel03]). Nowadays metaprogramming techniques are used more and more in modern C++ libraries, since their compile time evaluation allows more decisions and optimizations by the compiler. In generic programming, template metaprogramming techniques are used for mainly three purposes:

1. choosing or constructing a type in dependence of other types,

2. determining which properties a type has,

3. choosing an appropriate algorithm for a certain type.

In traditional object-oriented design, the first item was impossible at compile time while the latter two issues were treated with run time polymorphism. However as mentioned in Section 2.3.2, this approach often lacks performance. If we use static polymorphism for generic programming, we somehow must retrieve information about the type we are using, e.g. in order to choose a specialized algorithm and its return type.

Those constructs that compute compile-time information are also called *traits*. They can be seen as functions on the template level, which get types or compile-time constants as input parameters and generate types or compile-time constants as output. Since metaprogramming hasn't found its way into the C++ Standard yet, we use our own implementation of simple control structures like `Equal` and `IfElse`. In addition to that, we show how we use metaprogramming to get compile time type information.

### 3.5.1 Conditional structures

In order to realize simple control structure elements, we use the following metaprogramming classes. First of all the `Equal` class struct for checking whether two types are the same:

─────────── Equal template for distinct types ───────────
```
template <class FirstType, class SecondType>
struct Equal {
    static const bool value = false;
};
```

─────────── Equal template for equal types ───────────
```
template <class FirstType>
struct Equal<FirstType,FirstType> {
    static const bool value = true;
};
```

Then we need a construct to choose between (at last two) types, depending upon a condition (a boolean value). This is implemented with the `IfElse` class struct:

─────────────── If-then-else construct for true condition ───────────────

```
template <bool condition, class FirstType, class SecondType>
struct IfElse {
    typedef FirstType type;
};
```

─────────────── If-then-else construct for false condition ───────────────

```
template <class FirstType, class SecondType>
struct IfElse<false,FirstType,SecondType> {
    typedef SecondType type;
};
```

These constructs are used throughout the whole library for compile-time decisions.

### 3.5.2   Stored type lookup

Looking back at Section 3.4.1, we were faced with the problem to determine the return type of the get member functions. Here, we present the type lookup mechanism of the aggregate, that solves this problem.

Each Data layer class must export at least the types BaseType, MemoryType, NameType and size_type, then the StoredTypeLookup struct recursively ascends the encapsulated data layers until it matches the desired NameType. Then the member types memory_type, size_type and storage_type are defined.

─────────────── Stored type lookup ───────────────

```
template <class T, class NameType>
struct StoredTypeLookup
{
  typedef typename
  IfElse<Equal<typename T::NameType,NameType>::value,
         typename T::MemoryType,
         typename StoredTypeLookup<typename T::BaseType,
                                   NameType>::memory_type>::type
  memory_type;

  typedef typename
  IfElse<Equal<typename T::NameType,NameType>::value,
         typename T::size_type,
         typename StoredTypeLookup<typename T::BaseType,
                                   NameType>::size_type>::type
  size_type;

  typedef typename
  IfElse<Equal<typename T::NameType,NameType>::value,
         typename T::StorageType,
         typename StoredTypeLookup<typename T::BaseType,
                                   NameType>::storage_type>::type
  storage_type;
};
```

If NameType is not found in the whole data aggregate, the StoredTypeLookup is at the top of the hierarchy, and so we have a specialization for EmptyType (see Section 3.4.1) which defines the three member types as ErrorType. Trying to get (or set) values in the data aggregate that are associated with a NameType that is not contained in the aggegate leads to a compile time error.

──────────────── Stored type lookup for empty type ────────────────
```cpp
template <class NameType>
struct StoredTypeLookup<EmptyType,NameType>
{
  typedef ErrorType size_type;
  typedef ErrorType memory_type;
  typedef ErrorType storage_type;
};
```

The according **get** member functions now can use the type lookup to resolve the correct return type. All these lookups are done during the compilation time, so they don't increase the runtime of the program.

──────────────── Data aggregate get functions ────────────────
```cpp
template <class OtherName>
typename StoredTypeLookup<Data,OtherName>::size_type
getSize(OtherName m) const
{
  return b.getSize(m);
}
template <class OtherName>
typename StoredTypeLookup<Data,OtherName>::memory_type
getValue(OtherName m)
{
  return b.getValue(m);
}
};
```

### 3.5.3 Layer and layer config lookup

Sometimes, when we are dealing with a layered type, it can be useful to know which layers the type consist of, or at least, if a certain layer is included. If we know, that any type T is assembled using a layer L (maybe among others), then we know that T has the functionality implemented in L. The construct that was devised for this purpose is called LayerLookup:

──────────────── Layer lookup ────────────────
```cpp
template <class MatrixType, class Layer>
struct LayerLookup
{
  typedef typename
  IfElse<Equal<typename MatrixType::LayerName,Layer>::value,
         MatrixType::LayerName,
         typename LayerLookup<typename MatrixType::BaseLayer,
                              Layer>::type>::type type;
};
```

To terminate the structure we need a specialization for the empty type. Algorithms can now check in advance, if a layer is included. If not, the return type is `ErrorType`, otherwise the layer name type is returned.

```
———————————— Layer lookup for empty type ————————————
template <class Layer>
struct LayerLookup<EmptyType,Layer>
{
  typedef ErrorType type;
};
```

In certain situations, it is desirable to directly have access to the according layer config structs, that the type was built of, e.g. in the product matrix type generator (see Section 3.7.4). Especially, if the struct is a `FixedConfig`, one is interested to gain access to the encapsulated fixed constant.

The `LayerConfigLookup` seeks the `Layer` tag in the whole given `MatrixType` using the `LayerLookup` trait, and, if it exists, exports the according `LayerConfig` type in the member type `Config`. Otherwise, `ErrorType` is exported.

```
———————————— Layer config lookup ————————————
template <class MatrixType, class Layer>
struct LayerConfigLookup
{
  typedef typename LayerLookup<MatrixType,Layer>::layer HasLayer;
  typedef typename IfElse<Equal<HasLayer,ErrorType>::value,
                          ErrorType,
                          typename HasLayer::LayerConfig>::type Config;
};
```

### 3.5.4  Various matrix traits

For determining whether a certain matrix type is sparse (or dense or fixed), we need according compile-time functions that deliver the desired information.

To test if a type is a dense matrix (i.e. has its entries stored consecutively) we simply look up whether it contains the `DenseWeightedEdgeSources` layer.

```
———————————— IsDense trait ————————————
template <class MatrixType>
struct IsDense
{
  static const bool value =
  Equal<typename LayerLookup<MatrixType,
                             DenseWeightedEdgeSources>::type,
        DenseWeightedEdgeSources>::value;
};
```

For determining if a type is a fixed (dense) matrix, we have to take a closer look at the data categories of its layers.

```
─────────────────────────── IsFixed trait ───────────────────────────
template <class MatrixType>
struct IsFixed
{
  typedef typename LayerLookup<MatrixType,FirstTargets>::type
        HasFirstTargets;
  typedef typename LayerLookup<MatrixType,NeighbourhoodStarts>::type
        HasNeighbourhoodStarts;
  typedef typename FirstTargetsDataCategory<MatrixType,
                                        HasFirstTargets>::type
        HasFirstTargetssDataCategory;
  typedef typename NeighbourhoodStartsDataCategory<MatrixType,
                                        HasNeighbourhoodStarts>::type
        HasNeighbourhoodStartsDataCategory;
  typedef typename NeighbourhoodStartsFunctorCategory<MatrixType,
                               HasNeighbourhoodStartsDataCategory>::type
        HasNeighbourhoodStartsFunctorCategory;

  static const bool value =
  Equal<HasFirstTargetssDataCategory,fixed_tag>::value
        && (Equal<HasNeighbourhoodStartsDataCategory,functor_tag>::value
            || Equal<HasNeighbourhoodStartsDataCategory,static_tag>::value)
        && Equal<HasNeighbourhoodStartsFunctorCategory,fixed_linear_tag>::value;
};
```

### 3.5.5  Matrix expression chooser

The matrix expression chooser is a construct that determines the return type for product, sum and
difference expressions (in arbitrary combinations). The matrix expressions are explained in more detail in Section 3.7.

```
─────────────────── Matrix expression chooser ───────────────────

template <class Left,
         class Right,
         template <class,class,class> class SparseExpression,
         template <class,class,class> class DenseExpression,
         template <class,class,class,class> class SparseFunctor_,
         template <class,class,class,class> class DenseFunctor_,
         template <class,class,class,class> class FixedFunctor_>
struct MatrixExpressionChooser
{
  typedef typename Left::Orientation Orientation;
  typedef typename Left::WeightMemoryType WeightMemoryType;
  typedef FixedFunctor_<Left,Right,Orientation,WeightMemoryType>  FixedFunctor;
  typedef DenseFunctor_<Left,Right,Orientation,WeightMemoryType>  DenseFunctor;
  typedef SparseFunctor_<Left,Right,Orientation,WeightMemoryType> SparseFunctor;
  typedef DenseExpression<Left,
                          FixedFunctor,
                          Right> FixedResultExpression;
  typedef DenseExpression<Left,
```

```
                                  DenseFunctor,
                                  Right> DenseResultExpression;
      typedef SparseExpression<Left,
                               SparseFunctor,
                               Right> SparseResultExpression;
      typedef typename IfElse<IsDense<Left>::value && IsDense<Right>::value,
                              typename IfElse<IsFixed<Left>::value
                                              && IsFixed<Right>::value,
                                              FixedResultExpression,
                                              DenseResultExpression
                                              >::type,
                              typename IfElse<IsDense<Right>::value,
                                              DenseResultExpression,
                                              typename IfElse<IsDense<Left>::value,
                                                              DenseResultExpression,
                                                              SparseResultExpression
                                                              >::type
                                              >::type
                              >::type type;
    };
```

## 3.6 Type construction and generators

The intention of programming with layers is to offer a greater flexibility for the user of data structures, to avoid the redundancy of code (as well as that of computer memory) and to always have the most efficient implementation for a special purpose.

However, for users that are not familiar with mixin layers and the special concept of layer assembly it might be cumbersome to construct the type they want to use.

For this reason, we would like to have a *type generator*, that can automatically assemble a desired type. Before we introduce this template metaprogramming construct, we would like to describe how types are assembled manually.

### 3.6.1 Rules of type construction

The type construction underlies certain rules and restrictions, since not every layer combination makes sense, although it would be technically possible. In the following, we would like to give an outline of these rules and implications.

**Rules concerning the order of assembly**

Besides starting with the Base layer, we have the following precedence rules:

- First of all it should be stated, that the dimension layers are so essential that they should be included immediately after the Base layer. Which dimension layer comes first is however unimportant.

- NeighbourhoodStartsLayer, EdgeTargetsLayer, WeightValuesLayer and FirstTargetsLayer contain the basic data of a matrix type and should be used directly after the dimension layers. In any case, they *must* be used prior to any of the other layers, since they usually depend on the data provided here.

- The EdgeLayer requires the NeighbourhoodStartsLayer and the EdgeTargetsLayer.

- The `WeightedEdgeLayer` requires the `NeighbourhoodStartsLayer`, the `EdgeTargetsLayer` and the `WeightValuesLayer`.

- The (sparse) `SourceNodesLayer` requires the `NeighbourhoodStartsLayer` and the `EdgeTargetsLayer`.

- The (sparse) `RowWiseLayer` and `ColumnWiseLayer` require the `NeighbourhoodStartsLayer`, the `EdgeTargetsLayer` and the `WeightValuesLayer`.

- The `ConsecutiveSourceNodesLayer` requires the `NeighbourhoodStartsLayer` and the `FirstTargetsLayer`.

- The `ConsecutiveRowWiseLayer` and `ConsecutiveColumnWiseLayer` require the `NeighbourhoodStartsLayer`, the `FirstTargetsLayer` and the `WeightValuesLayer`.

- The `RandomAccessLayer` requires exactly one of `RowWiseLayer`, `ColumnWiseLayer`, `ConsecutiveRowWiseLayer` or `ConsecutiveColumnWiseLayer`.

- The `SliceLayer` syntactically doesn't need any other layer although its data refer to the weighted edges stored in the `WeightValuesLayer`.

- The `DiagonalLayer` needs the `SliceLayer`.

**Rules concerning the combination of layers**

- The `FirstTargetsLayer` and the `EdgeTargetsLayers` must be used mutually exclusive. The edge targets sequence only makes sense for matrices, where the edge targets numbering is not consecutive (a matrix with this property is usually called sparse).

- Also, when adding an orientation to the matrix type, one has to choose between either the `RowWiseLayer` or the `ColumnWiseLayer`. Using both, (although technically possible) would lead to overwriting and shadowing the types (and functions) of the first layer by the second layer in the hierarchy, disabling the first layer's functionality.

- Accordingly, the `ConsecutiveRowWiseLayer` and the `ConsecutiveColumnWiseLayer` are mutually exclusive.

- Of course, the layers designed for sparse matrices don't make any sense in a dense matrix type, and vice versa.

### 3.6.2 Type examples

In order to illustrate the rules of the type construction, we give a few example types. First, a simple sparse matrix that offer a row wise access to its data.

```
──────────────── Sparse matrix type ────────────────
typedef DataSequence<unsigned int,unsigned int>    IVT;
typedef DataSequence<double,unsigned int>          WVT;

typedef NormalConfig<unsigned int,Value>           DimConfig;
typedef NormalConfig<IVT,Value>                    IndexConfig;
typedef WeightConfig<WVT,Value,Value>              WeightValuesConfig;

typedef VerticalDimensionLayer<Base,DimConfig>       VDLayer;
typedef HorizontalDimensionLayer<VDLayer,DimConfig>  DLayer;
typedef NeighbourhoodStartsLayer<DLayer,IndexConfig> ETSLayer;
```

```
typedef EdgeTargetsLayer<ETSLayer,IndexConfig>        ETLayer;
typedef WeightValuesLayer<ETLayer,WeightValuesConfig> WVLayer;
typedef RowWiseLayer<WVLayer>                         RWLayer;
typedef Final<RWLayer>::Type                          RowWiseSparseMatrix;
```

Now we show, how a row wise oriented dense matrix type with random access can be assembled.

```
―――――――――――――― Dense matrix type ――――――――――――――
typedef FunctionSequence<linear<unsigned int,unsigned int> > LST;
typedef FixedValueSequence<unsigned int,unsigned int,0>      FST;
typedef DataSequence<double,unsigned int>                    WVT;

typedef NormalConfig<unsigned int,Value>              DimConfig;
typedef NormalConfig<LST,Value>                       LinearConfig;
typedef NormalConfig<FST,Value>                       FirstZeroConfig;
typedef WeightConfig<WVT,Value,Value>                 WeightValuesConfig;

typedef VerticalDimensionLayer<Base,DimConfig>               VDLayer;
typedef HorizontalDimensionLayer<VDLayer,DimConfig>          DLayer;
typedef NeighbourhoodStartsLayer<DLayer,LinearConfig>        DenseETSLayer;
typedef FirstTargetsLayer<DenseETSLayer,FirstZeroConfig>     DenseFTLayer;
typedef WeightValuesLayer<DenseFTLayer,WeightValuesConfig>   DenseWVLayer;
typedef ConsecutiveSourcesNodesLayer<DenseWVLayer>           DenseSNLayer;
typedef ConsecutiveRowWiseLayer<DenseSNLayer>                DenseRWLayer;
typedef RandomAccessLayer<DenseRWLayer>                      DenseRALayer;
typedef Final<DenseRALayer>::Type                            DenseMatrix;
```

Such a type as the above assembled dense matrix type is reasonable, if we don't know the size of the matrix at compile time (i.e. we would like to be able to change it at run time). In the other case, if the matrix size is completely fixed at compile time, we would have wasted memory for the edge target starts and first target sequences and the dimensions for each object. Especially when storing large amounts of such objects this would lead to a great memory overhead.

A solution is again closely related to the singleton design pattern (cf. [GHJV94]). Those properties that are common to all objects of a type should also be instantiated only once. This is achieved by declaring the according data as static (see also the treatment of fixed values in Section 3.3.3).

As an example, we want to construct a $3 \times 3$ dense matrix type. First, we replace the type DataSequence with FixedLengthDataSequence, leaving the rest unchanged:

```
―――――――――― A fixed length for the weight values sequence ――――――――――
#define DIM 3
typedef FixedLengthDataSequence<double,unsigned int,DIM*DIM>  WVT;
```

We do this in order to have all the data "owned" by an object of the according type. The DataSequence type only includes a size variable and a pointer to a memory block on the heap. This however could turn out badly when applying an algorithm to a very long sequence of such matrix objects. An example for this kind of algorithm is the matrix-vector multiplication for block matrices as they appear in Chapter 9. The DataSequence type then requires not only to store the pure matrix entries (in this case 9 doubles) but also a pointer.

Furthermore, dereferencing this pointer would lead to an address somewhere in the heap, not necessarily directly after the preceding matrix object. In other words, we would have a fragmented memory that e.g. wouldn't benefit from the pipelining techniques of modern microprocessors, and it would mislead any caching strategy.

Another advantageous side effect is that the default constructor of `FixedLengthDataSequence` already constructs the object with the correct size, which is extremely comfortable when allocating an array of such objects. When determining the size in bytes of this data type, with e.g.

```
int main(void) {
  cout << "sizeof(double)      : " << sizeof(double)      << endl;
  cout << "sizeof(WVT)         : " << sizeof(WVT)         << endl;
  cout << "sizeof(DenseMatrix) : " << sizeof(DenseMatrix) << endl;
}
```

we get the output

```
sizeof(double)      : 8
sizeof(WVT)         : 72
sizeof(DenseMatrix) : 92
```

on a Linux 32 bit Pentium 4 machine. Now we aim to reduce the size of the dense matrix type to the size of the pure data array `WVT` which is 9 times the size of a double precision floating point variable. We use the following defnitions:

```
———————————————— Fixed size matrix type ————————————————
typedef FixedLengthStaticFunctionSequence<fixed_linear<unsigned int,
                                           unsigned int,
                                           unsigned int,
                                           DIM>,unsigned
                                           int,DIM+1> > FLST;
typedef FixedValueFixedLengthSequence<unsigned int,
                           unsigned int,0,DIM> FZST;

typedef FixedConfig<unsigned int,DIM>             FDimConfig;
typedef NormalConfig<FLST,Static>                 FLinearConfig;
typedef NormalConfig<FZST,Static>                 FFirstZeroConfig;
typedef WeightConfig<WVT,Value,Value>             FLengthValueConfig;

typedef VerticalDimensionLayer<Base,FDimConfig>                  FixedVDLayer;
typedef HorizontalDimensionLayer<FixedVDLayer,FDimConfig>        FixedDLayer;
typedef NeighbourhoodStartsLayer<FixedDLayer,FLinearConfig>      FixedETSLayer;
typedef FirstTargetsLayer<FixedETSLayer,FFirstZeroConfig>        FixedFTLayer;
typedef WeightValuesLayer<FixedFTLayer,FLengthValueConfig>       FixedWVLayer;
typedef ConsecutiveSourcesNodesLayer<FixedWVLayer>               FixedSNLayer;
typedef ConsecutiveRowWiseLayer<FixedSNLayer>                    FixedRWLayer;
typedef RandomAccessLayer<FixedWESLayer>                         FixedRALayer;
typedef Final<FixedRALayer>::Type                                FixedMatrix;
```

Now this `FixedMatrix` type has the desired property, and an according program yields:

---

```
sizeof(FixedMatrix) : 72
```

---

Specifying sizes at compile time also has other advantages. Generic algorithms can determine (with traits – see Section 3.5 – at compile-time!) which data structure they have have to deal with and then dispatch a specialized variant of the algorithm (see e.g. Section 3.7.3).

### 3.6.3   A simple type generator

As we have seen in the previous examples, for constructing a type, it is necessary to

- define appropriate sequences,

- define appropriate config structs,

- and pass the config structs to the according layers and assemble them in the correct order.

This might seem as a circuituos way to gain a type, however, since we have so many possible combinations, we must somehow offer this functionality to the user. The philosophy is not so much

"The required sequences are a consequence of the properties of the desired type."

but rather

"The resulting type is a consequence of the utilized sequences."

Therefore, at the moment, we only supply a low level type generator, that merely relieves the user of caring about the order of assemby.

```
━━━━━━━━━━━━━━━━━━ Low level matrix type generator ━━━━━━━━━
template <class VerticalDimensionConfig,        //  1.
         class HorizontalDimensionConfig,       //  2.
         class NeighbourhoodStartsConfig,       //  3.
         class FirstTargetsConfig,              //  4.
         class EdgeTargetsConfig,               //  5.
         class EdgeConfig,                      //  6.
         class WeightValuesConfig,              //  7.
         class WeightedEdgeConfig,              //  8.
         class ConsecutiveSourceNodesConfig,    //  9.
         class ConsecutiveRowWiseConfig,        // 10.
         class ConsecutiveColumnWiseConfig,     // 11.
         class SourceNodesConfig,               // 12.
         class RowWiseConfig,                   // 13.
         class ColumnWiseConfig,                // 14.
         class RandomAccessConfig,              // 15.
         class AssignmentConfig>                // 16.
struct LowLevelMatrixGenerator
{
  typedef Base Layer0;
  //...
  typedef typename Final<Layer16>::Type type;
};
```

The typedef's in between have the form

```
typedef typename IfElse<Equal<LayerNameConfig,EmptyType>::value,
                        Layern,
                        LayerNameLayer<Layern,LayerNameConfig> >::type Layern+1;
```

if the layer *LayerName* has an own storage, and

```
typedef typename IfElse<Equal<LayerNameConfig,EmptyType>::value,
                        Layern,
                        LayerNameLayer<Layern> >::type Layern+1;
```

if it doesn't store own data. The syntactic usage of the generator is based on specifying the config structs, for the layers we want to include, as template arguments. If a template parameter is equal to EmptyType, the according layer is not inluded.

This generator is intended to offer the greatest flexibility for the type construction. For a more user-friendly type generation, one can add specialized generators, e.g. a sparse matrix type generator, a dense matrix type generator etc.

For the gcc 3.4.1 however, we experienced problems when using the above generator for block matrix types. The generator was used to build a dense matrix type with fixed dimensions, and this type was used as an entry type for generating a block sparse matrix. The latter however failed, the compiler crashed. Since increasing the maximum instantiation depth for template classes with the switch -ftemplate-depth-n also didn't fix the problem, we used the manual type construction from Section 3.6.2 as a workaround in this case.

## 3.7 Expression templates for matrix types

Originally invented for efficiently evaluating arbitrary vector expressions, we use an expression template technique for computing (sparse) matrix expressions like

$$A = B \cdot C \cdot D + E \cdot F - G, \tag{3.1}$$

with $B \in \mathbb{R}^{k \times l}$, $C \in \mathbb{R}^{l \times m}$, $D \in \mathbb{R}^{m \times n}$, $E \in \mathbb{R}^{k \times j}$, $F \in \mathbb{R}^{j \times n}$, and $G \in \mathbb{R}^{k \times n}$ being arbitrary (not necessarily quadratic) matrices.

The need for these type of matrix expressions arise in at least 3 places in our library:

1. The coarse level matrices $A_{l+1}$ have to be computed via the Galerkin product, see also formula (5.16): $A_{l+1} = R_l A_l P_l$.

2. For matrices like

$$F = \begin{pmatrix} A & B^T \\ B & C \end{pmatrix}$$

we would like to be able to easily compute[1] the Schur complement $S = BAB^T - C$.

3. Generally, we would like to be able to calculate a block matrix product $AB$,

$$A = \begin{pmatrix} A_{11} & \cdots & A_{1n} \\ \vdots & \ddots & \vdots \\ A_{m1} & \cdots & A_{mn} \end{pmatrix}, B = \begin{pmatrix} B_{11} & \cdots & B_{1k} \\ \vdots & \ddots & \vdots \\ B_{n1} & \cdots & B_{nk} \end{pmatrix},$$

where $A_{ij}$ and $B_{ij}$ are again matrices. In this case, the matrix-matrix multiplication algorithm needs a += operator.

---

[1]For many methods like Uzawa or pressure correction schemes, usually the Schur complement is not explicitly computed, because Krylov methods don't need the matrix to be explicitly available. Instead, it is sufficient to be able to compute the *effect* of the four matrices $B$, $A$,$B^T$, and $C$, applied to a vector. However this approach makes it impossible to apply a standard preconditioning method, nor does it allow an algebraic multigrid method. Therefore, it might be desirable to compute $S$ explicitly.

### 3.7.1   Sparse matrix expression templates concept

The problem with (sparse) matrix expressions like (3.1) is that we *have* to compute intermediate results like $CD$ before we can compute $B(CD)$ and we *have* to compute $EF$ before we can compute $EF + G$ etc. However, these temporary matrices can be much bigger (if $m \gg n$) or much smaller (if $m \ll n$) than the result matrix $A$.

What comes more is, that for a sparse matrix-matrix multiplication we don't know about the sparsity structure of the result matrix in advance. Thus for evaluating an expression like (3.1) we can't provide one object in the beginning that can hold all temporary results in between. This of course, is a major drawback, because it is one main idea behind expression templates. Against this have have no remedy, since it is mathematically unavoidable to compute the auxiliary results.

Allocating enough memory in advance turns out to be difficult. If too generously, it may result in waste of memory, or, if too tight, lead to frequent reallocating, which decreases the performance.

But there is no need to construct a complete matrix object for all these matrices in between. Instead we build a `MatrixExpression` object, which holds the sparsity structure and the values of the result, which may be a sum, a difference or a product of two matrices.

The distinction between a `MatrixExpression` object and a normal matrix object is that the former uses its own data structures independently of the implementation of the matrix objects's class. More precisely, it contains an vector of STL maps, which are nothing but (weighted) *red-black trees* (see also Section 5.3.2). This vector is used to store the result row entries and the according column indices. In the $n$-the component of this vector the $n$-the row of the result matrix is stored.

A (sparse) matrix object usually stores its data in a compressed format like the CRS (see Subsection 2.5.2), with three arrays containing all the matrix data (cf. Table 2.1).

However the (sparse) matrix-matrix multiplication routine implemented in our library doesn't immediately compute the complete CRS for the matrix product, since this would require the computation of the sparsity pattern in advance before applying the actual numeric operations. This would result not only in memory overhead, but also in several loops over the same data for each matrix-matrix product, which should be avoided. Instead the sparsity pattern and the matrix entries are computed on the fly and then stored in the maps. Several numerical experiments seem to support that this approach is beneficial.

Furthermore, we dispense with the allocation of memory for the intermediate matrix objects and copying data to them. We only work with the temporary data structures the `MatrixExpression` class provides. This has at least two benefits: We save at least *some* unnecessary memory alloctations and copying, and of course we have the possibility to write aribtrary long matrix expressions in a simple notation. Only at the end, when the whole matrix expression is evaluated, the resulting data is copied into the result matrix object, which is responsible of the appropriate copying/conversion method.

However, for the time being, the user is responsible for determining an appropriate result type. For sparse matrices, this is rather uncritical, since in the rare cases, where two sparse matrices are multiplied, it is sufficient to have one standard sparse result type. However, there may be cases, where the resulting matrix type differs from the participating types of the two factors. For example, when one type is sparse an the other is dense, or when multiplying two rectangular matrices with fixed dimension.

Thus, the optimal solution would be a general product matrix type generator, however, at the current state of development, the library offers no such general solution to this problem. Instead we do the following:

- If both factors are sparse (i.e. contain an `EdgeTargetsLayer`), we suggest to use again a standard (row-wise) sparse matrix.

- If one factor is sparse and the other is not (i.e. has a `FirstTargetsLayer`). This is a very rare case, however if it occurs, the resulting sparse matrix structure would be dense in most cases. However, in general, this is unpredictable, thus we have left this decision to the user.

- For expression of two dense matrix types, we have incorporated a product matrix type generator, that generates an appropriate product matrix type for most type combinations (see Section 3.7.4).

If we write a code like:

```
MatrixType A,B,C,D,E,F;
...
A = B*C*D + E*F - G;
```

the expression tree shown in Figure 3.7 will be built by the operators -, + and *. It will be evaluated when the = operator (a member of the `MatrixType` class) is called. The `compute()` method of the `MatrixExpression` object on the right side of the = sign is called and the expression tree is traversed from its root to its leaves, descending first to the right and then to the left (this is a pure and arbitrary implementation decision, of course it could have been done also first to the left and then to the right). If the algorithm descend to a leaf, nothing is done, if it descends to an operator `op`, the result of the expression 'left child op right child' is computed.

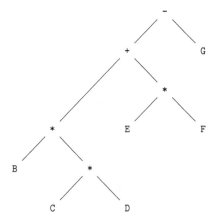

Figure 3.7: Expression tree

## 3.7.2 Participating classes and operators

### The `MatrixExpression` class

First and foremost, we have the `MatrixExpression` class, that is intended to represent the matrix expressions.

──────────── Matrix expression class ────────────
```
template <class Left, class Op, class Right>
class MatrixExpression
{
public:
    typedef typename Left::VerticalDimensionType VerticalDimensionType;
    typedef typename Right::HorizontalDimensionType HorizontalDimensionType;
    typedef RowWise  Orientation;
```

```
    typedef typename Left::index_type index_type;
    typedef typename Right::value_type value_type;
    typedef typename Right::WeightMemoryType WeightMemoryType;
private:
    typedef typename vector<map<index_type,value_type> > TmpWeightValuesContainer;
    typedef typename TmpWeightValuesContainer::iterator
                     TmpWeightValuesIterator;
public:
    typedef typename
      two_dim_map_indexed_iterator_adapter<TmpWeightValuesIterator> RowIterator;
private:
    Left&  left;
    Right& right;
    bool   computed;
    bool   providememory;
    TmpWeightValuesContainer* tmpvalues;
public:
    MatrixExpression(Left& l, Right& r)
    : left(l), right(r), computed(false), providememory(false), tmpvalues(0)
    {}
};
```

Within this class, the public types were defined in order to ensure that `MatrixExpression` can behave like a normal matrix class. Note that `MatrixExpression` is yet only designed to hold results which are row wise oriented.

The class stores references to the two involved operands of type `Left` and `Right`. The member `TmpWeightValuesContainer` is a pointer to the temporary data structure mentioned in Section 3.7.1.

If the stored values in the matrix type are not pointers, then the normal procedure would be the following: the = assignment operator of the matrix class calls the `compute()` function of the `MatrixExpression` class. This in turn computes the expression from the leaves of the expression tree recursively to its root. Then the values are copied from the root expression object by using the member functions `TmpWeightValues_begin()` and `TmpWeightValues_end()`. Thereafter, the `deleteTmp()` member function is called and frees the allocated memory for the temporary expression(s).

| return type | function name |
|---|---|
| void | compute() |
| void | deleteTmp() |
| void | useMemory() |
| TmpWeightValuesIterator | TmpWeightValues_begin() const |
| TmpWeightValuesIterator | TmpWeightValues_end() const |
| Left::VerticalDimensionType | verticalDimension() const |
| Right::HorizontalDimensionType | horizontalDimension() const |
| RowIterator | Row_begin() const |
| RowIterator | Row_end() const |

Table 3.1: Member functions of class `MatrixExpression`

The boolean variable `providememory` is only of interest when computing expressions with block matrices, or more precisely, if the `WeightMemoryType` is of type `Pointer`. If the member function `useMemory()` is called, `providememory` is set to true. This has the consequence that (in the *root* expression object) the allocated memory to which the pointers in the vectors of `TmpWeightValuesContainer` point to, won't be destroyed by the `deleteTmp()` function. The reason for this mechanism is that in this case, there is no need to physically copy the already allocated submatrices from the root expression object into the result matrix object. Instead, only the pointers are copied.

In addition to the publicly defined types, the member functions `Row_begin()`, `Row_end()`, `vertical-Dimension()`, and `horizontalDimension()`, were defined in order to provide a matrix interface to the involved operator given by the class `Op`. Table 3.1 gives a summary of the publicly provided member functions.

#### The `matrix_product` functor structure

The `matrix_product` structure acts as a functor that is given to the `MatrixExpression` class by the '`*`' operator.

```
──────────────── Matrix product functor ────────────────
template <class Matrix1Type, class Matrix2Type,
         class Orientation, class WeightMemoryType>
struct matrix_product
{
  template<class RowIterator>
  static void computeResult(Matrix1Type& A, Matrix2Type& B, RowIterator it)
  {
    matrix_product(A.Row_begin(), A.Row_end(),
               B.Row_begin(), it, WeightMemoryType());
  }
};
```

The `matrix_product` functor, as well as the `matrix_sum` and the `matrix_difference` functor solely has the static member function `computeResult`. It calls the template function `matrix_product`, that computes the sparse structure of the product and the new matrix entries on the fly by storing them in the according vector of STL maps (the auxiliary `*tmpvalues` in `MatrixExpression`).

In this default version, the functor implements a sparse matrix-matrix multiplication in which the two operands are *row wise* oriented. If at least one operand is oriented *column wise*, we need a specialization. Any combination of column wise and row wise oriented matrices would require an own specialization with an own algorithm, since the direction of traversal through the matrix is different each time. Thus, not all combinations are yet implemented. Table 3.2 gives an overview of the implemented algorithms.

|  | 2. operand row wise | 2. operand column wise |
|---|---|---|
| 1. operand row wise | implemented | not implemented |
| 1. operand column wise | implemented | not implemented |

Table 3.2: Implemented combinations of sparse matrix-matrix multiplication

The specialization for the variant with the first operand being column wise oriented is declared as:

```
──────────────── Matrix product functor ────────────────
template <class Matrix1Type, class Matrix2Type, class WeightMemoryType>
struct matrix_product<Matrix1Type,Matrix2Type,
                 ColumnWise,WeightMemoryType> {
  //...
};
```

The `transposed_matrix_product` template function is used instead to calculate the result within this implemenation.

### The `matrix_sum` functor structure

The `matrix_sum` structure is a functor that is given to the `MatrixExpression` class by the + operator.

```
─────────────── Matrix sum functor ───────────────
template <class Matrix1Type, class Matrix2Type,
         class Orientation, class WeightMemoryType>
struct matrix_sum {
  //...
}
```

The `generateResultStructure` member function uses the `generateMatrixSumPositions` template function to compute the sparsity pattern of the matrix sum A+B. The template function `matrix_sum` then computes the actual values of the sum and is used by the `computeResult` member function.

Again, we have restricted the implemented combinations of the row wise/column wise algorithms, see Table 3.3.

|  | 2. operand row wise | 2. operand column wise |
|---|---|---|
| 1. operand row wise | implemented | not implemented |
| 1. operand column wise | not implemented | partly implemented |

Table 3.3: Implemented combinations of sparse matrix-matrix addition

Note that the column wise/column wise matrix addition algorithm is the same as the row wise/row wise version. However, since the `MatrixExpression` class up to now only supports row wise result matrices, there would have to be at least a conversion routine from column wise to row wise somewhere in the functor structure or in the `MatrixExpression` class.

The `matrix_sum` template function makes use of a template metaprogramming technique. Its declaration looks like the following.

```
─────────────── Matrix sum function template ───────────────
template <class M1Iterator, class M2Iterator, class M3Iterator,
         class WeightMemoryType, class Positive2ndOperand>
inline void matrix_sum(M1Iterator matrix1_begin,
                       M1Iterator matrix1_end,
                       M2Iterator matrix2_begin,
                       M3Iterator matrix3_begin,
                       WeightMemoryType wt,
                       Positive2ndOperand positivesecond);
```

Depending now on the type of `Positive2ndOperand` respectively the `positivesecond` parameter it chooses different helper functions inside the function body. If `Positive2ndOperand` is of type `True`, then an addition is performed (by calling functions that do an addition of two values or assign a positive value). The function call looks like this:

```
───────────── Call from matrix sum functor ─────────────
matrix_sum(A.Row_begin(), A.Row_end(), B.Row_begin(), cit,
          WeightMemoryType(), True());
```

If `Positive2ndOperand` is of type `False`, then the 2nd operand is formally negated and a subtraction is performed (by calling functions that do a subtraction of two values or assign a negative value). Now since the type of `positivesecond` is known at compile time, the according functions can be inlined and optimized by the compiler.

#### The `matrix_difference` functor structure

The `matrix_difference` structure is a functor that is given to the `MatrixExpression` class by the - operator.

```
───────────── Matrix difference functor ─────────────
template <class Matrix1Type, class Matrix2Type,
         class Orientation, class WeightMemoryType>
struct matrix_difference
{
  //...
}
```

Here we can reuse the `generateMatrixSumPositions` template function for computing the sparsity pattern of the matrix difference since it is the same as for the sum.

The `computeResult` member function uses the `matrix_sum` template function as described above. It is called by

```
───────────── Call from matrix difference functor ─────────────
matrix_sum(A.Row_begin(), A.Row_end(), B.Row_begin(), cit,
          WeightMemoryType(), False());
```

The table of implemented row wise/column wise combinations is the same as for the `matrix_sum` functor.

#### The operators +, - and *

The operators +, - and * are implemented as template functions. Their purpose is to instantiate an object of the class `MatrixExpression` with the according template arguments for the left and right operand type and the operator type.

At this point we have to take care of the possible combinations of types that can instantiate a binary expression. Let op be an arbitrary operator type, `MatrixType1` and `MatrixType2` some arbitrary matrix types, and `MatrixExpression1` and `MatrixExpression2` some arbitrary expression types then there are the possibilities

- `MatrixType1 op MatrixType2`

- `MatrixExpression1 op MatrixType2`

- `MatrixType1 op MatrixExpression2`

- `MatrixExpression1 op MatrixExpression2`

For the * operator and the third possibility e.g., the implementation looks like this:

```
_____ The operator* for MatrixType * MatrixExpression _____
template <class Left, class Op, class Right, class RightRight>
MatrixExpression<Left,
                 matrix_product<Left,
                                MatrixExpression<Right,Op,RightRight>,
                                typename Left::Orientation,
                                typename Left::WeightMemoryType>,
                 MatrixExpression<Right,Op,RightRight> >
operator*(Left& A, MatrixExpression<Right,Op,RightRight> B)
{
  typedef typename Left::Orientation Orientation;
  typedef typename Left::WeightMemoryType WeightMemoryType;
  return MatrixExpression<Left,
                          matrix_product<Left,
                                         MatrixExpression<Right,Op,RightRight>,
                                         Orientation,
                                         WeightMemoryType>,
                          MatrixExpression<Right,Op,RightRight> >(A,B);
}
```

For the implementation of the other operators we refer to the library code for further details.

**The assignment layer**

To the sparse matrix expression template framework of course also belongs an assignment operator = which has to be a member function of the according matrix type. It is implemented in the
AssignmentLayer which is described in Section 3.3.7.

### 3.7.3 Dense matrix expression templates

In order to provide the same framework as for the sparse matrix types also for dense matrix expressions,
we have a introduced a dense matrix expression class. For the enabling of loop unrolling, we also have
implemented some special operators and functions for matrix types of fixed dimension.

However, for the time being, we only support the computation of binary/trinary dense matrix
expressions like:

- C = A+B

- C += A

- C += A+B

- C = A*B

- C += A*B

- C *= A

- C *= A+B

- and C *= A*B.

The reason for this restriction lies in the problem of allocation of memory for temporary results. When looking at the product of arbitrary rectangular matrices, if more than two factors are involved, we come across different dimensioned results in between. Moreover, these temporaries depend on the order of computation. For example consider the product

$$D = ABC, \qquad \text{with} \quad A \in \mathbb{R}^{1000 \times 3}, B \in \mathbb{R}^{3 \times 1000}, C \in \mathbb{R}^{1000 \times 4}.$$

The product $D$ is $\in \mathbb{R}^{1000 \times 4}$, however because of the associativity $(AB)C = A(BC)$, we can either have a temporary $AB$ in $\mathbb{R}^{1000 \times 1000}$ or $BC$ in $\mathbb{R}^{3 \times 4}$, depending on the order of calculation. Regarding that the computational cost for multiplying an $n \times m$ with an $m \times k$ matrix, is $O(nmk)$ we would have a total effort of 7000000 floating point operations in the first case contrasting to 24000 in the second case.

Thus, a complete expression templates library would have to incorporate an algorithm for dense matrix product expressions that minimizes the temporary results. For matrix types where all dimensions are known at compile time, this would result in the need for a template metaprogramming optimization algorithm, which is beyond the scope of this thesis (an according algorithm can e.g. be found in [Sed01]).

Furthermore, the result types for arbitrary combination of matrix types should be taken into account. Here certain rules have to be applied, e.g. the result of a sparse/dense product is again sparse, etc.

However, one can say that matrix products with more than two operands are relatively rare in numerical computing, and therefore we can get along with the above restrictions.

The dense matrix expression class very much resembles the sparse matrix expression class, with the exception that it hasn't got own memory to store temporary results.

──────────────── Dense matrix expression class ────────────────

```
template <class Left, class Op, class Right>
class DenseMatrixExpression
{
public:
    typedef typename Left::VerticalDimensionType VerticalDimensionType;
    typedef typename Right::HorizontalDimensionType HorizontalDimensionType;
    typedef RowWise  Orientation;
    typedef typename Left::index_type index_type;
    typedef typename Right::value_type value_type;
    typedef typename Right::WeightMemoryType WeightMemoryType;

private:
    const Left&  left;
    const Right& right;
public:
    DenseMatrixExpression(const Left& l, const Right& r)
        : left(l), right(r)
    {}
};
```

### 3.7.4 Dense product matrix type generator

For dense matrix types the struct `ProductTypeGenerator` can generate an appropriate result matrix type for the product of two matrix types, say `Type1` and `Type1` that include the `FirstTargetsLayer` in their layer hierarchy. The result type then is defined in the member type called `result_type`.

```
———————————— Dense product matrix generator ————————————
template <class Type1, class Type2>
struct ProductTypeGenerator
{
  typedef ... result_type;
};
```

This means, that

  LayerLookup<Type1,FirstTargets>::name  and  LayerLookup<Type2,FirstTargets>::name

must be equal to FirstTargets, otherwise the result type is ErrorType. The LayerConfigLookup trait is used to determine the layer config structs for the two dimension layers, the first targets, the neighbourhood starts and the weight values layer of both types. A trait called

DenseProductSequenceConfig

chooses all the according sequences in dependence on these config structs, such that the resulting matrix type can accomodate the matrix product. Finally, the matrix type is assembled using the LowLevelMatrixGenerator (cf. Section 3.6.3). For further details, we refer to the library class text, file "Generators.hh".

## 3.8 Matrix-vector operation

A major operation in numerical linear algebra is the matrix-vector multiplication. It is used intensively in Krylov subspace methods like Conjugate Gradient or GMRES (see [Saa03]).

Let us first describe shortly the architecture for matrix-vector operations in our library. Afterwards we give a performance measurement in comparison with a C library.

### 3.8.1 Concept

Two major matrix-vector operations are supplied: addmul and submul. The function addmul computes $y := y + Ax$, where $x$ and $y$ are vectors and $A$ is a matrix, whereas submul does the same for $y := y - Ax$. The template function below is the entry point for addmul. From here, it is dispatched to the according functions, in dependence on the involved types.

```
———————————— Additive matrix vector product entry point ————————————
template <class Matrix, class InVector, class OutVector>
inline void addmul(const Matrix& A, const InVector& x, OutVector& y)
{
  typedef numericalfunctors::_addmul<typename Matrix::value_type,
                                     typename InVector::value_type,
                                     typename OutVector::value_type,
                                     typename OutVector::value_type>
                  AddMulFunctor;
  typedef typename LayerLookup<Matrix,Partition>::name HasPartition;
  typedef typename IfElse<IsFixed<Matrix>::value,Fixed,ErrorType>::type FixType;
  matrix_vector_dispatch(A,x,y,AddMulFunctor(),HasPartition(),FixType());
}
```

If the matrix type is partitioned, the parallel variant of matrix_vector_dispatch is called. It uses as many threads as there are partitions (stripes) in the matrix. If there are no partitions and the matrix size is not fixed, the standard matrix-vector operation with the _addmul functor is called:

```
──────────────── Standard matrix vector product dispatch ────────────────
template <class Matrix, class InVector, class OutVector, class Functor>
inline void matrix_vector_dispatch(const Matrix&    A,
                                   const InVector&  x,
                                   OutVector&       y,
                                   const Functor&   f,
                                   const ErrorType& nothread,
                                   const ErrorType& notfixed)
{
  typedef typename MatrixTraits<Matrix>::Orientation Orientation;
  matrix_vector_operation(A,x,y,f,Orientation());
}
```

The actual algorithm is implemented in `matrix_vector_operation`, here shown for row-wise oriented matrices. It works for sparse and dense matrices.

```
──────────────── Standard matrix vector operation ────────────────
template <class Matrix, class InVector, class OutVector, class Functor>
inline void matrix_vector_operation(const Matrix&    A,
                                    const InVector&  x,
                                    OutVector&       y,
                                    const Functor&   f,
                                    RowWise          r)
{
  typedef typename Matrix::ConstMajorIterator ConstMajorIterator;
  typedef typename ConstMajorIterator::const_iterator const_iterator;
  for (ConstMajorIterator cit = A.Row_begin(); cit != A.Row_end(); ++cit)
  {
    for (const_iterator rit = cit.begin(); rit != cit.end(); ++rit)
      f(*rit,x[rit.index()],y[cit.index()]);
  }
}
```

The `addmul` and `submul` functors are provided to increase the code reusability – the matrix vector operation algorithm above is the same for both operations.

The Functor type specifies what the algorithm in `matrix_vector_operation` has to do with the matrix and vector entries. For example, the `_addmul` functor by default assumes that the entries are again matrices/vectors:

```
──────────────── addmul functor ────────────────
template <class Argument1, class Argument2, class Argument3, class Result>
struct _addmul
{
  Result& operator()(const Argument1& a, const Argument2& x, Argument3& y) const
  {
    return addmul(a,x,y);
  }
};
```

Only the specialized functor for scalar `double` entries directly carries out a computation:

```
——————————— Specialized addmul functor ———————
template <class Argument2, class Argument3, class Result>
struct _addmul<double,Argument2,Argument3,Result>
{
  ResultType& operator()(const double& a, const Argument2& x, Argument3& y) const
  {
    return y += a * x;
  }
};
```

This fine grained function architecture ensures flexibility when using different matrix types, especially each thinkable block-matrix type is supported. That it also delivers high performance is shown in the next section.

### 3.8.2   Benchmark

In the following, we apply the addmul operation to a block stiffness matrix stemming from the discretization of a 2D Stokes problem as described in 10.2. The according matrix sizes are displayed in Table 3.4. Note that at any time, 9 double nonzero entries are grouped together in a $3 \times 3$ matrix.

| $h$ | 1/64 | 1/128 | 1/256 |
|---|---|---|---|
| overall matrix dimension | 12675 | 49923 | 198147 |
| overall nonzeros | 261513 | 1039113 | 4142601 |
| nonzero $3 \times 3$ blocks | 29057 | 115457 | 460289 |

Table 3.4: Matrix properties for the Stokes problem

We compare the run times for a loop over a 10000 calls to addmul with the according function blanc_mv_mul from the *BLANC* library (*Blockwise Linear Algebra and Numerical Computations in C*, see [Pri96]), which is a highly tuned library written in C for numerical linear algebra (and which is one of the few libraries available that is capable of dealing with such a matrix format).

| library test case | operation | compiler | switches | $h = 1/64$ | $h = 1/128$ | $h = 1/256$ |
|---|---|---|---|---|---|---|
| | | | | time in sec. | | |
| BLANC(1) | blanc_mv_mul | gcc | G1 | 12.6 | 50.3 | 227 |
| BLANC(2) | blanc_mv_mul | gcc | G2 | 13.7 | 54.5 | 234 |
| MiLTON(1) | universal addmul | g++ | G1 | 24.3 | 99.2 | 394 |
| MiLTON(2) | universal addmul | g++ | G2 | 24.2 | 98.7 | 368 |
| MiLTON(3) | specialized addmul | g++ | G1 | 14.2 | 56.4 | 224 |
| MiLTON(4) | specialized addmul | g++ | G2 | 14.1 | 56.2 | 223 |
| MiLTON(5) | specialized addmul | g++ | G3 | 7.6 | 29.7 | 118 |

Table 3.5: CPU times for 10000 matrix-vector multiplications

Figure 3.8 compares the CPU run times for the different test cases that are listed in Table 3.5. First of all, we can see that the common unspecialized version of addmul that works for all types of matrices is relatively slow, compared to the BLANC routines. However when using the specialized

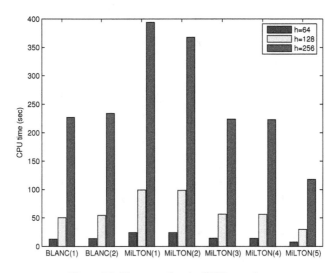

Figure 3.8: Test cases for the GNU compiler

version for fixed sized matrices (which is only used where such a matrix type is encountered by the dispatcher function matrix_vector_dispatch) we can see, that our C++ library is nearly on par with the C code.

The speedup is due to the possibilities for the compiler to enforce loop unrolling for loops with a small constant number of iterations, which is enabled by the -funroll-loops compiler switch for the GNU compiler (see Table 3.6).

| | G1 | G2 | G3 |
|---|---|---|---|
| | -O3 | -O3 | -O3 |
| | | -funroll-loops | -funroll-loops |
| switches | | -fpeel-loops | -fpeel-loops |
| | | | -finline-limit=400 |

Table 3.6: Utilized compiler switches

If one looks at the BLANC library and the code for blanc_mv_mul, one could question why our approach couldn't be even faster, because BLANC doesn't set the dimension of the $3 \times 3$ block matrix entries to be fixed at compile time. Thus, for the compiler, loop unrolling and vectorization would be easier to do in MiLTON.

The reason for this lies in the inlining strategies of the compiler. One has to ensure that really small functions are inlined, however we have to make sure, that the assembled functions are not too big for the CPU cache. Adjusting now the inline-limit to a value between 200 and 600 finally generates a code that is twice as fast as the original BLANC C code.

The -finline-limit switch controls a threshold value (measured in pseudo instructions) that determines the size of functions, that are inlined. The optimal value however depends on the hardware, the cache and register sizes. The above was carried out on a Pentium 4 machine (cf. Appendix B), but one can a observe similar behaviour e.g. on AMD Athlon machines.

In Figure 3.9 we have plotted the execution times for the smallest matrix ($h = 1/64$), for different values of the inline limit. According to the gcc manual, the default value is 600, however it makes a difference, if one supplies the switch -finline-limit=600 or leaves it out.

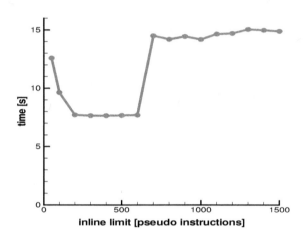

Figure 3.9: Running times in dependence of the inline limit

Concludingly, it can be stated, that an abstract programming approach in C++ can be very competitive regarding the performance, but with the additional gain of greater flexibility and reusability when e.g. compared to C libraries. Furthermore, we observe again, that in most cases, compilers are better optimizers than programmers, and that the decisions about what to optimize should be left to the compiler.

However, in order to be capable of doing so, the compiler should be provided with small building blocks, rather than monolithic code. It would be the next task for compiler constructors, to adjust the inlining-level and automatically synchronize it with the underlying hardware architecture.

# Part II

# AMG for scalar problems

# Chapter 4

# Scalar partial differential equations

The numerical solution of partial differential equations is still one of the most challenging problems in scientific computing. They arise from a wide range of real-world-problems in areas such as meteorology, aerodynamics, nuclear physics and even economic topics like capital markets. Thus, they are the motivation for developing fast numerical algorithms in order to provide more detailed simulations of mathematical models and to give a better understanding or even to allow forecasts for the underlying scientific problem.

In the following we introduce elliptic partial differential equations and describe the difficulties and strategies to solve them. Especially – in the next chapter – we will investigate the behaviour of algebraic multigrid, applied to linear systems arising from the finite element discretizations of scalar boundary value problems

$$(Lu)(x) = f(x), \quad x \in \Omega \subset \mathbb{R}^d,$$

where $u, f : \Omega \to \mathbb{R}$, and $L$ is a linear elliptic differential operator, and $d \in \mathbb{N}$ is the space dimension.

## 4.1 Convection-diffusion-reaction equations

A typical elliptic scalar partial differential equation is the stationary convection (or advection) diffusion reaction equation.

**Definition 4.1.1** (Convection-diffusion-reaction problem). *Find* $u : \mathbb{R}^d \to \mathbb{R}$, *such that*

$$-\nu \Delta u + \mathbf{b} \cdot \nabla u + cu = f \quad in \ \Omega \in \mathbb{R}^d, \tag{4.1}$$

*with* $0 < \nu \in \mathbb{R}$, $\mathbf{b} : \Omega \to \mathbb{R}^d$, $c : \Omega \to \mathbb{R}$, $f : \Omega \to \mathbb{R}$ *and appropriate boundary conditions on* $\partial\Omega$.

It can be transformed into a weak formulation by multiplying the equation with test functions $v \in V := W_0^{1,2}(\Omega)$ and integrating over the domain $\Omega$. The according variational formulation for homogenous Dirichlet boundary conditions then consists of finding $u \in V$ such that

$$a(u, v) = f(v), \quad \forall \ v \in V \tag{4.2}$$

with

$$a(u, v) := \nu(\nabla u, \nabla v) + (\mathbf{b} \cdot \nabla u, v) + (cu, v), \tag{4.3}$$
$$f(v) := (f, v), \tag{4.4}$$

using the standard scalar products

$$(u, v) := (u, v)_{L^2(\Omega)} := \int_\Omega uv \, dx, \quad (\nabla u, \nabla v) := \sum_{i=1}^d \int_\Omega \frac{\partial u}{\partial x_i} \frac{\partial v}{\partial x_i} dx.$$

71

This scalar problem can be interpreted as a model for describing the concentration (or the temperature) $u$ of a substance in a liquid, which is contained in a reservoir $\Omega$, under the influence of a certain amount of diffusion $\nu$, a convection field $\mathbf{b}$, and a chemical reaction indicated by $c$. Often, the problem occurs without the reaction term, then it is simply referred to as the convection-diffusion problem.

For the existence and uniqueness of a solution, $a(\cdot, \cdot)$ has to satisfy the conditions of the famous theorem of Lax-Milgram.

**Definition 4.1.2** (Coercivity). *The bilinear form $a : V \times V \longrightarrow \mathbb{R}$ is called $V$-elliptic or coercive, if there exists a $\gamma > 0$ with*

$$a(v, v) \geq \gamma \|v\|_V^2, \qquad \forall \ v \in V. \tag{4.5}$$

**Theorem 4.1.3** (Lax-Milgram Lemma). *Let $a(\cdot, \cdot) : V \times V \longrightarrow \mathbb{R}$ be a bounded, coercive bilinear form in the Hilbert space $V$, and $f : V \longrightarrow \mathbb{R}$ a bounded linear form. Then the variational formulation (4.2) has a unique solution $u \in V$.*

**Lemma 4.1.4.** *Let*

$$\mathbf{b} \in L^\infty(\Omega)^d, \quad c \in L^\infty(\Omega), \quad f \in L^2(\Omega),$$

*then $a(\cdot, \cdot)$ is a bounded bilinear form in $W_0^{1,2}(\Omega) \times W_0^{1,2}(\Omega)$ and $f(\cdot)$ is a bounded linear form in $W_0^{1,2}(\Omega)$. Furthermore, $a(\cdot, \cdot)$ is coercive in $W_0^{1,2}$ under the conditions*

$$\nabla \mathbf{b} \in L^\infty(\Omega)^d \qquad and \qquad c - \frac{1}{2}\nabla \cdot \mathbf{b} \geq 0,$$

*when homogenous Dirichlet boundary conditions are applied.*

*Proof.* The coercivity can be shown by partial integration of the convection part and using the equivalence of the seminorm $|\cdot|_{W^{1,2}}$ and $\|\cdot\|_{W^{1,2}}$ in $W_0^{1,2}(\Omega)$. A complete proof can be found e.g. in [QV97], where also other boundary conditions are considered. $\qquad\square$

The Lax-Milgram theorem now ensures the solvability of (4.2). It is also possible to extend the above result to inhomogenous boundary conditions.

## 4.2 Standard Galerkin approximation

In order to give a numerical solution to (4.2), we introduce a discrete approximation by the standard Galerkin[1] approach. Given a finite-dimensional subspace $V_h \subset V$, we restrict the problem to the following discrete formulation. Find $u_h \in V_h$ such that

$$a(u_h, v_h) = f(v_h), \qquad \forall \ v_h \in V_h. \tag{4.6}$$

Let now $n := \dim V_h$ and $\{\phi_1, \ldots, \phi_n\}$ be a basis of $V_h$, then (4.6) is equivalent to the linear system

$$A\mathbf{u} = \mathbf{f}, \tag{4.7}$$

with $\mathbf{u} = (u_i)_{i=1}^n \in \mathbb{R}^n$ and

$$A = (a_{ij})_{i,j=1}^n \in \mathbb{R}^{n \times n}, \quad a_{ij} = a(\phi_j, \phi_i) \tag{4.8}$$

$$\mathbf{f} = (f_i)_{i=1}^n \in \mathbb{R}^n, \qquad f_i = f(\phi_i). \tag{4.9}$$

Note that the condition (4.5) guarantees, that $A$ is positive definite, and therefore (4.7) has a unique solution $\mathbf{u}$. The choice of $V_h$ and its basis functions is crucial for the structure of $A$. Ideal would be a orthonomal basis of $V_h$ with respect to $a(\cdot, \cdot)$, which however isn't trivial for (4.2) and

---

[1]Named after *Boris Grigorievich Galerkin* (1871–1945), Belarussian engineer and mathematician.

arbitrary domains $\Omega$. Functions with a small support however at least lead to a sparse matrix $A$. The according discrete subspaces are the *finite element spaces*.

In our program system $\mathcal{PNS}$, we use a *triangulation* of $\overline{\Omega}$, meaning a set $T_h = \{T_1, \ldots, T_M\}$ of $M$ disjoint triangles $(d = 2)$ or tetrahedrons $(d = 3)$ $T_i$ with

$$\bigcup_{i=1}^{M} T_i = \overline{\Omega} \tag{4.10}$$

and piecewise linear $(P_1)$ finite elements to discretize the problem.

## 4.3  Stabilization of convection diffusion problems

For absent reaction $(c \equiv 0)$ and decreasing diffusion $(\nu \to 0)$ the problem (4.2) becomes convection dominated and looses its elliptic property, resulting in a nearly singular discrete problem, since the positive definiteness is solely grounded on $\nu$. Problems with iterative solvers are the consequence, because their convergence rates directly depend on the condition of the matrix. Furthermore, the resulting discrete solutions then exhibit strong oscillations. Therefore, for practical applications, one needs to apply a stabilization method, that strengthens the ellipticity of the bilinear form.

Let in the following (4.3) - (4.4) be again discretized using a finite element space $V_h \subset V$, with an according triangulation $T_h$, leading to a discrete problem as in (4.6).

The Streamline Diffusion/SUPG stabilization method (originally introduced in [HB79]), for example, adds artificial diffusion only in the direction of the convection $\mathbf{b}$.

**Definition 4.3.1** (SUPG method). *The streamline upwind Petrov Galerkin (SUPG) or streamline diffusion method is defined as finding $u_h \in V_h$, such that*

$$a_{SUPG}(u_h, v_h) = f_{SUPG}(v_h), \qquad \forall \quad v_h \in V_h,$$

*with*

$$a_{SUPG}(u_h, v_h) := a(u_h, v_h) + \sum_{i=1}^{M} \delta_{T_i}(-\nu\Delta u_h + b \cdot \nabla u_h + cu_h, b \cdot \nabla v_h)_{T_i}, \tag{4.11}$$

$$f_{SUPG}(v_h) := f(v_h) + \sum_{i=1}^{M} (f, b \cdot \nabla v_h)_{T_i} \tag{4.12}$$

Here $(\cdot, \cdot)_{T_i}$ is the local $L^2$-scalar product on the triangle/tetrahedron $T_i$:

$$(u, v)_{T_i} := (u, v)_{L^2(T_i)} = \int_{T_i} uv \, dx.$$

Especially for piece linear elements, where we have vanishing second order derivatives, and for $c = 0$ we see, that the SUPG method adds a small diffusive part to the variational formulation.

In the Galerkin least-squares method (see [HFH89]), the stabilization term is tested not only with the convection part but with the whole differential operator.

**Definition 4.3.2** (GLS method). *The Galerkin least squares (GLS) method is defined as finding $u_h \in V_h$, such that*

$$a_{GLS}(u_h, v_h) = f_{GLS}(v_h), \qquad \forall \quad v_h \in V_h,$$

*with*

$$a_{GLS}(u_h, v_h) := a(u_h, v_h) + \sum_{i=1}^{M} \delta_{T_i}(-\nu\Delta u_h + b \cdot \nabla u_h + cu_h, -\nu\Delta v_h + b \cdot \nabla v_h + cv_h)_{T_i}, \tag{4.13}$$

$$f_{GLS}(v_h) := f(v_h) + \sum_{i=1}^{M} (f, -\nu\Delta v_h + b \cdot \nabla v_h + cv_h)_{T_i} \tag{4.14}$$

Both of the above methods enhance the diffusive part of the bilinear form and therefore strengthen the positive definiteness of the stiffness matrix $A$. In $\mathcal{PNS}$ the stabilization parameter for both methods is chosen as

$$\delta_{T_i} := \frac{h_{T_i}^2}{2\nu}(1 + Pe_{T_i}^2)^{-\frac{1}{2}}, \tag{4.15}$$

where $h_{T_i} := \operatorname{diam}(T_i)$ and

$$Pe_{T_i} := \|b\|_{\infty,T_i}\frac{h_{T_i}}{\nu} \tag{4.16}$$

is the local *Peclet number* on element $T_i$. The Peclet number can be seen as a measure for the relation of convection and diffusion. A possible definition for the whole equation could be the following:

**Definition 4.3.3.** *Problem (4.1) is called*

$$\text{purely convection dominated} \quad \textit{if} \quad \min_{i=1,\ldots,M} Pe_{T_i} > 1 \tag{4.17}$$

$$\text{purely diffusion dominated} \quad \textit{if} \quad \max_{i=1,\ldots,M} Pe_{T_i} \leq 1. \tag{4.18}$$

Of course, mixtures of these types can occur, since $Pe_{T_i}$ is only a local measure, that can vary over the domain. For stability proofs and error estimations of the above stabilization methods, we refer to [RST96].

# Chapter 5

# Algebraic multilevel methods

Since algebraic multigrid is heavily inspired by the concept of geometric multigrid and uses many terms thereof, it is hardly possible to describe the idea behind the former without first presenting the idea of the latter. But we will keep things as short as possible.

This chapter will give a brief overview first of geometric multigrid and then introduce the approach of algebraic multigrid.

## 5.1 Geometric multigrid

The foundations of (geometric) multilevel or multigrid methods were laid by Fedorenko[1] [Fed61] and Bakhvalov [Bak66] in the 1960's and further developed by Brandt (e.g. in [Bra73]) in the 1970's. It was only in the 1980's when they became more popular since increasing CPU speed and larger memories then allowed to tackle bigger problems.

The motivation of geometric multigrid arose from the observation that simple solvers – splitting methods like Jacobi or Gauß-Seidel (see Section 8.2.1) – have a smoothing effect on the error of the approximate solution.

### 5.1.1 Smoothing

Let $x = A^{-1}b$ denote the exact solution and $x^{(k)}$ the approximation at step $k$. Remember that the according iteration reads

$$x^{(k)} := (I - M^{-1}A)x^k + M^{-1}b,$$

and thus, if $e^{(k)} := x^{(k)} - x$ is the error in the $k$-th step we have for step $k + 1$:

$$e^{(k+1)} = x^{(k+1)} - x = x^k - x - M^{-1}(Ax^k - b) = (I - M^{-1}A)e^k.$$

So the error components are damped with the iteration matrix $I - M^{-1}A$. Looking, for example, at a simple boundary value problem like the 2-dimensional Poisson equation

$$-\Delta u = f, \quad \text{in } \Omega := (0,1) \times (0,1) \tag{5.1}$$

$$u = 0, \quad \text{on } \partial\Omega, \tag{5.2}$$

---

[1] *Radii Petrovich Fedorenko*, a Russian mathematician at the Keldysh Institute for Applied Mathematics, is always cited as the inventor of multi-level methods. Interestingly however in an article by Saad [Sv00], it is mentioned that the British engineer and mathematician *Richard Vynne Southwell* (1888–1970) in 1935 [Sou35] already had the the basic idea of a two-level method.

discretized using finite differences on a structured $(N \times N)$ grid produces a linear system $Ax = b$ with a symmetric positive definite stiffness matrix

$$A = \frac{1}{h^2} \begin{pmatrix} T_N & -I_N & & \\ -I_N & \ddots & \ddots & \\ & \ddots & \ddots & -I_N \\ & & -I_N & T_N \end{pmatrix}, \tag{5.3}$$

with $h = \frac{1}{N+1}$ and

$$T_N = \begin{pmatrix} 4 & -1 & & \\ -1 & \ddots & \ddots & \\ & \ddots & \ddots & -1 \\ & & -1 & 4 \end{pmatrix} \in \mathbb{R}^{N \times N}.$$

Solving this linear system with the (damped) Jacobi [2] method using the relaxation parameter $\omega = \frac{1}{2}$ yields the iteration

$$x^{(k+1)} = (I - \frac{1}{2}D^{-1}A)x^{(k)} + \frac{1}{2}D^{-1}b, \tag{5.4}$$

As the component $u_{ij}$ of the discrete solution at grid point $(i,j)$, $i,j = 1, \ldots, N$ corresponds to the $n$-th component of the solution vector $x$ (with $n = i * N + j$) we have

$$u_{ij} = x_n \quad \text{for} \quad n = i * N + j.$$

Analogously, we get $f_{ij} = b_n$ for $n = i * N + j$. Hence, for the $n$-th component of the vector $x^{(k+1)}$ in (5.4) we get

$$x_n^{(k+1)} = u_{ij}^{(k+1)} = \frac{1}{2}u_{ij}^{(k)} + \frac{1}{8}\left(u_{i-1,j}^{(k)} + u_{i+1,j}^{(k)} + u_{i,j-1}^{(k)} + u_{i,j+1}^{(k)}\right) + \frac{1}{8}h^2 f_{ij},$$

and for the $n$-th component of the error $x_n^{(k+1)}$:

$$e_n^{(k+1)} = u_{ij}^{(k+1)} - u_{ij} = \frac{1}{2}\left(e_{ij}^{(k)} + \frac{1}{4}\left(e_{i-1,j}^{(k)} + e_{i+1,j}^{(k)} + e_{i,j-1}^{(k)} + e_{i,j+1}^{(k)}\right)\right). \tag{5.5}$$

In (5.5) the new component of the error vector is formed by the (weighted) average over the neighbouring points – this means that small oscillations are reduced quickly. The local information transport is very quick, whereas the global information transport (if $N$ is very large) is quite slow – which is why this method is a good smoother, but a poor solver.

**Remark 5.1.1.** *Another approach is to look at the eigenvectors of the iteration matrix $I - M^{-1}A$. They are the same as those of $A$ which in turn correspond to the discrete points of the eigenfunctions of the boundary value problem (5.1) – (5.2). Now the low and middle-frequent eigenfunctions (and thus the eigenvectors) belong to eigenvalues of $I - M^{-1}A$ which are close to 1 in contrast to the high frequent eigenvectors belonging to eigenvalues which are close to zero.*

As a consequence of this, we only need to find a way to smooth the lower frequencies of the error as well, to have a good solver.

---

[2]Originally, the German mathematician *Carl Gustav Jacob Javobi* (1804–1851) in [Jac45] invented this iterative method, because the exact Gaussian elimination method was tedious and error-prone for large linear systems.

## 5.1.2 Coarse grid correction

Since partial differential equations are posed on a geometric domain $\Omega$ they are usually discretized using a grid of a certain mesh width, say $h$. Now it lies near to approximate the lower frequencies of the error with a dicretization on a coarser level, for instance on a grid of width $2h$. On that level the same type of smoothing as above can be applied, and its low frequencies in turn can be smoothed on coarser grids recursively, which gives the classic multigrid method.

Precisely, we need a *hierarchy of grids*

$$\Omega_{l_{\max}} \subset \Omega_{l_{\max}-1} \subset \cdots \Omega_1 \subset \Omega_0 \subset \Omega,$$

where $\Omega_i \subset \Omega_j$ means that $\Omega_j$ includes all points of $\Omega_i$. On each level $l$ the problem is discretized using the finite element space $V_l$ which consists of the according polynomial elements defined on grid $\Omega_l$, so we get a sequence of linear systems

$$A_l x_l = b_l, \quad \text{with} \quad A_l \in \mathbb{R}^{n_l \times n_l}, n_l = \dim V_l \tag{5.6}$$

where $b_l \in \mathbb{R}^{n_l}$ is the discrete version of the right hand side $f$ and $x_l \in \mathbb{R}^{n_l}$ the discrete approximation of $u$ on level $l$. Especially we set $A = A_0$, $b = b_0$ and $x = x_0$.

Since fine grids are often generated through the refinement of a simpler coarse grid, such hierarchies may be produced at no extra costs, if some rules are heeded.

Between the grids we need of course appropriate transfer operators for the interpolation.

**Definition 5.1.2** (Restriction, Prolongation). *The restriction from a finer level $l$ to the coarser level $l+1$ is denoted by*

$$R_l : V_l \longrightarrow V_{l+1},$$

*while the reverse mapping from level $l+1$ to level $l$*

$$P_l : V_{l+1} \longrightarrow V_l,$$

*which has to be some suitable interpolation, is called the* prolongation.

Usually we have $R_l \in \mathbb{R}^{n_{l+1} \times n_l}$, $P_l \in \mathbb{R}^{n_l \times n_{l+1}}$ and $R_l = c(P_l)^T$ with some constant $c$. Generally the prolongation is chosen such that a point $p \in \Omega_l$ is interpolated through its neighbouring points which lie in $\Omega_{l+1}$.

**Remark 5.1.3.** *When the domain $\Omega$ has a simple geometry like a rectangle and is discretized using structured grids with regular refinement, all works very nicely. But if the domain is more complex and if we have unstructured grids generated by an adaptive refinement, then the construction of proper transfer operators is anything but trivial.*

## 5.1.3 The algorithm

Let $S_l$ be the smoother on level $l$ and the sequence of linear equations as in (5.6) be given. Then, after $k$ iterations with $S_l$, the error is $e_l^{(k)} = x_l^{(k)} - x_l \iff x_l = x_l^{(k)} - e_l^{(k)}$ and thus $e_l^{(k)}$ would be the optimal correction for our current approximation $x_l^{(k)}$. Since now for the residual $r_l^{(k)}$ the following relation holds

$$r_l^{(k)} = A_l x_l^{(k)} - b_l = A_l e_l^{(k)} \tag{5.7}$$

we approximate $e_l^{(k)}$ now by restricting $r_l^{(k)}$ on the coarser level $l+1$:

$$r_{l+1} := R_l r_l^{(k)}, \tag{5.8}$$

where we solve the equation

$$A_{l+1} e_{l+1} = r_{l+1}. \tag{5.9}$$

The result $e_{l+1}$ is prolongated again to level $l$ and then used to update our current solution $x_l^{(k)}$:

$$x_l^{(k,new)} := x_l^{(k)} - P_l e_{l+1}. \tag{5.10}$$

As this simple coarse-grid correction does not automatically guarantee convergence, additional smoothing is required after the correction (*post-smoothing*) or before (*pre-smoothing*).

**Definition 5.1.4** (Two-grid-cycle, Multigrid-cycle). *The process described above is called* two-grid-cycle *if only two levels are involved and the system on the coarsest level is solved exactly. If this process is again used recursively to solve (5.9), it is called a* multigrid-cycle.

Finally we can summarize these ideas in the following general multigrid algorithm. The parameters $\nu_1, \nu_2$ control the number of pre- and post-smoothing steps, while $\gamma_l$ determines the recursion pattern of the cycle:

$$\gamma_l \equiv 1 \quad : \quad \text{V-cycle,}$$
$$\gamma_l \equiv 2 \quad : \quad \text{W-cycle,}$$
$$\gamma_l = l \quad : \quad \text{F-cycle.}$$

Furthermore, let $\mathsf{Smoother}_l(A_l, x_l, b_l)$ be a function that applies the smoother $S_l$ once to the System $A_l x_l = b_l$.

---

**Algorithm 1:** $\mathsf{MGCycle}_l(A_l, x_l, b_l)$

---

Input: Matrix $A_l$, vector $b_l$, smoother $S_l$, parameters $\nu_1, \nu_2, \gamma_l$,
initial approximation $x_l$
Output: An approximation $x_l$ to $A_l^{-1} b_l$
if $l = l_{\max}$ then
    $x_l \leftarrow A_l^{-1} b_l$
else
    for $i = 1$ to $\nu_1$ do
        $x_l \leftarrow \mathsf{Smoother}_l(A_l, x_l, b_l)$
    end
    $r_{l+1} \leftarrow R_{l+1}(A_l x_l - b_l)$
1    $e_{l+1} \leftarrow 0$
    for $i = 1$ to $\gamma_l$ do
        $e_{l+1} \leftarrow \mathsf{MGCycle}_{l+1}(A_{l+1}, e_{l+1}, r_{l+1})$
    end
    $x_l \leftarrow x_l - P_l e_{l+1}$
    for $i = 1$ to $\nu_2$ do
        $x_l \leftarrow \mathsf{Smoother}_l(A_l, x_l, b_l)$
    end
end

---

**Remark 5.1.5.** *Algorithm 1 is the basic algorithm for all multigrid methods – even algebraic multigrid methods rely on this procedure since it is the core principle of every multigrid idea.*

**Remark 5.1.6.** *The runtime complexity of one multigrid-cycle is proportional to the total number of unknowns on the finest mesh, $n_0$, if*

$$\sum_{l=0}^{l_{\max}} n_l \leq C n_{l_0}, \tag{5.11}$$

*with a constant $C$ independent of $n_0$. This is because the number of nonzeros in $A$ is $O(n_0)$ when $A$ comes from some discretization (FEM, FDM, FVM) of a PDE. The above equation is a reasonable condition, since the meshsize on a level $l + 1$ should be significantly smaller than on level $l$.*

**Remark 5.1.7.** *To get a sensible solving algorithm, we apply several multigrid-cycles,*

$$x^{(k)} := \mathsf{MGCycle}_0(A, x^{(k-1)}, b)$$

*until $x^{(k)}$ satisfies some stopping criterion. In order to improve the initial value $x^{(o)}$, we might use the so-called nested iterations: The system is solved directly on the coarsest level, i.e. $x_{l_{\max}} := A_{l_{\max}}^{-1} b_{l_{\max}}$, then prolongated to the next level ($l = l_{\max} - 1$), where some smoothing steps are applied, then again prolongated, and so on, until we get some $x^{(o)}$ on the finest level, where the normal multigrid solving algorithm can be started as above.*

### 5.1.4 Convergence results

In order to show the convergence of a multigrid method, one needs to ensure that the smoother $S_l$ really reduces the high-frequent error and that the error can be approximated on the coarser level as decribed through equations (5.8) – (5.10). The standard convergence theory for geometric multigrid is based on the following two properties.

**Definition 5.1.8** (Smoothing property). *The condition*

$$\|A_l S_l^{\nu_1}\| \le C_S \eta(\nu_1) h^{-\alpha}, \tag{5.12}$$

*with some function $\eta$ with $\eta(\nu_1) \to 0$ for $\nu_1 \to \infty$ and $\alpha > 0$ is called* smoothing property.

**Definition 5.1.9** (Approximation property). *The condition*

$$\|A_l^{-1} - P_l A_{l-1}^{-1} R_{l+1}\| \le C_A h^{-\alpha} \tag{5.13}$$

*is called* approximation property.

For symmetric scalar problems there are already convergence results available as e.g. in [Hac85] or [Man88]. Fewer results are available for nonsymmetric scalar problems like the convection-diffusion equation. For this type of problem Reusken was one of the first to show convergence for the the the two-grid method and the W-cycle with damped Jacobi and Gauss-Seidel smoothing for finite differences [Reu00]. A similar result for a finite element discretization is given in [OR03].

Derived originally for elliptic problems, the (geometric) multigrid method delivers good results as well for other types of problems. For many cases, it only needs a constant number of multigrid-cycles to converge, independently of the meshsize $h$, which results in an overall runtime complexity of $O(n_0)$.

### 5.1.5 Disadvantages

Geometric multigrid are however not the optimal method in every case. For example, they show a lack of performance if the data of the underlying boundary value problem is not smooth enough. This is mainly due to the construction of the prolongation, which simply interpolates between points, and does not take into account the special properties of the (discretized) differential operator which forms the stiffness matrix $A$. As a first remedy, operator-dependend transfer operators have been developed by e.g. Alcouffe et al. [ABDP81] and de Zeeuw [dZ90].

In addition, as mentioned above, multigrid methods are not easy to implement independently of the problem. The interpolation is a crucial point, especially if we deal with complex geometries and unstructured grids. Adaptive mesh refinement with green refinement e.g. yields meshes that are not hierarchical and so are not applicable to the above approach.

Generally we need geometrical information about the underlying problem which can be missing

- because our software doesn't allow access to the geometry information for some reason, maybe it's because we have a legacy system whose mesh-generator is not capable of providing us with hierarchical grids or it is a third party product for which we don't even have the source code

- or because the linear system does not stem from a discretized PDE at all, so we have no finite element spaces and no mesh information - e.g. optimization problems.

Speaking now in terms of computer science for geometric multigrid, the interface between the solver and the FEM-software doesn't only consist of the linear system $Ax = b$, but also contains the meshes $\Omega_0, \ldots, \Omega_{l_{\max}}$. Thus, a geometrical multigrid method is *no* black box solver.

## 5.2   Algebraic multigrid for scalar problems

As we have seen from the last section there is a need for purely algebraic black-box solvers and indeed several methods have been developed over the last twenty years. We will subsume them under the term *algebraic multilevel methods*. All these methods have in common, that they try to give an approximation to the solution of the linear system

$$Ax = b, \quad A = A_0 \in \mathbb{C}^{n \times n}, b = b_0 \in \mathbb{C}^n \tag{5.14}$$

by reducing the coefficient matrix $A_0$ to a significantly smaller matrix $A_1 \in \mathbb{C}^{m \times m}$ with $m < n$ (and appropriate smaller right-hand side $b_1$). This is then repeated recursively leading to different *levels* $A_l x_l = b_l$ of equations (thus the name).

Various methods fall under this category, among which are the following main variants:

- The "classical" AMG, that was first introduced by the work of Brandt et al. [BMR84] and Ruge/Stueben [RS87]. It is based on partitioning the variables on each level into two sets by using strong connection relations imposed by the matrix.

- Algebraic multigrid merely based on graph information ([Bec99], [Kic98]).

- Aggregation based AMG ([VMB94], [SS95]), were the variables are seperated into several aggregates, which are then represented by one coarse level variable. An improvement hereof is the smoothed aggregation ([VMB95]) that includes a smoothing step into the construction of the coarse level operators.

- AMGe based on element agglomeration ([JV01]) uses element stiffness matrices to generate a better measure for the coarsening of the variables.

- Algebraic multilevel incomplete factorizations e.g. ARMS ([SS02]), AMLP ([Kra04]), AMLI ([AL98]), ILU-MG ([BS99]) where the original matrix is reordered and approximately factorized into block matrices.

In this thesis however, we will concentrate on the classical AMG approach and investigate its application to nonsymmetric problems. For $A \in \mathbb{C}^{n \times n}$, $D = \mathrm{diag}(A)$, and $x \in \mathbb{C}^n$ we will use

$$\|x\|_A := \sqrt{|x^* A x|}$$
$$\|x\|_D := \sqrt{|x^* D x|}$$
$$\||x\||_A := \sqrt{|x^* A^* D^{-1} A x)|},$$

which are proper norms if $A$ and $D$ are positive definite (semi-norms if they are positive semi-definite). Furthermore, if $A \in \mathbb{R}^{n \times n}$, $A = (a_{ij})_{i,j=1}^n$ we refer to its positive or the negative entries by writing

$$a_{ij}^- = \begin{cases} a_{ij} & \text{if } a_{ij} < 0 \\ 0 & \text{else} \end{cases} \quad \text{and} \quad a_{ij}^+ = \begin{cases} 0 & \text{if } a_{ij} \leq 0 \\ a_{ij} & \text{else} \end{cases}.$$

### 5.2.1   Towards geometry independent multigrid

Algorithm 1 doesn't make use of any mesh information, so the main goal of an algebraic multigrid algorithm is to generate a hierarchical system of levels as in (5.6) and corresponding transfer matrices – without using multiple grids. Given these sequence of equations, and of course appropriate smoothers, the multigrid cycle can be applied without any modification.

Prior to the multgrid cycle iteration, the *AMG preprocess* now is responsible for generating the coarser levels:

**Definition 5.2.1** (AMG preprocess).
*Repeat for level $l = 0, \ldots$ until the linear system on level $l$ is small enough to use an exact solver:*

1. *Generate a $C/F$-Splitting : Given a level $l$ with matrix $A_l \in \mathbb{C}^{n_l \times n_l}$ we identify those variables $i \in \Omega_l := \{1, \ldots, n_l\}$ that should be approximated by other (neighbouring) variables on a coarser level. These variables are gathered in a set $F_l$, while the rest, which are going to be the next coarse level variables, are put into a set $C_l := \Omega_l \setminus F_l$ and thus the dimension of the next level is $n_{l+1} := \#[C_l]$.*

2. *Define the weighted interpolation $P_l \in \mathbb{C}^{n_{l+1} \times n_l}$ as the prolongation operator in dependency of the entries in $A_l$. Then the restriction will be set to*

$$R_l = (P_l)^*. \tag{5.15}$$

3. *Finally compute the next coarse level matrix with the Galerkin principle (Galerkin product) :*

$$A_{l+1} := R_l A_l P_l. \tag{5.16}$$

Assuming we have a given $C/F$-splitting, we can re-order the variables and equations of (5.14), such that the variables belonging to $F$ are sorted before the ones belonging to $C$. Then we can also use the following notation:

$$A_l x = \begin{pmatrix} A_{FF} & A_{FC} \\ A_{CF} & A_{CC} \end{pmatrix} \begin{pmatrix} x_F \\ x_C \end{pmatrix} = \begin{pmatrix} b_F \\ b_C \end{pmatrix} = b, \tag{5.17}$$

as well as

$$P_l = \begin{pmatrix} P_{FC} \\ P_{CC} \end{pmatrix}, \quad R_l = \begin{pmatrix} R_{CF} & R_{CC} \end{pmatrix},$$

where $P_{CC} = R_{CC} = I$ is the identity matrix. With $D_{FF}$ we will denote the diagonal of $A_{FF}$, with $D_{CC}$ the diagonal of $A_{CC}$.

The above construction in Definition (5.2.1) has some advantages especially when dealing with symmetric (Hermitian) positive definite matrices, as the following lemmas state.

**Lemma 5.2.2.** *Let $A = A_0 \in \mathbb{C}^{n \times n}$, and the coarse level matrices be formed by (5.16) for $l = 0, \ldots, l_{\max}$.*

1. *If $A$ is Hermitian, and the relation (5.15) holds, then $A_l$ is again Hermitian for $l = 1, \ldots, l_{\max}$.*

2. *If $A^{-1}$ exists and the prolongation (and restriction) matrices on each level have full rank (i.e. $\operatorname{rank}(P_l) = \operatorname{rank}(R_l) = n_{l+1}$), then $A_l^{-1}$ exists for $l = 1, \ldots, l_{\max}$. Especially, if $A$ is positive definite $A_l$ is positive definite again for all $l$.*

*Proof.* Clearly, if $A_l$ is Hermitian, $A_{l+1}$ is again Hermitian. The second proposition follows from $\operatorname{rank}(P_l) = n_{l+1}$, and thus we have $\dim(\operatorname{Range}(P_l)) = n_{l+1} \implies \dim(\operatorname{Null}(P_l)) = 0 \implies \operatorname{rank}(A_{l+1}) = n_{l+1}$. In particular, the positive definiteness of $A_l$ implies that of $A_{l+1}$. $\square$

Hence, it is reasonable assuming $R_l = (P_l)^*$ to have maximal rank in the following.

**Lemma 5.2.3.** *Let $A, A^{-1} \in \mathbb{C}^{n \times n}$.*

1. *The coarse level correction operator for a two-level cycle*

$$T_l := I_l - P_l A_{l+1}^{-1} R_l A_l \tag{5.18}$$

*on each level $l$ is a projection.*

2. *Moreover, if $A$ is also Hermitian, $T_l$ is an orthogonal projection with respect to the bilinear form $(\cdot, \cdot)_{A_l}$.*

*Proof.* $T_l$ is a projection:

$$
\begin{aligned}
T_l^2 &= (I_l - P_l A_{l+1}^{-1} (P_l)^* A_l)^2 \\
&= I_l - 2 P_l A_{l+1}^{-1} (P_l)^* A_l + P_l A_{l+1}^{-1} \underbrace{(P_l)^* A_l P_l}_{=A_{l+1}} A_{l+1}^{-1} (P_l)^* A_l \\
&= I_l - P_l A_{l+1}^{-1} (P_l)^* A_l = T_l.
\end{aligned}
$$

If $A = A^*$, we get

$$
\begin{aligned}
T_l^* A_l &= (I_l - P_l A_{l+1}^{-1} (P_l)^* A_l)^* A_l \\
&= A_l - A_l^* P_l A_{l+1}^{-*} (P_l)^* A_l \\
&= A_l (I_l - P_l A_{l+1}^{-1} (P_l)^* A_l) = A_l T_l,
\end{aligned}
$$

and therefore $T_l$ is self-adjoint with respect to $(\cdot, \cdot)_{A_l}$. Thus, for $u, w \in \mathbb{C}_l^n$ we have

$$((I_l - T_l)u, T_l w)_{A_l} = (T_l (I_l - T_l)u, w)_{A_l} = (T_l u - T_l u), w)_{A_l} = 0.$$

Furthermore, because $(I_l - T_l) = P_l A_{l+1}^{-1} (P_l)^* A_l$ and

$$\mathrm{Range}(P_l A_{l+1}^{-1} (P_l)^* A_l) = \mathrm{Range}(P_l), \tag{5.19}$$

it follows that

$$\mathrm{Range}(I_l - T_l) = \mathrm{Range}(P_l) = \mathrm{Null}(T_l) \perp \mathrm{Range}(T_l). \tag{5.20}$$

$\square$

**Lemma 5.2.4.** *Let $A$ be positive definite and the coarse levels be defined as in (5.16). Then for any two consecutive levels $l$ and $l + 1$ and any $w \in \mathbb{C}^{l+1}$ the following equation holds:*

$$\|P_l w\|_{A_l} = \|w\|_{A_{l+1}}. \tag{5.21}$$

*Proof.* This follows immediately from

$$\|P_l w\|_{A_l}^2 = w^* \underbrace{(P_l)^* A_l P_l}_{=A_{l+1}} w = \|w\|_{A_{l+1}}^2.$$

$\square$

### 5.2.2 Convergence theory for symmetric problems

Typical convergence results exploit the orthogonality of $T_l$ and thus are only available for the symmetric (Hermitian) case.

**Definition 5.2.5.** *An iterative method for (5.14) that produces an approximation $x^{(k+1)}$ to the exact solution $x$ in the $k - th$ step out of a previous approximation $x^{(k)}$ is said to have the convergence factor $\eta \in [0, 1)$ if*

$$\|x - x^{(k+1)}\| \le \eta \|x - x^{(k)}\|.$$

The following theorem now motivates further definitions and shows a simple convergence result for the V-cycle.

**Theorem 5.2.6.** *Let $A = A_0 \in \mathbb{C}^{n \times n}$ be Hermitian positive definite and let the prolongation (and restriction) matrices as defined in (5.15) on each level have full rank. For the smoothers $S_l$ and all $e_l$ the following conditions may hold*

$$\|S_l e_l\|_{A_l}^2 \le \|e_l\|_{A_l}^2 - \delta_1 \|T_l e_l\|_{A_l}^2, \tag{5.22}$$

$$\|S_l e_l\|_{A_l}^2 \le \|e_l\|_{A_l}^2 - \delta_2 \|T_l S_l e_l\|_{A_l}^2 \tag{5.23}$$

*for all levels $l = 0, \ldots, l_{\max}$ with some constants $\delta_1, \delta_2 > 0$ being independent of $e_l$ and $l$. Assume that at least one pre-smoothing step as well as one post-smoothing step is carried out. Then $\delta_1, \delta_2 < 1$ and if smoothing on the coarsest level has the convergence factor $\eta < 1$ then for the convergence factor $\eta_l$ of the V-cycle on level $l$ the following inequality holds:*

$$\eta_l \le \max\left(\eta, \sqrt{\frac{1 - \delta_1}{1 + \delta_2}}\right). \tag{5.24}$$

*Proof.* As the start of the induction, we see that the proposition is true for $l_{\max}$. Assume now, that the convergence factor for the V-cycle on level $l + 1$ is $\eta_{l+1} \in [0, 1)$. For level $l$ we now denote the V-cycle coarse level correction operator with $\tilde{T}_l$. The V-cycle approximate solution (on level $l + 1$) of (5.9) will be named $\tilde{e}_{l+1}$ and the exact solution of (5.9) is denoted with $e_{l+1}$. Then the error on level $l$ *after* a V-cycle coarse level correction is

$$\tilde{T}_l e_l = e_l - P_l \tilde{e}_{l+1} = e_l - P_l e_{l+1} + P_l(e_{l+1} - \tilde{e}_{l+1}) = T_l e_l + P_l(e_{l+1} - \tilde{e}_{l+1}). \tag{5.25}$$

Now because of (5.21) we have

$$\|P_l(e_{l+1} - \tilde{e}_{l+1})\|_{A_l} = \|e_{l+1} - \tilde{e}_{l+1}\|_{A_{l+1}} \le \eta_{l+1} \|e_{l+1}\|_{A_{l+1}} = \eta_{l+1} \|P_l e_{l+1}\|_{A_l}$$

since $\tilde{e}_{l+1} = \tilde{e}_{l+1}^{(1)}$ and $\tilde{e}_{l+1}^{(0)} = 0$ (see also line 1 in algorithm 1). Due to (5.19) and (5.20) we can now state

$$\begin{aligned}
\|\tilde{T}_l e_l\|_{A_l}^2 &= \|T_l e_l\|_{A_l}^2 + \|P_l(e_{l+1} - \tilde{e}_{l+1})\|_{A_l}^2 \\
&\le \|T_l e_l\|_{A_l}^2 + \eta_{l+1}^2 \|P_l e_{l+1}\|_{A_l}^2 \\
&= \|T_l e_l\|_{A_l}^2 + \eta_{l+1}^2 \left(\|e_l\|_{A_l}^2 - \|T_l e_l\|_{A_l}^2\right).
\end{aligned}$$

Applying the first assumption (5.22) and then the last estimation to $S_l e_l$ instead of $e_l$ yields

$$\begin{aligned}
\|S_l \tilde{T}_l S_l e_l\|_{A_l}^2 &\le \|\tilde{T}_l S_l e_l\|_{A_l}^2 - \delta_1 \|T_l \tilde{T}_l S_l e_l\|_{A_l}^2 = \|\tilde{T}_l S_l e_l\|_{A_l}^2 - \delta_1 \|T_l S_l e_l\|_{A_l}^2 \\
&\le \|T_l S_l e_l\|_{A_l}^2 + \eta_{l+1}^2 \left(\|S_l e_l\|_{A_l}^2 - \|T_l S_l e_l\|_{A_l}^2\right) - \delta_1 \|T_l S_l e_l\|_{A_l}^2,
\end{aligned} \tag{5.26}$$

because from (5.25) and (5.20) follows $T_l \tilde{T}_l = T_l$. Substituting now $\|T_l S_l e_l\|_{A_l}^2 / \|S_l e_l\|_{A_l}^2 := \alpha$ in (5.26) and applying the second assumption (5.23) leads to

$$\begin{aligned}
\|S_l \tilde{T}_l S_l e_l\|_{A_l}^2 &\le \left(\alpha(1 - \eta_{l+1}^2 - \delta_1) + \eta_{l+1}^2\right) \|S_l e_l\|_{A_l}^2 \\
&\le \frac{\alpha(1 - \eta_{l+1}^2 - \delta_1) + \eta_{l+1}^2}{1 + \alpha \delta_2} \|e_l\|_{A_l}^2.
\end{aligned}$$

Since $T_l$ is a projection, we have $\|T_l S_l e_l\|^2_{A_l} < \|S_l e_l\|^2_{A_l} \Rightarrow \alpha < 1$. So for the convergence factor $\eta_l$ on level $l$ we get

$$\eta_l = \max_{0 \leq \alpha \leq 1} \frac{\alpha(1 - \eta^2_{l+1} - \delta_1) + \eta^2_{l+1}}{1 + \alpha \delta_2} = \max\left(\eta^2_{l+1}, \frac{1 - \delta_1}{1 + \delta_2}\right).$$

$\square$

A similar result for the W-cycle is presented in [Man88].

### 5.2.3   Algebraic smoothness for nonsymmetric problems

The conditions (5.22) and (5.23) of the last theorem show us the dependence between smoothing and coarse grid correction and lead to a characterization of smooth error in the algebraic sense. An error $e_l$ for which $\|T_l e_l\|_{A_l} \ll \|e_l\|_{A_l}$ is obviously well approximated on the coarser level $l+1$ but the smoother $S_l$ fails to reduce $e_l$ significantly, as we still have $\|S_l e_l\|_{A_l} \approx \|e_l\|_{A_l}$. Thus, errors with $S_l e_l \approx e_l$ will be called *algebraically smooth* – they mainly consist of eigenvectors corresponding to eigenvalues of $S_l$ which are close to one.

**Remark 5.2.7.** *Here lies a major difference between geometric and algebraic multigrid. In geometric multigrid, the coarse levels are fixed – they emerge from given discretizations, and smoothing and interpolation is chosen accordingly. In algebraic multigrid the smoothing is fixed, and the coarse levels (i.e. the interpolations) have to be constructed such that algebraically smooth errors can be approximated well on them.*

Obviously, the conditions

$$\|S_l e_l\|^2_{A_l} \leq \|e_l\|^2_{A_l} - \alpha_1 \|\|e_l\|\|^2_{A_l}, \tag{5.27}$$

$$\|T_l e_l\|^2_{A_l} \leq \beta_1 \|\|e_l\|\|^2_{A_l}, \tag{5.28}$$

and

$$\|S_l e_l\|^2_{A_l} \leq \|e_l\|^2_{A_l} - \alpha_2 \|\|S_l e_l\|\|^2_{A_l}, \tag{5.29}$$

$$\|T_l e_l\|^2_{A_l} \leq \beta_2 \|\|e_l\|\|^2_{A_l}, \tag{5.30}$$

imply (5.22) respectively (5.23) with $\delta_1 = \alpha_1/\beta_1$ and $\delta_2 = \alpha_2/\beta_2$.

**Definition 5.2.8** (Algebraic smoothing and approximation property). *In the algebraic multigrid context, condition (5.27) respectively (5.29) will be called* smoothing property, *while (5.28) and (5.30) will be referred to as* approximation property.

In [RS87], Theorem 4.2 and 4.4, it is shown that Gauss-Seidel as well as Jacobi relaxation satisfy the conditions (5.27) and (5.29) for symmetric positive definite matrices.

In order to characterize smooth error we first state the following lemma.

**Lemma 5.2.9.** *Let $A \in \mathbb{C}^{n \times n}$. If $a_{ii} > 0$, $i = 1, \ldots, n$ then*

$$\|e\|^2_A \leq \|e\|_D \|\|e\|\|_A, \quad \forall e \in \mathbb{C}^n. \tag{5.31}$$

*Proof.* Using the Cauchy-Schwarz inequality, we get:

$$\|e\|^2_A = |e^* A e| = |e^* D^{\frac{1}{2}} D^{-\frac{1}{2}} A e| \leq \|D^{\frac{1}{2}} e\|_2 \|D^{-\frac{1}{2}} A e\|_2 = \|e\|_D \|\|e\|\|_A.$$

$\square$

If now $e = e_l$ is a smooth error with $\|Se\|_A \approx \|e\|_A$ we have $0 \approx \|Se\|^2_A - \|e\|^2_A \leq -\alpha_1 \|\|e\|\|^2_A \Longrightarrow \|\|e\|\|^2_A \approx 0$. For a relatively large error $e$, this means $\|\|e\|\|_A \ll \|e\|_A$, and combined with Lemma 5.2.9, it yields $\|e\|_A \ll \|e\|_D$.

**Smooth error in the real case**

Looking at the consequences this property has for real matrices, for arbitrary $A \in \mathbb{R}^{n \times n}$ with $a_{ii} > 0$ for $i = 1, \ldots, n$, we get

$$\frac{1}{2} \sum_{i=1}^{n} \sum_{j=1}^{n} (-a_{ij})(e_i - e_j)^2 + \frac{1}{2} \sum_{i=1}^{n} \left( \sum_{j=1}^{n} a_{ij} + \sum_{j=1}^{n} a_{ji} \right) e_i^2 = e^T A e$$

$$\leq |e^T A e| = \|e\|_A^2 \tag{5.32}$$

$$\ll \|e\|_D^2 = \sum_{i=1}^{n} a_{ii} e_i^2.$$

In the case when the row and column sums are negligible, or at least not negative, i.e. $\sum_{j=1}^{n} a_{ij} + \sum_{j=1}^{n} a_{ji} \gtrsim 0$, this simplifies to

$$\frac{1}{2} \sum_{i=1}^{n} \sum_{j=1}^{n} (-a_{ij})(e_i - e_j)^2 \ll \sum_{i=1}^{n} a_{ii} e_i^2, \tag{5.33}$$

and if we further assume $a_{ij} < 0$ for $i = 1, \ldots, n$ and every $j \neq i$, we get on the average for each variable $i$:

$$\frac{1}{2} \sum_{\substack{j=1 \\ j \neq i}}^{n} \frac{(-a_{ij})}{a_{ii}} \frac{(e_i - e_j)^2}{e_i^2} \ll 1. \tag{5.34}$$

This, of course, is a heuristic approach, but it triggers the observation that if $\frac{-a_{ij}}{a_{ii}}$ is quite large, the difference between the $i$-th and the $j$-th error component has to be relatively small. The circumstance, that $\frac{-a_{ij}}{a_{ii}}$ is large (compared to other entries in the row $i$) is often referred to as a *large negative connection* from $i$ to $j$ (cf. Definition 5.2.22).

**Remark 5.2.10.** *The above assumptions are certainly true for M-matrices, and if A is also symmetric, one only has to ensure that the row sums are $\geq 0$. Note that the matrix from (5.3) has this property as well as many other stiffness matrices arising from finite difference and finite element schemes. Note also, that A doesn't need to be symmetric nor positive definite to derive this inequality.*

**Smooth error in the complex case**

Regarding the complex matrix $A \in \mathbb{C}^{n \times n}$, we need also to take into account the matrix $\bar{A}$. If $A_{Her} := \frac{1}{2}(A + A^*)$ is the Hermitian part of $A$, we define $\hat{A} := A_{Her} + \bar{A}_{Her}$ and we get similarly to the above:

$$\frac{1}{2} \sum_{i=1}^{n} \sum_{j=1}^{n} -\hat{a}_{ij} |e_i - e_j|^2 + \sum_{i=1}^{n} \left( \sum_{j=1}^{n} \hat{a}_{ij} \right) |e_i|^2 = e^* A_{Her} e + e^* \bar{A}_{Her} e$$

$$\leq |e^* A_{Her} e| + |e^* \bar{A}_{Her} e| = \|e\|_{A_{Her}}^2 + \|e\|_{\bar{A}_{Her}}^2$$

$$\ll 2\|e\|_D^2 = 2 \sum_{i=1}^{n} a_{ii} |e_i|^2,$$

with

$$\hat{a}_{ij} = \frac{1}{2}(a_{ij} + \bar{a}_{ij} + a_{ji} + \bar{a}_{ji}). \tag{5.35}$$

Again positive diagonal elements were assumed. Since $\hat{a}_{ij} \in \mathbb{R}$, we look at the case $\sum_{j=1}^{n} \hat{a}_{ij} \gtrsim 0$ and $\hat{a}_{ij} < 0$ for $i, j = 1, \ldots, n$ and $j \neq i$, using the mean value for each variable $i$:

$$\frac{1}{4} \sum_{\substack{j=1 \\ j \neq i}}^{n} \frac{-\hat{a}_{ij}}{a_{ii}} \frac{|e_i - e_j|^2}{|e_i|^2} \ll 1. \tag{5.36}$$

**Essentially positive type matrices**

A generalization of matrices with only negative off-diagonal entries (such as M-matrices) are matrices of *essentially positive type* introduced in [Bra86].

**Definition 5.2.11** (Essentially positive type). *A matrix* $A = (a_{ij})_{i,j=1}^n \in \mathbb{R}^{n \times n}$ *is called of* essentially positive type *if there is a constant* $c > 0$ *such that for all* $e \in \mathbb{R}^n$,

$$\sum_{i=1}^n \sum_{j=1}^n (-a_{ij})(e_i - e_j)^2 \geq c \sum_{i=1}^n \sum_{j=1}^n (-a_{ij}^-)(e_i - e_j)^2 \tag{5.37}$$

This type of matrices can be characterized as perturbed M-matrices with positive off-diagonal elements which are small compared to the negative entries. If now (5.37) is applied to (5.33) we can still see, that smooth error varies slowly in the direction of large negative connections.

## 5.2.4   Interpolation for nonsymmetric problems

Considering now the prolongation and restriction operators $P_l$ and $R_l$, it follows from the above remarks, that they should be chosen such that the approximation properties (5.28) and (5.30) are fulfilled by the operator $T_l$. As in [RS87] we would like the prolongation to be of the following form.

**Definition 5.2.12** (Prolongation matrix). *Assume that we have a* $C/F$-*Splitting (cf. Definition 5.2.1) given on level* $l$. *Let* $\varphi : C_l \to \Omega_{l+1} := \{1, \ldots, n_{l+1}\}$ *be a mapping that renumbers the marked coarse variables for the next level. The general prolongation matrix* $P_l = (p_{ik}) \in \mathbb{C}^{n_{l+1} \times n_l}$ *from level* $l+1$ *to level* $l$ *is defined as*

$$p_{ik} := \begin{cases} w_{ik} & \text{if} \quad i \in F_l \quad \text{and} \quad \varphi^{-1}(k) \in \mathcal{P}_i^l \\ 1 & \text{if} \quad i \in C_l \quad \text{and} \quad \varphi^{-1}(k) = i \\ 0 & \text{else} \end{cases} \tag{5.38}$$

*with the according interpolation weights* $w_{ik} \in \mathbb{C}, w_{ik} \neq 0$ *and the interpolation variables* $\mathcal{P}_i^l \subset C_l$ *which contribute to the interpolation of* $i$.

It is evident, that this kind of prolongation matrix has the full rank $n_{l+1}$. The importance of the correct interpolation is shown in the next statements concerning the two-level convergence.

**Lemma 5.2.13.** *Let* $A_l \in \mathbb{C}^{n_l \times n_l}$ *have positive diagonal elements. For* $e_l \in \mathbb{C}^{n_l}$ *the interpolation* $P_l$ *may satisfy*

$$\min_{e_{l+1}} \|e_l - P_l e_{l+1}\|_{D_l}^2 \leq \tau \|e_l\|_{A_l}^2, \tag{5.39}$$

*with* $\tau$ *being independent of* $e_l$. *Then for the operator* $T_l$ *holds the following:*

$$\|T_l x\|_{A_l}^2 \leq \tau \|\|T_l x\|\|_{A_l}^2 \tag{5.40}$$

*for all* $x \in \mathbb{C}^{n_l}$.

*Proof.* First let $e_l \in \text{Range}(T_l)$. This means that there is a $x \in \mathbb{C}^{n_l}$ with $T_l x = e_l$. Hence we have for arbitrary $e_{l+1} \in \mathbb{C}^{n_{l+1}}$

$$\begin{aligned} |(e_l - P_l e_{l+1})^* A_l e_l| &= |e_l^* A_l e_l - e_{l+1}^* (P_l)^* A_l T_l x| \\ &= |e_l^* A_l e_l - e_{l+1}^* \big( (P_l)^* A_l - \underbrace{(P_l)^* A_l P_l}_{=A_{l+1}} A_{l+1}^{-1} (P_l)^* A_l \big) x| \\ &= |e_l^* A_l e_l| = \|e_l\|_{A_l}^2. \end{aligned}$$

By applying now the Cauchy-Schwarz inequality, we get

$$
\begin{aligned}
\|e_l\|_{A_l}^2 &= |(e_l - P_l e_{l+1})^* D_l^{\frac{1}{2}} D_l^{-\frac{1}{2}} A_l e_l| \\
&\leq \|D_l^{\frac{1}{2}}(e_l - P_l e_{l+1})\|_2 \|D_l^{-\frac{1}{2}} A_l e_l\|_2 \\
&= \|e_l - P_l e_{l+1}\|_{D_l} \|e_l\|_{A_l}.
\end{aligned}
$$

Using now the assumption (5.39) yields (5.40). $\qquad\square$

This directly leads to a convergence result for the two-level cycle with post-smoothing only.

**Theorem 5.2.14** (Two-level convergence). *Let $A_l \in \mathbb{C}^{n_l \times n_l}$ have only positive diagonal elements and let the property (5.27) be satisfied for the smoother $S_l$ with $\alpha := \alpha_1 > 0$. If $T_l$ satisfies the conditions*

$$
\|T_l e\|_{A_l}^2 \leq \tau \|\|T_l e\|\|_{A_l}^2 \tag{5.41}
$$

$$
\|T_l\|_{A_l} =: \gamma < \frac{\tau}{\tau - \alpha} \tag{5.42}
$$

*with $\tau > 0$ independent of $e \in \mathbb{C}^{n_l}$, then $\tau \geq \alpha$ and the two-level (algebraic) multigrid cycle involving the levels $l$ and $l+1$ converges with a convergence factor of $\sqrt{\gamma(1 - \alpha/\tau)}$ when using post-smoothing.*

*Proof.* With the same argumentation as in [Stü99], Theorem 4.1 we immediately get for $e \in \mathbb{C}^{n_l}$

$$
\|S_l T_l e\|_{A_l}^2 \leq \|T_l e\|_{A_l}^2 - \alpha_1 \|\|T_l e\|\|_{A_l}^2 \leq (1 - \frac{\alpha}{\tau})\|T_l e\|_{A_l}^2 \leq (1 - \frac{\alpha}{\tau})\gamma \|e\|_{A_l}^2.
$$

$\qquad\square$

**Remark 5.2.15.** *Note that for Lemma 5.2.13 and Theorem 5.2.14 we didn't need the symmetry nor the positive definiteness of $A_l$. Instead, the critical condition is now the boundedness of $\|T_l\|_{A_l}$ in (5.42). If $A_l$ is symmetric, $T_l$ is an orthogonal projection (cf. Lemma 5.2.3) and we have $\|T_l\|_{A_l} = 1$, which permits the proofs usually found in the literature.*

The crucial question is the decision, whether a variable $i$ might be interpolated by neighbouring variables, so that it can be neglected on a coarser level. Since we don't have access to the mesh, we only have the matrix as the source of information about our problem. But if $A$ was assembled as a stiffness matrix from a finite element method (or FDM, FVM), all the geometrical information is represented somehow in the matrix. The neighbourhood of a variable $i$ is therefore formulated in terms of matrix entries. Let in the following $A \in \mathbb{C}^{n \times n}$ be a matrix with entries $(a_{ij})_{i,j=1}^n$.

**Definition 5.2.16** (Neighbourhood). *The neighbourhood of a variable $i \in \Omega = \{1, \ldots, n\}$ with respect to a matrix $A \in \mathbb{R}^{n \times n}$ is defined as*

$$
\mathcal{N}_i(A) := \{j \in \Omega \mid i \neq j, \, a_{ij} \neq 0\}.
$$

*If it is unambiguous, which matrix is meant, we simply write $\mathcal{N}_i$. The elements of $\mathcal{N}_i$ are called* neighbours *of $i$. Accordingly, we define the sets of* negative *and* positive neighbours*, $\mathcal{N}_i^-$ and $\mathcal{N}_i^+$, as*

$$
\mathcal{N}_i^- := \{j \in \mathcal{N}_i \mid a_{ij} < 0\}, \qquad\qquad \mathcal{N}_i^+ := \{j \in \mathcal{N}_i \mid a_{ij} > 0\}.
$$

Note that the property "is neighbour of" is only symmetric if the sparse pattern $\mathcal{M}(A)$ is symmetric, which is the case for FEM (FDM,FVM) discretizations.

**Definition 5.2.17** (Sparse pattern). *The* sparse pattern *$\mathcal{M}(A) = (m_{ij})_{i,j=1}^n \in \{0,1\}^{n \times n}$ of $A$ is a matrix whose entries are defined as*

$$
m_{ij} = \begin{cases} 1 & \text{if } a_{ij} \neq 0, \\ 0 & \text{else.} \end{cases}
$$

**Direct interpolation**

A first type of interpolation for matrices $A \in \mathbb{R}^{n \times n}$ with $a_{ij} \leq 0$, $i \neq j$, and $a_{ii} > 0$, $i = 1, \ldots, n$ is defined in [Stü99] as follows

**Definition 5.2.18** (Direct interpolation). *The interpolation weights in 5.38 are chosen as*

$$w_{ik} := \frac{-\alpha_i a_{ik}}{a_{ii}}, \qquad \text{with} \qquad \alpha_i := \frac{\sum_{j \in \mathcal{N}_i} a_{ij}}{\sum_{k \in \mathcal{P}_i} a_{ik}}$$

*with $\mathcal{P}_i \subseteq C \cap \mathcal{N}_i$.*

In the following, we show, that this interpolation satisfies the approximation property (5.39).

**Theorem 5.2.19.** *Let $A \in \mathbb{R}^{n \times n}$ with $a_{ij} \leq 0$, $i \neq j$, and $a_{ii} > 0$, $i = 1, \ldots, n$, as well as*

$$\delta_i \sum_{j=1}^{n} a_{ji} \geq \sum_{j=1}^{n} a_{ij} \quad \text{with some} \quad \delta_i \geq 1 \quad \text{for each} \quad i \in F \tag{5.43}$$

*and*

$$\sum_{j=1}^{n} a_{ij} \geq 0 \quad \text{for} \quad i = 1, \ldots, n. \tag{5.44}$$

*Furthermore, assume there is a $C/F$-Splitting with a $\mu \geq 2$ such that, for each $i \in F$, there is a set $\emptyset \neq \mathcal{P}_i \subseteq C \cap \mathcal{N}_i$ with*

$$\sum_{k \in \mathcal{P}_i} |a_{ik}| \geq \frac{2}{\mu} \sum_{j \in \mathcal{N}_i} |a_{ij}|. \tag{5.45}$$

*Then the direct interpolation satisfies property (5.39) with $\tau := \mu \delta_{\max}$,*

$$\delta_{\max} := \max_{i=1, \ldots, n} \delta_i. \tag{5.46}$$

*Proof.* First of all, let $e_l \in \mathbb{R}^n$. For the $C/F$-Splitting we choose a permutation matrix $\Pi \in \mathbb{R}^{n \times n}$ such that the $F$-variables are sorted before the $C$-variables as in (5.17) and set

$$\Pi e_l := \begin{pmatrix} e_F \\ e_C \end{pmatrix},$$

resulting in

$$\|e_l - P_l e_C\|_{D_l}^2 = \|\Pi e_l - \Pi P_l e_C\|_{D_l}^2 = \left\| \begin{pmatrix} e_F \\ e_C \end{pmatrix} - \begin{pmatrix} P_{FC} \\ P_{CC} \end{pmatrix} e_C \right\|_{D_l}^2 = \|e_F - P_{FC} e_C\|_{D_{FF}}^2$$

Now we can estimate

$$\min_{e_{l+1}} \|e_l - P_l e_{l+1}\|_{D_l}^2 \leq \|e_F - P_{FC} e_C\|_{D_{FF}}^2 = \sum_{i \in F} a_{ii} \Big( e_i - \sum_{k \in \mathcal{P}_i} w_{ik} e_k \Big)^2$$

$$= \sum_{i \in F} a_{ii} \Big( \sum_{k \in \mathcal{P}_i} w_{ik}(e_i - e_k) + (1 - \sum_{k \in \mathcal{P}_i} w_{ik}) e_i \Big)^2$$

$$\leq \sum_{i \in F} a_{ii} \Big( \sum_{k \in \mathcal{P}_i} w_{ik}(e_i - e_k)^2 + (1 - \sum_{k \in \mathcal{P}_i} w_{ik}) e_i^2 \Big), \tag{5.47}$$

using Jensen's Inequality and regarding

$$0 < w_{ik} \leq 1 \quad \text{and} \quad a_{ii} \Big( 1 - \sum_{k \in \mathcal{P}_i} w_{ik} \Big) = \sum_{j=1}^{n} a_{ij} \geq 0 \quad \Longrightarrow \quad 0 < 1 - \sum_{k \in \mathcal{P}_i} w_{ik} \leq 1.$$

Condition (5.45) now is equivalent to $\tau \geq 2\alpha_i$, and remembering that $a_{ii}w_{ik} = -\alpha_i a_{ik}$, we have $a_{ii}w_{ik} \leq \frac{\tau}{2}(-a_{ik})$. Using now (5.43) and then (5.32), we get

$$(5.47) \leq \sum_{i \in F}(\sum_{k \in \mathcal{P}_i} \frac{\tau}{2}(-a_{ik})(e_i - e_k)^2 + \sum_{k=1}^{n} a_{ik}e_k^2)$$

$$\leq \tau \sum_{i \in F}(\sum_{k \in \mathcal{P}_i} \frac{1}{2}(-a_{ik})(e_i - e_k)^2 + \frac{\delta_i}{2} \sum_{k=1}^{n}(a_{ik} + a_{ki})e_i^2)$$

$$\leq \mu \delta_{\max} \|e\|_A^2.$$

$\square$

Note that this result holds even for nonsymmetric matrices, as long as (5.43) is fulfilled.

**Remark 5.2.20.** *One can show that for example convection diffusion reaction problems discretized with finite differences yield stiffness matrices, that have the above property (5.43). For example on $\Omega = (0,1) \times (0,1)$ using an equidistant grid with mesh width $h$, constant $\nu$, $\mathbf{b} = (b_1, b_2)^T > 0$, $c$, the according matrix fulfills (5.43) with*

$$\delta_{\max} \leq 1 + \frac{2\|\mathbf{b}\|_\infty h}{2\nu + ch^2}. \tag{5.48}$$

**General interpolation**

If we choose now the general interpolation with

$$\alpha_i = \frac{\sum_{j \in \mathcal{N}_i} a_{ij}^-}{\sum_{k \in \mathcal{P}_i} a_{ik}^-} \quad \text{and} \quad \beta_i = \frac{\sum_{j \in \mathcal{N}_i} a_{ij}^+}{\sum_{k \in \mathcal{P}_i} a_{ik}^+}, \tag{5.49}$$

setting the interpolation weights to

$$w_{ik} := \begin{cases} -\alpha_i a_{ik}/a_{ii} & \text{for } k \in \mathcal{P}_i^- \\ -\beta_i a_{ik}/a_{ii} & \text{for } k \in \mathcal{P}_i^+ \end{cases} \tag{5.50}$$

it is shown in [Stü99], Theorem 4.6, that if $A$ is symmetric, this satisfies assumption (5.39) of Lemma 5.2.13 and thus guaranties at least the two-level convergence. The concrete choice of the interpolation variable set $\mathcal{P}_i$ is deferred until the end of the next subsection.

### 5.2.5 Strong couplings and coarse variable selection

In order to give a criterion that allows us to decide which variables are more important and which can be neglected (in the sense that they can be interpolated by the others) we look again at the estimates (5.33) and (5.34) for the real case, $A \in \mathbb{R}^{n \times n}$. If $-a_{ij}$ is relatively large, compared to other entries in row $i$, the error in the $i$-th component differs only slightly from that in the $j$-th component. This motivates the following definition of strong (negative) connections between variables.

**Definition 5.2.21** (Strong negative coupling). *Let $A \in \mathbb{R}^{n \times n}$. A variable $i \in \Omega = \{1, \ldots, n\}$ is said to be* strongly negatively coupled *(or connected) to another variable $j$, if*

$$-a_{ij} \geq \theta \max_{\substack{k \neq i \\ k=1,\ldots,n}} |a_{ik}|,$$

*where $\theta$ is threshold value between 0 and 1 (we will also refer to it as the coupling or coarsening parameter).*

For complex matrices we suggest to consider

$$-\hat{a}_{ij} \geq \theta \max_{\substack{k \neq i \\ k=1,\ldots,n}} |\hat{a}_{ik}|,$$

where $\hat{a}_{ij}$ is defined as in (5.35). Note that the relationship of $i$ being strongly negatively connected to $j$ is normally not symmetric, not even for symmetric matrices. Therefore, another useful definition is

**Definition 5.2.22** (Strong neighbourhood). *The* strong (negative) neighbourhood *of a variable* $i \in \Omega = \{1,\ldots,n\}$ *is defined as*

$$\mathcal{S}_i := \mathcal{S}_{i,\theta} := \{j \in \mathcal{N}_i \,|\, i \text{ is strongly negatively coupled to } j\}.$$

*The elements of* $\mathcal{S}_i$ *will also be called* strong (negative) neighbours *of* $i$. *The* strong transpose (negative) neighbourhood *of a variable* $i$ *is the set of variables which are strongly negatively connected to* $i$:

$$\mathcal{S}_i^T := \{j \in \Omega \,:\, i \in \mathcal{S}_j\}.$$

*Since the coarsening parameter* $\theta$ *is fixed for the whole matrix (and indeed mostly even fixed for the whole coarsening process), we will normally omit it.*

We should keep in mind the equivalence

$$j \in \mathcal{S}_i^T \Longleftrightarrow i \in \mathcal{S}_j.$$

The idea of coarsening is now the following. Assume that we have chosen a variable $i$ to become a coarse level variable. Then all variables that are strongly negatively connected to $i$ will get $F$-variables. Then the next $C$-variable is chosen and so on. To ensure a uniform distribution of $C$- and $F$-variables a measure $\lambda_i$ was introduced in [Stü99] to indicate how valuable a variable $i$ is as a $C$-variable:

$$\lambda_i := \#\big[\mathcal{S}_i^T \cap U\big] + 2\#\big[\mathcal{S}_i^T \cap F\big] \tag{5.51}$$

where $U$ is the set of variables which are not yet inserted into $C$ or $F$. It tries to measure the importance of $i$ for the set $C$, by first considering how many $F$-variables (namely $\#\big[\mathcal{S}_i^T \cap U\big]$) it would yield, but then also even stronger taking into account the $F$ to $F$ connectivity it would produce. This concrete measure is a mere heuristical approach, other definitions are possible, like

$$\lambda_i := \#\big[\mathcal{S}_i^T\big] + \#\big[\mathcal{S}_i^T \cap F\big] \tag{5.52}$$

which was used in [GNR98]. However, $\#\big[\mathcal{S}_i^T \cap U\big]$ is a more realistic value than $\#\big[\mathcal{S}_i^T\big]$ which gives no information about how many $F$-variables $i$ would yield currently. But on the other hand, (5.52) is easier to implement, since it requires fewer update loops than (5.51). We summarize the ideas in the following algorithm.

---

**Algorithm 2: Splitting process**

---

Input: $\Omega_l = \{1, \ldots, n_l\}$, $\mathcal{S}_i$, $\mathcal{S}_i^T$ for $i = 1, \ldots, n_l$
Output: A splitting of the variables with $\Omega_l = F \cup C$, $F \cap C = \varnothing$
$F \leftarrow \varnothing$
$C \leftarrow \varnothing$
$U \leftarrow \Omega_l$
for $i \in U$ do
    Compute the measures $\lambda_i$
end
1  while $U \neq \varnothing$ do
2     Choose $i$ with $\lambda_i = \max_{k \in U} \lambda_k$
     $C \leftarrow C \cup \{i\}$
     $U \leftarrow U \setminus \{i\}$
3     for $j \in H := \mathcal{S}_i^T \cap U$ do
       $F \leftarrow F \cup \{j\}$
     end
     $U \leftarrow U \setminus H$
     for $k \in (\mathcal{S}_i \cup \bigcup_{j \in H} \mathcal{S}_j) \cap U$ do
       Update the measures $\lambda_k$
     end
end

---

Note that for the measure (5.52) it would be sufficient to update only the $\lambda_k$ with

$$k \in \bigcup_{j \in H} \mathcal{S}_j \cap U.$$

Now we are able to define the set $\mathcal{P}_i^-$ of interpolation variables as

$$\mathcal{P}_i^- := C \cap \mathcal{S}_i. \tag{5.53}$$

For $\mathcal{N}_i^+ = \emptyset$ we set $\mathcal{P}_i^+ = \emptyset$ and $\beta_i = 0$. If $\mathcal{N}_i^+$ is not empty, but only contains relatively small entries (compared to the absolute values of the negative entries) we again set $\mathcal{P}_i^+ = \emptyset$, $\beta_i = 0$ and modify (5.50) by adding these positive entries to the diagonal before computing $w_{ik}$:

$$w_{ik} = \frac{\alpha_i a_{ik}}{a_{ii} + \sum_{j \in \mathcal{N}_i} a_{ij}^+}, \tag{5.54}$$

with $\alpha_i$ defined as in (5.49). This interpolation reflects the properties of essential positive type matrices (cf. [Stü99] showing that this type of interpolation satifies the approximation property (5.39)). If $\mathcal{N}_i^+$ contains large positive elements, i.e. the set

$$\mathcal{S}_i^+ := \{j \in \mathcal{N}_i \mid a_{ij} \geq \theta^+ \max_{k \neq i} |a_{ik}|\}$$

with $\theta^+ > 0$ is not empty, then we have to modify the splitting such that each $F$-variable that has both strong negative and positive couplings is interpolated from both types of connections in $C$. That is, we have to ensure, that $C \cap \mathcal{S}_i^+ \neq \emptyset$ for these points $i$.

However, in most cases of interest here, (5.54) is sufficient for an accurate interpolation.

## 5.2.6 An example

We would now like to look on an example of the scalar convection diffusion problem (4.1) in order to show the effect of the AMG coarsening especially under the influence of convection. For this we take

$$-\nu \Delta u + \mathbf{b} \cdot \nabla u = f \quad \text{in } \Omega := (0,1) \times (0,1)$$
$$u = 0 \quad \text{on } \partial\Omega,$$

and set $f \equiv 1$ and $\mathbf{b} = (b_1, b_2)^T \in \mathbb{R}^2$, with the constants $b_1, b_2 > 0$. For the simplicity of the presentation we discretize this problem with finite differences, on an equidistant grid with mesh width $h = 1/(N + 1)$, using backward (upwind) differences.

This leads to the matrix

$$A = \frac{1}{h^2} \begin{pmatrix} T_N & -\nu I_N & & \\ -(\nu + hb_2)I_N & \ddots & & \ddots \\ & \ddots & & \ddots & -\nu I_N \\ & & & -(\nu + hb_2)I_N & T_N \end{pmatrix} \in \mathbb{R}^{N^2 \times N^2},$$

with

$$T_N = \mathrm{tridiag}(-(\nu + hb_1), 4\nu + h(b_1 + b_2), -\nu) \in \mathbb{R}^{N \times N}.$$

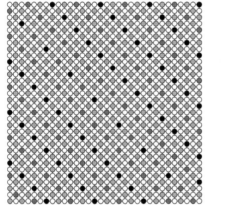

Figure 5.1: Diagonal convection, coarsening structure, $\nu = 1$

Figure 5.2: Diagonal convection, coarsening structure, $\nu = 10^{-6}$

Figures 5.1 and 5.2 illustrate the different behaviour of the coarsening strategy in dependance of the amount of diffusion. The intensity of the colour of the points indicate on wich level they still reside. The white points are coarsened away on the first level, becoming $F$-points. The darkest points are the remaining variables on the coarsest level. Here, 3 levels were generated, with $\theta = 0.5$.

For both computations we have set $\mathbf{b} = (1, 1)^T$, $h = 1/33$, $f \equiv 1$. For $\nu = 1$ the diffusion part dominates the equation and yields a uniform coarsening in *all* directions, whereas for $\nu = 10^{-6}$, we have a dominant convection resulting in a coarsening along the streamlines.

Taking a closer look at the coarsening process for the convection dominated problem, we see now that the sets $\mathcal{S}_i$ and $\mathcal{S}_i^T$ are chosen in the following way:

$$
\mathcal{S}_i = \begin{cases} \{2, N+1\} & i = 1 \\ \{i-1\} & i = 2, \ldots, N \\ \{i-N\} & i = kN + 1, \ k = 1, \ldots, N - 1 \\ \{i-1, i-N\} & \text{else.} \end{cases} \qquad \text{upstream direction}
$$

$$
\mathcal{S}_i^T = \begin{cases} \{2, 1+N\} & i = 1 \\ \{1, 3, 2+N\} & i = 2 \\ \{i+N\} & i = kN, \ k = 1, \ldots, N - 1 \\ \{i+1\} & i = N^2 - N + 1, \ldots, N^2 - 1 \\ \emptyset & i = N^2 \\ \{i+1, i+N\} & \text{else.} \end{cases} \qquad \text{downstream direction}
$$

The numbering of the grid starts with 1 in the lower left corner, $N$ is at the lower right corner, and so on, ending with $N^2 - N + 1$ in the upper left and $N^2$ in the upper right corner.

One now can easily see that Algorithm 2 coarsens in the downstream direction of the convection field $\mathbf{b}$ when the coarsening parameter $\theta$ is bounded as in (5.55). On the other hand, it groups together those points which lie orthogonal to the streamlines induced by $\mathbf{b}$. These are the points which carry the important information to interpolate the other points.

This approach can be applied also if we loosen the restriction of positive vector fields $\mathbf{b} \in \mathbb{R}^2$. Arbitrary constant convection fields and even non constant vector fields $\mathbf{b} = \mathbf{b}(x, y)$ (using forward differences where the according convection component $b_i$ is negative) yield similar results.

The actual solving/iteration process consists of standard V-cycles with SSOR smoothing ($\omega = 1.0$). The stopping criterion was the reduction of the residual by a factor of $10^{-6}$.

Note that for the convection dominated problem with $\mathbf{b} \equiv (1, 1)^T$ AMG turns out to be nearly an exact solver - it only needs one V-cycle step to reduce the residual by more than $10^{-15}$. This is due to the fact, that in this case, the lexicographical ordering of the unknowns is optimal for SOR/SSOR-type smoothers. A convection field $\mathbf{b}$ that points in the opposite direction or is not constant at all, may considerably slow down the performance of the algorithm. For those cases, we suggest to apply a *downwind numbering* algorithm from e.g. [BW95] or [HP97] in a preprocess before we apply the actual splitting algorithm, in order to find a numbering which is more suited for the smoother.

For the diffusion dominated case, the direction of coarsening is not that easy to detect for the algorithm, resulting in a need for more multigrid cycles in order to reduce the residual by the same amount as in the convection dominated case. However for constant vector fields $\mathbf{b} = (b_1, b_2)^T \in \mathbb{R}^2$, $b_1, b_2 \neq 0$ we can enforce the coarsening along the streamlines (at least for the first level) even in this case, by choosing $\theta$ between the following bounds:

$$
\frac{\nu}{\nu + b_{\min}} < \theta \leq \frac{\nu + b_{\min}}{\nu + b_{\max}}, \tag{5.55}
$$

where $b_{\max} := \max\{|b_1|, |b_2|\}$, $b_{\min} := \min\{|b_1|, |b_2|\}$. Especially for small $h$ this choice turns out to be advantageous as one sees in Table 5.1

| h | | $\theta = 0.25$ | $\theta = 0.5$ | $\theta = 0.55$ |
|---|---|---|---|---|
| $\frac{1}{128}$ | setup time [s] | 1.55 | 1.62 | 2.64 |
| | solve time [s] | 6.13 | 3.18 | 1.18 |
| | cycles | 46 | 22 | 5 |
| $\frac{1}{256}$ | setup time [s] | 6.3 | 7.0 | 12.0 |
| | solve time [s] | 53.46 | 24.75 | 6.3 |
| | cycles | 93 | 39 | 6 |
| $\frac{1}{512}$ | setup time [s] | 25.63 | 27.3 | 44.14 |
| | solve time [s] | 378.25 | 138.57 | 30.93 |
| | cycles | 163 | 55 | 8 |

Table 5.1: The effect of $\theta$ on diffusion dominated problems, $\nu = 1$

## 5.3 Complexity of the AMG preprocess

In this section we would like to investigate the time and memory complexity of the AMG specific algorithms. This includes especially the coarse variable selection and the multiplication of sparse matrices which are essential ingredients of the AMG preprocess (cf. Definition 5.2.1).

### 5.3.1 $C/F$-Splitting process

First we take a closer look at the coarsening process and its involved components.

**Definition 5.3.1.** *For the level $l$ let*

$$
\begin{array}{ll}
n := n_l & \text{be the dimension of the current matrix } A_l, \\
r_i := \#[\mathcal{N}_i] & \text{the number of nonzero entries in its } i\text{-th row,} \\
c_i & \text{the number of nonzero entries in its } i\text{-th column,} \\
s_i := \#[\mathcal{S}_i] & \text{the number of strong (negative) neighbours of } i, \\
s_i^T := \#[\mathcal{S}_i^T] & \text{the number of variables which have } i \text{ as a strong neighbour.}
\end{array}
$$

*Furthermore, $r_{av} = \sum_{i=1}^{n} r_i/n$ denotes the average number of nonzero entries in its rows and $r_{\max} := \max_{i=1,\ldots,n} r_i$ the maximal number of entries in a row. Similarly we define $c_{\max}, s_{\max}, s_{\max}^T, etc.$*

#### Preliminaries

We will use the symbols and notation of Section 5.2. Before we can apply Algorithm 2 we have to compute the sets $\mathcal{S}_i$ and $\mathcal{S}_i^T$ for every $i$ in $\Omega = \{1, \ldots, n\}$. Note that both sets can be computed in the same loop with $\sum_{i=1}^{n} 2r_i = 2nr_{av}$ comparisons (and as many assignments in the worst case).

Concerning the coarsening algorithm itself, first the weights $\lambda_i$ (cf. (5.51)) have to be computed. Since in the beginning, it is $U = \Omega$ and $F = \emptyset$, we have $\lambda_i = \#[\mathcal{S}_i^T]$, for $i = 1, \ldots, n$, requiring $n$ assignments only, since the cardinality of the sets $\mathcal{S}_i^T$ should be computed on the fly by the above procedure. The first maximal $\lambda_i$ is obtained while setting the initial weights.

#### Generating the $C/F$-Splitting and updating the weights

Setting $i$ as a $C$-variable and all $j \in \mathcal{S}_i^T$ as F-variables should require not more than $1 + \#[\mathcal{S}_i^T]$ assignments if an array $v$ of length $n$ is held for storing the splitting, e.g. like:

$$
v[i] = \begin{cases} "true" & i \in C, \\ "false" & i \in F. \end{cases}
$$

After assigning the new $C$- and $F$-variables, the according weights must be updated. Of course only the weights for which $\lambda_i$ has changed must be treated. If $i_{\max}$ is the variable chosen to be the new $C$-Variable (in line 2 of Algorithm 2) and $H_{i_{\max}} := \mathcal{S}_{i_{\max}}^T \cap U$ (cf. line 3 of the algorithm) the weights for all variables $i$ with

$$i \in T_{i_{\max}} := (\mathcal{S}_{i_{\max}} \cup \bigcup_{j \in H_{i_{\max}}} \mathcal{S}_j) \cap U \qquad (5.56)$$

have to be computed newly. Let $\lambda_i^{(k)}$ be the weight of variable $i$ and $U^{(k)}$, $F^{(k)}$ the according sets after the $k$-th iteration of the while loop beginning in line 1 of algorithm 2. Then the weights after the $(k+1)$-th iteration of the loop are:

$$\lambda_i^{(k+1)} = \#[\mathcal{S}_i^T \cap U^{(k+1)}] + 2\#[\mathcal{S}_i^T \cap F^{(k+1)}]$$

We are now looking for an update formula to compute $\lambda_i^{(k+1)}$ in terms of $U^{(k)}$, $F^{(k)}$, rather than $U^{(k+1)}$ and $F^{(k+1)}$. This is evaluated in the following lemma.

**Lemma 5.3.2.** *For the weights* $\lambda_i^{(k+1)}$, $i \in \Omega$ *the following relation holds:*

$$\lambda_i^{(k+1)} = \lambda_i^{(k)} + \#[\mathcal{S}_i^T \cap \mathcal{S}_{i_{\max}}^T \cap U^{(k)}] - \sigma_i(i_{\max}),$$

*with*

$$\sigma_i(j) = \begin{cases} 1 & j \in \mathcal{S}_i^T, \\ 0 & else. \end{cases}$$

*Proof.* First we look at the according sets and observe:

(i.)

$$\begin{aligned}
\mathcal{S}_i^T \cap U^{(k+1)} &= \mathcal{S}_i^T \cap (U^{(k)} \setminus (\mathcal{S}_{i_{\max}}^T \cup \{i_{\max}\})) \\
&= \mathcal{S}_i^T \cap \left(U^{(k)} \setminus ((\mathcal{S}_{i_{\max}}^T \cap U^{(k)}) \cup \{i_{\max}\})\right) \\
&= (\mathcal{S}_i^T \cap U^{(k)}) \setminus ((\mathcal{S}_{i_{\max}}^T \cap U^{(k)}) \cup \{i_{\max}\}) \\
&= (\mathcal{S}_i^T \cap U^{(k)}) \setminus \left(\mathcal{S}_i^T \cap ((\mathcal{S}_{i_{\max}}^T \cap U^{(k)}) \cup \{i_{\max}\})\right) \\
&= \underbrace{(\mathcal{S}_i^T \cap U^{(k)})}_{=:A_i} \setminus \left(\underbrace{(\mathcal{S}_i^T \cap \mathcal{S}_{i_{\max}}^T \cap U^{(k)})}_{=:B_i} \cup (\mathcal{S}_i^T \cap \{i_{\max}\})\right).
\end{aligned}$$

Since $B_i$ is a subset of $A_i$ and $\mathcal{S}_i^T \cap \{i_{\max}\}$ consists only of $i_{\max}$ if $i_{\max} \in \mathcal{S}_i^T$ and is empty otherwise, we can write the cardinality of the set as

$$\#[\mathcal{S}_i^T \cap U^{(k+1)}] = \#[\mathcal{S}_i^T \cap U^{(k)}] - \#[\mathcal{S}_i^T \cap \mathcal{S}_{i_{\max}}^T \cap U^{(k)}] - \sigma_i(i_{\max}).$$

(ii.)

$$\begin{aligned}
\mathcal{S}_i^T \cap F^{(k+1)} &= \mathcal{S}_i^T \cap \left(F^{(k)} \cup (\mathcal{S}_{i_{\max}}^T \cap U^{(k)})\right) \\
&= \underbrace{(\mathcal{S}_i^T \cap F^{(k)})}_{=:D_i} \cup \underbrace{(\mathcal{S}_i^T \cap \mathcal{S}_{i_{\max}}^T \cap U^{(k)})}_{=B_i}
\end{aligned}$$

The sets $B_i$ and $D_i$ are disjoint (because $F^{(k)}$ and $\mathcal{S}_{i_{\max}}^T \cap U^{(k)}$ are disjoint), and thus we can write

$$\#[\mathcal{S}_i^T \cap F^{(k+1)}] = \#[\mathcal{S}_i^T \cap F^{(k)}] + \#[\mathcal{S}_i^T \cap \mathcal{S}_{i_{\max}}^T \cap U^{(k)}].$$

Combining now (i.) and (ii.) completes the proof. $\qquad\square$

In the worst case, all variables whose weights have to updated, are yet undecided. Thus, for the cardinality of $T_{i_{\max}}$ we have

$$\#[T_{i_{\max}}] \leq \#[\mathcal{S}_{i_{\max}}] + \sum_{j \in H_{i_{\max}}} \#[\mathcal{S}_j] \leq s_{\max} + s_{\max}^T s_{\max}, \tag{5.57}$$

since

$$\#[H_{i_{\max}}] \leq \#[\mathcal{S}_{i_{\max}}^T] \leq s_{\max}^T. \tag{5.58}$$

Now for each $i \in T_{i_{\max}}$ we have to compute $\#[\mathcal{S}_i^T \cap \mathcal{S}_{i_{\max}}^T \cap U^{(k)}] - \sigma_i(i_{\max})$. This can be done with at most $2(\#[\mathcal{S}_i^T] + \#[\mathcal{S}_{i_{\max}}]) + 1$ operations. Therefore, the computational cost of one iteration of the while loop is bounded by

$$4(s_{\max} s_{\max}^T + s_{\max}(s_{\max}^T)^2) + s_{\max} + s_{\max} s_{\max}^T. \tag{5.59}$$

Now the number of variables erased from $U$ at each loop iteration is at least 1 and at most $1 + s_{\max}$. Thus, the number of loop iterations is bounded above by $n$ and below by $n/(1 + s_{\max})$. Summarizing the results, we can state the following

**Lemma 5.3.3.** *The computational cost for updating the weights during the splitting process is bounded above by*

$$n(s_{\max} + 5 s_{\max} s_{\max}^T + 4 s_{\max}(s_{\max}^T)^2). \tag{5.60}$$

### Finding the next variable with maximal weight

The last problem, we have to deal with, is to find the next variable with maximal weight $\lambda_{\max}$. That this can be a problem might become clear if we claim two requirements for the $C/F$-Splitting process:

- Setting/accessing a weight $\lambda_i$ must be possible in constant time $O(1)$.

- Finding a maximal weight $\lambda_{\max} = \max_{i \in U} \lambda_i$ must be possible in a time significantly smaller than $O(n)$.

Just storing the $\lambda_i$'s in an array fulfills the first requirement, but not the second. If we use a data structure like a priority queue, where updating a weight automatically causes the variable $i$ to move up/down in the queue (according to its new weight), then we can fulfill the second requirement, but not the first.

As a way out of this dilemma, we propose a kind of combination of both data structures. This is possible due to the observation that the values for the weights have the upper bound

$$\lambda_i \leq 2 s_{\max}^T, \quad \forall i \in \Omega, \tag{5.61}$$

and therefore many variables have the same weight. Thus, first of all, we store the weight of each variable $i$ in an array $\lambda$ of length $n$ (with $\lambda[i] = \lambda_i$). Then we group together all variables that have the same weight in an own linked list. Since there can be maximal $2 s_{\max}^T + 1$ of such lists (including zero weight), we store them in an array, say $w$, which we address by the weights $\lambda[i]$, meaning that at $w[\lambda[i]]$ we find all variables with the according weight.

Accessing and updating the weight for a vaiable $i$ in the array $\lambda$ can now be done in constant time $(\lambda[i] := \lambda_i^{new})$. Updating the weight for $i$ in $w$ now consists of accessing the linked list $w[\lambda_i]$ (constant time), finding the variable $i$ (we will get to this immediately), then removing $i$ out of this list (constant time) and finally inserting it into the list $w[\lambda_i^{new}]$ (constant time).

Finding the variable $i$ in the list $w[\lambda_i]$ would normally be of time $O(n)$ or $O(\log n)$ if we keep it sorted, unless we use an auxiliary data array $p$ of length $n$ that stores a pointer (or iterator in modern programming languages) to the element $i$. So $p[i]$ indicates the position of $i$ in $w[\lambda_i]$, which can thus be located in constant time.

Now we have shown that accessing and updating a weight can be realized in $O(1)$ time complexity (and $O(n)$ memory complexity). Finding a maximal new weight now simply consists of finding (any) element from the topmost non-empty list in $w$, which can be done in a maximal time of $O(2s_{\max}^T + 1)$.

Of course, one has to point out, that variables $i$, which are marked as $C$ or $F$ variables, are removed from their according list in $w$. Their weight in $\lambda[i]$ might then be set to a negative value to indicate this.

**Complexity of the $C/F$-Splitting process**

Concludingly, we have proven the following theorem, which is an extension of Lemma 5.3.3.

**Theorem 5.3.4** (Complexity of the $C/F$-Splitting process). *The time complexity of the splitting procedure described in Algorithm 2 is*

$$n(s_{\max} + 5s_{\max}s_{\max}^T + 4s_{\max}(s_{\max}^T)^2 + 2s_{\max}^T + 1). \tag{5.62}$$

Since in the FEM context, the number of neighbours of a node depends only on the degree of the used elements and not on the mesh width $h$, the values of $r_{\max}$ and $c_{\max}$ are independent of $n$ (indeed, they are equal for structured meshes). Furthermore, we note that $s_{\max} \leq r_{\max}$ and $s_{\max}^T \leq c_{\max}$ and therefore we have a linear complexity of the splitting procedure which we want to note down in a corollary.

**Corollary 5.3.5.** *For matrices arizing from finite element discretizations, the time complexity of the $C/F$-Splitting procedure is bounded above by*

$$O(n(3r_{\max} + 5(r_{\max})^2 + 4(r_{\max})^3 + 1)) = O(n(r_{\max})^3) = O(n). \tag{5.63}$$

*Moreover, the memory consumption is also of order $O(n)$.*

### 5.3.2 Sparse matrix-matrix multiplication

Since it is a rarely found routine in matrix libraries, we shortly want to look at the way the product of two sparse matrices is computed in our library as well as the according time and space complexity.

Let $A \in \mathbb{R}^{n \times m}$, $B \in \mathbb{R}^{m \times k}$ be arbitrary sparse matrices. As it is exposed in Section 3.7.2, the sparsity structure of $AB$, is computed and stored in a temporary data structure.

**Generation of the product sparsity pattern**

The algorithm for multiplying two sparse matrices depends on their ordering and orientation. For example, for two row wise oriented matrices, we just need random access on the rows of $B$, then the most efficient ordering of the loops is depicted in Algorithm 3.

---

**Algorithm 3:** Sparse matrix multiplication for two row-wise oriented matrices

Input: Row wise oriented sparse matrices $A \in \mathbb{R}^{n \times m}$, $B \in \mathbb{R}^{m \times k}$
Output: Sets $\bar{\mathcal{N}}_i(C)$, $i = 1, \ldots, n$, representing the sparsity pattern of the product $AB$
for $i = 1, \ldots, n$ do
    for $j \in \bar{\mathcal{N}}_i(A)$ do
        for $l \in \bar{\mathcal{N}}_j(B)$ do
1           $\bar{\mathcal{N}}_i(C) := \bar{\mathcal{N}}_i(C) \cup l$
2           $c_{il} := c_{il} + a_{ij}b_{jl}$
        end
    end
end

---

The problems with, respectively the requirements for, the set $\bar{\mathcal{N}}_i(C)$ in line 1 are the following:

1. We don't know in advance how big the set is going to be.

2. The data structure that implements the set has to ensure that it doesn't store dublicates of an index $l$ (stemming from different rows $j$ of $B$).

3. At the end of the procedure, the indices in the data structure for $\bar{\mathcal{N}}_i(C)$ should be ordered increasingly.

Two possibilities come into question. One would be to use *linked lists* with ordered inserting: the new insert position is determined by a binary search, leading to inserting costs of approximately $O(\log(\#[\bar{\mathcal{N}}_i(C)]))$. Another would be to use *red-black trees*.

We made the decision for the latter one, since the run-time for inserting is approximately the same as for linked lists[3], however it promised to be easier to implement, since we can directly use a `std::set` resp. `std::map` from the C++ STL . These data structures are implemented as red-black trees, and thus inserting a variable $l$ into the set $\bar{\mathcal{N}}_i(C)$ costs $O(\log(\#[\bar{\mathcal{N}}_i(C)]))$. The `operator[]()` of `std::map` allows us to combine the two lines 1 and 2 in Algorithm 3 into one line of code.

In the worst case, the sets $\bar{\mathcal{N}}_j(B)$ are disjoint for all $j \in \bar{\mathcal{N}}_i(A)$. Then the number of variables added to $\bar{\mathcal{N}}_i(C)$ will be

$$m_i := \sum_{j \in \bar{\mathcal{N}}_i(A)} \#[\bar{\mathcal{N}}_j(B)].$$

**Lemma 5.3.6.** *The time complexity of Algorithm 3 is bounded above by*

$$O(\log(\Pi_{i=1}^n m_i!)). \tag{5.64}$$

*Proof.* With $m_i$ being the number variables added in the two inner loops for each row $i$ of $A$, we immediately have:

$$\sum_{i=1}^n \sum_{j=1}^{m_i} O(\log(j)) = \sum_{i=1}^n O(\log(m_i!)) = O(\log(\prod_{i=1}^n m_i!)).$$

$\square$

Note that the space requirement is $O(\sum_{i=1}^n m_i)$ integer values.

In this thesis we are especially interested in the complexity of the Galerkin product $P^T A P$ (cf. Definition 5.2.1), where $A \in \mathbb{R}^{n \times n}$ is a matrix stemming from a finite element discretization and $P \in \mathbb{R}^{n \times k}, k < n$, the according prolongation matrix.

From now on, we abbreviate $\bar{\mathcal{N}}_j := \bar{\mathcal{N}}_j(A)$, $C_j := C \cap \bar{\mathcal{N}}_j$ and $F_j := F \cap \bar{\mathcal{N}}_j$. If we consider direct interpolation only, then we have that $\mathcal{P}_j \subset \bar{\mathcal{N}}_j$ for $j \in F$. For $j \in C$ the set $\mathcal{P}_j$ even only consists of one element. If the splitting Algorithm 2 was applied successfully, i.e. after its termination, the set $U$ is empty, then all $F$-variables are strongly negative coupled with at least one $C$-variable. In any case, since $F$-variables are interpolated through surrounding $C$-variables, we have that

$$\#[\bar{\mathcal{N}}_j(P)] = \#[\mathcal{P}_j] < \#[\bar{\mathcal{N}}_j].$$

Moreover, it is $\mathcal{P}_j = C \cap S_j \subset C_j = \bar{\mathcal{N}}_j \setminus F$. Defining

$$p_{\max} := \max_{1 \le i \le n} \#[\mathcal{P}_j] \le \max_{1 \le i \le n} \#[C_j] =: r_C,$$

and

$$r_F := \max_{1 \le i \le n} \#[F_j],$$

yields

$$m_i = \#[C_i] + \sum_{j \in F_i} \#[\mathcal{P}_j] \le r_C + r_F p_{\max} \le r_C + r_F r_C < r_{\max} + r_{\max}^2.$$

---

[3]The according costs (tree rotations included) are of order $O(\log(\#[\bar{\mathcal{N}}_i(C)]))$, see e.g. [CLRS01]

Inserting this in the result from the last lemma leads to an amount of

$$O(n \log((r_{\max} + r_{\max}^2)!)) \tag{5.65}$$

for an upper bound. Taking a closer look on $m_i$ and setting $\tilde{r} := r_{\max} + \varepsilon = r_C + r_F$, with some $\varepsilon > 0$ we might also estimate

$$r_C + r_F r_C = \tilde{r}q + (\tilde{r})^2(q - q^2) < (\tilde{r} + (\tilde{r})^2)q,$$

with $q = \frac{r_C}{\tilde{r}}$. In practice, we often have $\tilde{r} \approx r_{\max}$ and the quotient $q$ then is an indicator for the amount of coarsening. In this case, (5.65) becomes

$$O(n \log(((r_{\max} + r_{\max}^2)q)!)) = O(n\rho \log \rho). \tag{5.66}$$

with the constant

$$\rho = (r_{\max} + r_{\max}^2)q. \tag{5.67}$$

Now we would like to take a look on the product $P^T B$, where $B = AP$ is already computed. Since we store the transpose of $P$ as a column wise oriented matrix, we first examine the general algorithm for generating such a sparsity pattern. In order to formulate the method, we use the transpose neighbourhood (cf. 5.2.16).

**Definition 5.3.7** (Transpose neighbourhood). *For $A \in \mathbb{R}^{n \times m}$ we define the* transpose neighbourhood *of a variable $i \in \Omega = \{1, \ldots, m\}$ as*

$$\bar{\mathcal{N}}_i^T = \bar{\mathcal{N}}_i^T(A) := \{j \in \{1, \ldots, n\} \mid a_{ji} \neq 0\}.$$

It is of course $\bar{\mathcal{N}}_i^T(A) = \bar{\mathcal{N}}_i(A^T)$. The following prodedure varies only in the way it exploits the iteration directions of its matrices – mathematically it is the same as the last one.

---

**Algorithm 4: Sparse matrix multiplication for column-wise/row-wise oriented matrices**

---

Input: One column wise oriented sparse matrix $A \in \mathbb{R}^{n \times m}$,
one row wise oriented sparse matrix $B \in \mathbb{R}^{m \times k}$
Output: Sets $\bar{\mathcal{N}}_j(C)$, $j = 1, \ldots, n$, representing the sparsity pattern of the product $C = AB$
for $i = 1, \ldots, m$ do
    for $j \in \bar{\mathcal{N}}_i^T(A)$ do
        for $l \in \bar{\mathcal{N}}_i(B)$ do
            $\bar{\mathcal{N}}_j(C) := \bar{\mathcal{N}}_j(C) \cup l$
            $c_{il} := c_{il} + a_{ij}b_{jl}$
        end
    end
end

---

As said above, similar considerations as for Algorithm 3 lead to the same costs for this algorithm since merely the loops are interchanged. If we assume, that the left matrix has at least one entry in every row, then for $P^T B$, $B = AP$, this leads to a complexity of

$$\sum_{i=1}^{k} O(\log(k_i!)) \quad \text{with} \quad k_i := \sum_{j \in \bar{\mathcal{N}}_i^T(P)} \#[\bar{\mathcal{N}}_j(AP)].$$

The question now is, how big is the set $\bar{\mathcal{N}}_i^T(P) = \bar{\mathcal{N}}_i(P^T)$ ? Closely related is: how many $F$-variables interpolate from $i$ ? This number is bounded above by $r_F$. Thus we have

$$\bar{\mathcal{N}}_i^T(P) \leq r_F + 1,$$

and therefore

$$k_i = \sum_{j \in \tilde{\mathcal{N}}_i(P)} m_j \le (r_F + 1)(r_C + r_F r_C) = (r_F + 1)^2 r_C.$$

And so the complexity is of order

$$O(k \log(((r_F + 1)^2 r_C)!)),$$

or in terms of $\tilde{r}$ and $q$:

$$O(k \log(r'!)), \qquad \text{with} \qquad r' = (\tilde{r}(1 - q) + 1)^2 q \tilde{r}.$$

And because of

$$r' \le \tilde{r}^3 (1 - (1 - q)^3),$$

we have the following result

**Lemma 5.3.8.** *The time complexity of Algorithm 4 for generating the matrix product $P^T B$ with $B = AP$, $A \in \mathbb{R}^{n \times n}$ where $P \in \mathbb{R}^{n \times k}$ is a prolongation matrix, is bounded above by*

$$O(k \rho \log \rho). \tag{5.68}$$

*with the constant $\rho := \tilde{r}^3 (1 - (1 - q)^3)$.*

Since $q < 1$ and $k = n \cdot \dfrac{\#[C]}{\#[C] + \#[F]}$, we can summarize the results in

**Proposition 5.3.9** (Complexity of the Galerkin product). *The complexity of the Galerkin product $P^T AP$ as defined in (5.16), with $A \in \mathbb{R}^{n \times n}$ and $P \in \mathbb{R}^{n \times k}$ is of order*

$$O(n \tilde{r}^3 \log \tilde{r}^3). \tag{5.69}$$

# Chapter 6

# Numerical Results

## 6.1 The AMG method

Let us first specify the AMG method we apply for the practical computations. The AMG solver system is implemented on the base of the MiLTON matrix library. Though different other smoothers like Jacobi, Gauss-Seidel, SOR are available, we only use the SSOR method for smoothing since it offers a greater stability and better convergence properties for our scalar problems. First attempts with Jacobi and simple Gauss-Seidel smoothers didn't lead to satisfying results. In all cases for the scalar problems, exactly one post-smoothing and one pre-smoothing step is applied.

Furthermore, we choose the direct interpolation as described in Section 5.2.4, with the modification of Formula (5.54). For convection diffusion reaction problems covered in this chapter, this type of interpolation has turned out to be sufficient.

We generate 5 levels for each problem size and then use a SuperLU (cf. [DEG$^+$99]) exact sparse LU decomposition to solve the equation on the coarsest level.

For the numerical tests and parameter search, we use nested iterations to compute a first approximation $x_0$ of the solution. Hereof, a start residual $r_0 := Ax_0 - b$ is computed, which is then reduced with standard V-cycles until $\|r_k\|_2/\|r_0\|_2 < 10^{-6}$.

## 6.2 Convection diffusion problems

In this section the behaviour of AMG applied to convection diffusion equations shall be studied. We will start with two-dimensional problems, investigating the effect of convection on the solution process. Afterwards we will also take a look on a three-dimensional example.

We use the $\mathcal{PNS}$ (cf. the manual in [AMOG99]) program system for the finite element discretization.

### 6.2.1 2D examples

First of all, we consider the problem:

Find $u(x, y) : \mathbb{R}^2 \to \mathbb{R}$, such that

$$-\nu\Delta u + \mathbf{b} \cdot \nabla u = f \quad \text{in } \Omega \in \mathbb{R}^2, \tag{6.1}$$

with $\nu \in \{1, 10^{-2}, 10^{-4}, 10^{-6}\}$,

$$\mathbf{b}(x, y) := \begin{pmatrix} (2y - 1)(1 - (2x - 1)^2) \\ 4y(2x - 1)(y - 1) \end{pmatrix}, \tag{6.2}$$

and $f(x, y) := 0$. The domain $\Omega$ is set to the unit square $\Omega = (0, 1) \times (0, 1)$. Furthermore we prescribe the following dirichlet boundary conditions:

$$u = -0.5 \quad \text{on} \quad \{(0\ y)^T : 0 \le y \le 1\}$$
$$u = \phantom{-}0.5 \quad \text{on} \quad \{(1\ y)^T : 0 \le y \le 1\}$$
$$u = \phantom{-}0 \quad \text{else.}$$

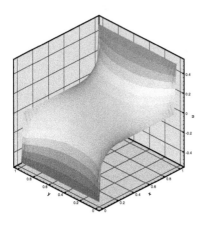

Figure 6.1: 2D convection diffusion, solution for $\nu = 1$

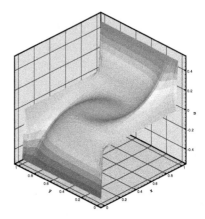

Figure 6.2: 2D convection diffusion, solution for $\nu = 10^{-2}$

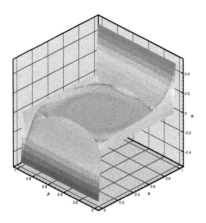

Figure 6.3: 2D convection diffusion, solution for $\nu = 10^{-4}$

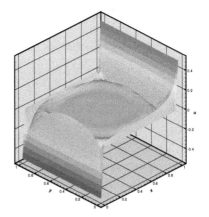

Figure 6.4: 2D convection diffusion, solution for $\nu = 10^{-6}$

The plots in Figures (6.1) to (6.4) show the discrete solution at $h = 1/32$ for the different values of $\nu$. With dominating diffusion at $\nu = 1$ and $\nu = 1/100$ the fullfilment of the boundary conditions doesn't cause bigger problems. As the diffusion decreases ($\nu = 10^{-4}$ and $\nu = 10^{-6}$ ) we observe oscillations at $x = 0$ and $x = 1$.

The reason for this behaviour becomes clearer if we look at solution of the reduced problem ($\nu = 0$)

$$\mathbf{b} \cdot \nabla w = f, \tag{6.3}$$

in $\Omega$, which is a constant zero for $f \equiv 0$. For $\varepsilon \to 0$ one would expect that the solution $w$ of (6.3) converges to the solution $u$ of (6.1). However, at $x = 0$ and $x = 1$ this leads to problems, since the boundary conditions need to be satisfied.

Therefore, for $\varepsilon \longrightarrow 0$ we observe parabolic boundary layers (see e.g. [RST96]) at $x = 0$ and $x = 1$, because the convection field $\mathbf{b}$ is constructed in such a way that it runs everywhere parallel to the boundary.

The convection dominated problems, especially at $\nu = 10^{-6}$, are a serious challenge for every numerical solver, since the condition of the system matrix increases as $\nu$ and $h$ are getting smaller. Without according stabilization schemes like SUPG or GLS, that strengthen the positive definite part of the matrix, such discrete problems are hardly solvable – most iterative solvers heavily depend on the matrix condition number.

Thus, besides discretizing the problem with linear ($P_1$) finite elements, we use GLS (cf. Section 4.3) as a stabilization method. For all problems, we have chosen the stabilization parameter $\delta_{T_i}$ simply as suggested in formula (4.15) in Chapter 4. Some properties of the resulting stiffness matrices generated by the $\mathcal{PNS}$-system for different mesh widths are depicted in Table 6.1. We will treat the problem with different mesh widths on structured grids and investigate the convergence rates and $h$-dependency of the AMG solver.

| $h$ | 1/8 | 1/16 | 1/32 | 1/64 | 1/128 | 1/256 | 1/512 | 1/1024 |
|---|---|---|---|---|---|---|---|---|
| number of variables | 81 | 289 | 1089 | 4225 | 16641 | 66049 | 263169 | 1050625 |

Table 6.1: Mesh widths and matrix dimensions for the 2D convection diffusion problem

**The effect of the strong coupling parameter $\theta$ on the coarsening process**

First of all and before looking at the convergence and performance of the overall solution process, we investigate the influence of the parameters on the AMG preprocess. On the following pages, we would like to study the impact of the coupling parameter $\theta$ on the generated hierarchy of levels. The parameter $\theta$ is varied in the range of

$$\Theta := \{\theta \in (0, 1) \mid \theta = \frac{j}{10}; \ j = 2, \ldots, 8\}. \tag{6.4}$$

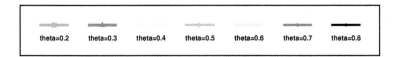

Figure 6.5: Legend: coupling parameter colouring

The colours in Figure 6.5 are used to distinguish the curves for different $\theta$. We examplarily show the properties of the coarse level hierarchies for the mesh width $h = 1/1024$ and the four diffusion parameters from $\nu = 1$ to $\nu = 10^{-6}$ in the Figures 6.6 – 6.9. The lower set of curves in these figure shows the dimensions of the generated matrices on the level $i = 1, \ldots, 5$, where level 0 is the base stiffness matrix assembled by $\mathcal{PNS}$. The upper set of curves indicates the nonzero entries of the according matrices.

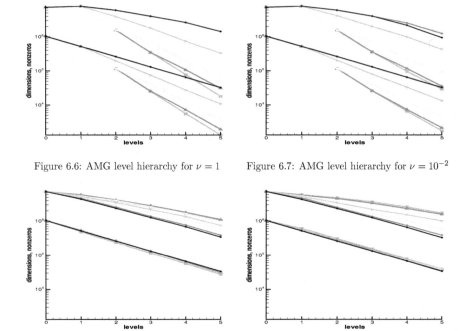

Figure 6.6: AMG level hierarchy for $\nu = 1$      Figure 6.7: AMG level hierarchy for $\nu = 10^{-2}$

Figure 6.8: AMG level hierarchy for $\nu = 10^{-4}$      Figure 6.9: AMG level hierarchy for $\nu = 10^{-6}$

Looking back at Definition 5.2.21, $\theta = 0$ would mean to choose every (negative) coupling to be included in $\mathcal{S}_{i,\theta}$ and thus $\mathcal{S}_{i,\theta}^T$ would also be the biggest possible set (for non-negative $\theta$). For M-matrices for example, we would have $\mathcal{S}_{i,0}^T = \mathcal{S}_{i,0}$. Generally, for arbitrary $A \in \mathbb{R}^{n \times n}$, $1 \leq i \leq n$, $\theta_1, \theta_2 \in \mathbb{R}$, $\theta_1 < \theta_2$, we have

$$\mathcal{S}_{i,\theta_1} \subseteq \mathcal{S}_{i,\theta_2} \quad \text{and} \quad \mathcal{S}_{i,\theta_1}^T \subseteq \mathcal{S}_{i,\theta_2}^T.$$

The other extremal case, $\theta > 1$, would lead to $\mathcal{S}_i$ and $\mathcal{S}_i^T$ being empty. Between these two extremes, the coarsening algorithm generates the C/F-splitting. Because of line 3 in Algorithm 2 (Section 5.2.5), we can predict a tendency to generate a stronger coarsening (at least in terms of dimension reduction), meaning a smaller set $C(\theta)$, the smaller the value for $\theta$ is.[1] And indeed, we can recognize this behaviour in the diagrams, especially for the diffusion dominated cases in the Figures 6.6 and 6.7. At this point however, we must keep in mind that for a matrix $A_l$ on level $l$ and different $\theta_1 \neq \theta_2$ ($\Longrightarrow C(\theta_1) \neq C(\theta_2)$) we have from then on different coarse level matrices $A_k$ for $k > l$. Thus the levels are not directly comparable.

For the overall runtime of the AMG solver however, not only the dimension of the matrix is important, but also the amount of nonzero entries, and its relation to the dimension, i.e. the sparsity of the matrix, since this directly influences the matrix-matrix-multiplication algorithm. Therefore, included in the Tables 6.2 to 6.5, is also the average number of nonzero row entries

$$r_{avg} := \frac{1}{l_{\max} + 1} \sum_{i=0}^{l_{\max}} \frac{nnz_i}{n_i}, \tag{6.5}$$

---

[1] Here, with $C(\theta)$, we denote the set $C$ that results from Algorithm 2 using the coarsening parameter $\theta$.

in addition to the amount of time in seconds, the whole AMG setup process needs for computing all five levels and the sparse LU decomposition of the matrix on the coarsest level via the SuperLU (see [DEG+99]) method.

For structured meshes (regular triangulization) like the ones used here, each point has six neighbours in the inner part of the domain, thus we have 7 row entries (with the diagonal entry), left alone at the boundary.

We see that for diffusion dominated problems (Figures 6.6 and 6.7 and Tables 6.2 and 6.3) first of all the reduction from the first to the second level is nearly the same for every problem. This is because no value for $\theta$ can really identify an upstream direction, since the convection is too weak compared with the diffusion. From the second level on, the coarsening, especially the dimension reduction is more drastically, the smaller $\theta$ is. We can see this also at the extreme form of this type of equation, the Poisson problem. A small $\theta$ leads to a coarsening in *all* directions, however also to bigger sets $\mathcal{P}_i$, because an $F$-variable is then also interpolated from *all* directions. Therefore we also have more entries in the prolongation matrix $P$ and thus more entries in the next coarse level matrix, which means (many) more connections than the 7 on the initial finite element mesh.

On the other hand, a great number of these new neighbours can be coarsened away easily – the more, the smaller $\theta$ is. And indeed, we can see, that the number of variables on level 1 is about half of the number of variables on level 0. For small $\theta$, the number of variables on level 2 is even only a *quarter* of the number of variables on level 1. Here, bigger values for $\theta$ lead to a weaker reduction of the unknowns, resulting in a longer setup time.

For convection dominated problems (Figures 6.8 and 6.9 and Tables 6.4 and 6.5), there is however a different picture. First of all, this type of equation, with nearly absent diffusion, produces off-diagonal

| | $h = 1/32$ | | $h = 1/64$ | | $h = 1/128$ | | $h = 1/256$ | | $h = 1/512$ | | $h = 1/1024$ | |
|---|---|---|---|---|---|---|---|---|---|---|---|---|
| $\theta$ | $r_{avg}$ | time | $r_{avg}$ | time | $r_{avg}$ | time | $r_{avg}$ | time | $r_{avg}$ | time | $r_{avg}$ | time |
| 0.2 | 8.5 | 0.04 | 10.2 | 0.13 | 11.4 | 0.56 | 12.3 | 2.28 | 12.6 | 9.30 | 12.8 | 38.12 |
| 0.3 | 8.6 | 0.03 | 10.4 | 0.13 | 11.3 | 0.50 | 12.4 | 2.04 | 13.1 | 8.35 | 13.3 | 33.78 |
| 0.4 | 9.2 | 0.03 | 12.0 | 0.13 | 12.9 | 0.52 | 13.7 | 2.09 | 14.1 | 8.61 | 14.3 | 34.78 |
| 0.5 | 11.0 | 0.03 | 14.0 | 0.13 | 15.5 | 0.56 | 19.0 | 2.37 | 20.5 | 9.95 | 20.6 | 42.25 |
| 0.6 | 18.4 | 0.04 | 22.7 | 0.17 | 24.9 | 0.77 | 25.9 | 3.38 | 26.5 | 15.52 | 26.7 | 133.19 |
| 0.7 | 18.4 | 0.04 | 22.7 | 0.18 | 24.9 | 0.78 | 25.9 | 3.38 | 26.5 | 15.49 | 26.7 | 104.58 |
| 0.8 | 18.4 | 0.04 | 22.7 | 0.17 | 24.9 | 0.77 | 25.9 | 3.37 | 26.5 | 16.00 | 26.7 | 130.89 |

Table 6.2: AMG setup for the 2D problem, $\nu = 1$

| | $h = 1/32$ | | $h = 1/64$ | | $h = 1/128$ | | $h = 1/256$ | | $h = 1/512$ | | $h = 1/1024$ | |
|---|---|---|---|---|---|---|---|---|---|---|---|---|
| $\theta$ | $r_{avg}$ | time | $r_{avg}$ | time | $r_{avg}$ | time | $r_{avg}$ | time | $r_{avg}$ | time | $r_{avg}$ | time |
| 0.2 | 11.0 | 0.03 | 11.3 | 0.12 | 12.9 | 0.55 | 12.4 | 2.28 | 13.1 | 9.41 | 13.5 | 38.05 |
| 0.3 | 9.6 | 0.02 | 12.2 | 0.11 | 13.3 | 0.51 | 13.3 | 2.09 | 13.1 | 8.42 | 13.6 | 33.75 |
| 0.4 | 11.4 | 0.03 | 13.4 | 0.13 | 13.6 | 0.51 | 14.9 | 2.13 | 14.1 | 8.60 | 15.2 | 35.07 |
| 0.5 | 9.8 | 0.03 | 13.0 | 0.12 | 13.8 | 0.54 | 16.9 | 2.35 | 18.9 | 10.01 | 21.6 | 43.61 |
| 0.6 | 9.7 | 0.03 | 11.4 | 0.11 | 14.7 | 0.56 | 18.9 | 2.78 | 23.8 | 13.81 | 26.3 | 86.49 |
| 0.7 | 8.9 | 0.03 | 10.4 | 0.10 | 13.0 | 0.51 | 16.5 | 2.60 | 21.4 | 13.00 | 25.5 | 80.21 |
| 0.8 | 7.9 | 0.02 | 9.3 | 0.09 | 11.1 | 0.43 | 14.1 | 2.24 | 18.2 | 11.52 | 23.0 | 65.52 |

Table 6.3: AMG setup for the 2D problem, $\nu = 10^{-2}$

| $\theta$ | $h = 1/32$ | | $h = 1/64$ | | $h = 1/128$ | | $h = 1/256$ | | $h = 1/512$ | | $h = 1/1024$ | |
|---|---|---|---|---|---|---|---|---|---|---|---|---|
| | $r_{avg}$ | time | $r_{avg}$ | time | $r_{avg}$ | time | $r_{avg}$ | time | $r_{avg}$ | time | $r_{avg}$ | time |
| 0.2 | 12.5 | 0.03 | 18.1 | 0.14 | 21.4 | 0.61 | 22.0 | 2.73 | 22.1 | 12.97 | 21.1 | 64.07 |
| 0.3 | 11.8 | 0.03 | 16.8 | 0.12 | 19.9 | 0.54 | 20.8 | 2.36 | 20.9 | 11.21 | 19.9 | 56.62 |
| 0.4 | 11.9 | 0.03 | 15.1 | 0.12 | 16.2 | 0.52 | 17.7 | 2.17 | 18.2 | 10.04 | 17.6 | 47.85 |
| 0.5 | 10.4 | 0.03 | 13.1 | 0.10 | 14.0 | 0.43 | 14.7 | 1.85 | 15.0 | 8.38 | 15.1 | 38.48 |
| 0.6 | 9.5 | 0.03 | 10.4 | 0.10 | 10.7 | 0.39 | 11.4 | 1.57 | 11.9 | 6.85 | 12.3 | 30.16 |
| 0.7 | 7.7 | 0.02 | 9.0 | 0.09 | 9.3 | 0.35 | 9.6 | 1.42 | 9.8 | 5.87 | 10.0 | 24.96 |
| 0.8 | 7.5 | 0.02 | 8.1 | 0.08 | 8.6 | 0.33 | 8.8 | 1.31 | 8.9 | 5.51 | 9.1 | 23.31 |

Table 6.4: AMG setup for the 2D problem, $\nu = 10^{-4}$

| $\theta$ | $h = 1/32$ | | $h = 1/64$ | | $h = 1/128$ | | $h = 1/256$ | | $h = 1/512$ | | $h = 1/1024$ | |
|---|---|---|---|---|---|---|---|---|---|---|---|---|
| | $r_{avg}$ | time | $r_{avg}$ | time | $r_{avg}$ | time | $r_{avg}$ | time | $r_{avg}$ | time | $r_{avg}$ | time |
| 0.2 | 12.5 | 0.03 | 18.3 | 0.13 | 20.2 | 0.62 | 22.0 | 2.80 | 22.0 | 14.77 | 22.2 | 94.73 |
| 0.3 | 11.7 | 0.03 | 17.1 | 0.12 | 19.7 | 0.55 | 21.3 | 2.41 | 21.4 | 12.00 | 22.0 | 73.19 |
| 0.4 | 12.0 | 0.03 | 15.1 | 0.11 | 16.3 | 0.50 | 18.2 | 2.18 | 19.0 | 10.16 | 19.1 | 56.93 |
| 0.5 | 10.3 | 0.03 | 13.1 | 0.11 | 14.0 | 0.44 | 14.6 | 1.85 | 15.2 | 8.25 | 15.4 | 42.41 |
| 0.6 | 9.1 | 0.03 | 10.1 | 0.09 | 10.7 | 0.38 | 11.2 | 1.61 | 11.4 | 6.72 | 11.6 | 28.42 |
| 0.7 | 8.2 | 0.02 | 8.9 | 0.08 | 9.2 | 0.34 | 9.4 | 1.42 | 9.5 | 5.88 | 9.6 | 24.26 |
| 0.8 | 7.5 | 0.02 | 8.2 | 0.08 | 8.5 | 0.32 | 8.7 | 1.32 | 8.8 | 5.47 | 8.9 | 22.27 |

Table 6.5: AMG setup for the 2D problem, $\nu = 10^{-6}$

entries, that vary stronger in their order of magnitude. As in the FDM context (see Section 5.2.6), the strong negative connections lie more in the upstream direction. The SUPG or GLS stabilization even enhances this, it adds positive portions to the diagonal and negative values to the off-diagonal entries. The smaller now the value for $\theta$ is, the bigger are the sets $\mathcal{S}_i$, however they don't include the neighbours that lie in downstream direction unless $\theta = O(\nu)$. This the reason, why the dimension reduction doesn't differ much between the considered values out of $\Theta$ from (6.4).

In this situation, a value for $\theta$ that is close to 1 causes the algorithm to select only the maximal negative neighbour to be in $\mathcal{S}_i$, which thus is the one that lies the most clearly in the upstream direction (within the restrictions of the underlying grid). Consequently, if the vector field $\mathbf{b}$ doesn't change too much locally (which is certainly true for constant or sufficiently smooth $\mathbf{b}$, if $h$ is small enough) the $\mathcal{S}_i$ consists only of the downstream nodes. This extreme coarsening might have the slight drawback, that most $F$-variables are interpolated from only one $C$-variable, however it has the advantage that the arising coarse levels are more sparse and the according SOR/SSOR smoother is better able to reduce the error, last but not least, because of the better numbering of the variables.

**The effect of relaxation on the solution process**

On the next two pages, in Tables 6.6 – Table 6.7, we can see the effect of the relaxation parameter $\omega \in (0, 2)$ of the SSOR smoother and the coupling parameter $\theta \in (0, 1)$ from the AMG coarsening preprocess on the amount of multigrid-cycles the algorithm needs to reduce the first residual by a factor of $10^{-6}$.

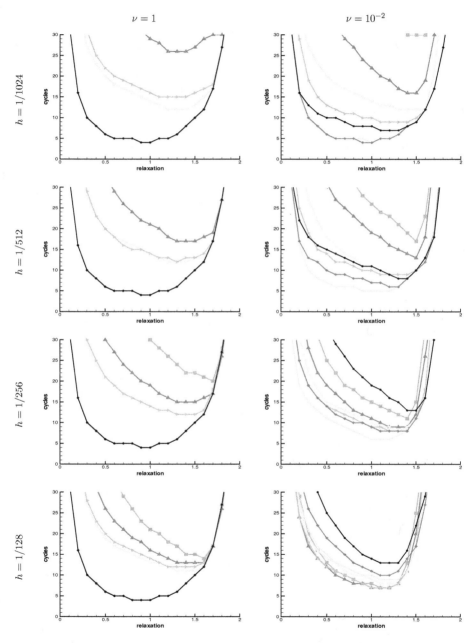

Table 6.6: SSOR smoothing for $\nu = 1, 10^{-2}$, $h = \frac{1}{128}, \ldots, \frac{1}{1024}$

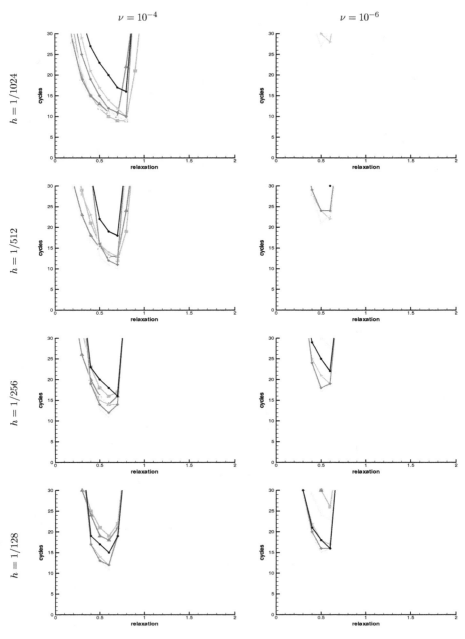

Table 6.7: SSOR smoothing for $\nu = 10^{-4}, 10^{-6}$, $h = \frac{1}{128}, \ldots, \frac{1}{1024}$

The relaxation was restricted to the discrete set

$$\{\omega \in (0,2)|\ \omega = \frac{j}{10}, j = 1,\dots,19\} \tag{6.6}$$

In the tables, from the left to the right, the diffusion parameter varies from $\nu = 1$ to $\nu = 10^{-6}$, and from the bottom to the top of the page, the mesh width changes form $h = 1/128$ to $h = 1/1024$.

First of all, we can see, that diffusion-dominated problems ($\nu = 1$, $\nu = 10^{-2}$) exhibit a relatively good-natured convergence behaviour. The method converges for a relatively wide range of values for $\omega$ (Table 6.6).

Although the optimal relaxtion parameter $\omega_{opt}$ is in most cases greater than 1, which would mean an over-relaxation, we still have the convergence for $\omega = 1$ in all cases, meaning that a standard symmetric Gauss-Seidel smoother would also be sufficient. Furthermore the choice of $\theta$ doesn't seem to be critic, we observe convergence for all considered values.

For convection dominated problems ($\nu = 10^{-4}$, $\nu = 10^{-6}$) however, the situation is different. First of all, the range of possible values for $\omega$ is slightly smaller, or at least, the spectrum is shifted to the left in the diagrams, resulting in the need for an explicit under-relaxation, with $\omega_{opt}$ lying between 0.6 and 0.9. This aligns with the fact, that convection dominated problems require under-relaxation when treated with a stand-alone SOR or SSOR *solver* (see e.g. [Pri96]).

Especially if $\omega$ is chosen too large, then there isn't any value for $\theta$ that the method converges with. The standard symmetric Gauss-Seidel smoothing can't always guarantee convergence for convection dominated problems. These problems are also more sensitive to changes of $\theta$, we can observe big differences in the convergence speed (Table 6.7). However, we see that smoothing is possible for the convection-dominated problems, if the relaxation parameter is chosen properly.

**Convergence speed of the AMG method**

In order to judge the performance of the AMG method we first compare it to a Krylov subspace method that is widely used in this context, a GMRES($m$) solver, with restart length $m = 20$, in combination with a SSOR preconditioner ($\omega = 0.7$). It is implemented in the BLANC library, which is the sparse matrix numerical linear algebra library used by $\mathcal{PNS}$.

It should be mentioned, that the ILU(0) preconditioner exhibited a worse convergence rate in connection with the GMRES solver. This is the reason for using the SSOR preconditioner instead. For the measurement of the residual $r \in \mathbb{R}^n$ we use the norm

$$\|r\|_{L^2} := \sqrt{\frac{1}{n}\sum_{i=1}^{n} r_i^2}. \tag{6.7}$$

In Figures 6.10 and 6.11 we exemplarily see the convergence rate of the two methods for $\nu = 10^{-6}$ at the two finest mesh-widths, $h = \frac{1}{512}$ and $h = \frac{1}{1024}$. We have plotted the relative residual norm $\|r_k\|_{L^2}/\|r_0\|_{L^2}$, where $r_0$ is the initial residual and $r_k$ the residual after the $k$-th iteration step. The setup cost of the GMRES solver and the SSOR preconditioner are relatively cheap, such that the iteration starts nearly immediately (red curves). The AMG setup time[2] however is comparatively high, roughly 4 sec. for $h = \frac{1}{512}$ and 15 sec. at $h = \frac{1}{1024}$. Thus its iteration starts later, but then with a better convergence rate (green curve).

---

[2]Note that in contrast to Table 6.5, here, 6 levels were generated, resulting in a smaller matrix on the coarsest level and therefore smaller setup costs for the SuperLU decomposition.

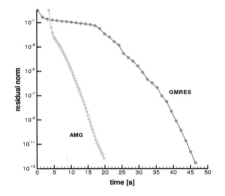

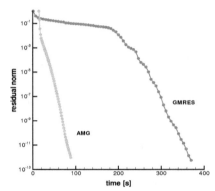

Figure 6.10: Convergence of GMRES vs. AMG for $h = \frac{1}{512}$

Figure 6.11: Convergence of GMRES vs. AMG for $h = \frac{1}{1024}$

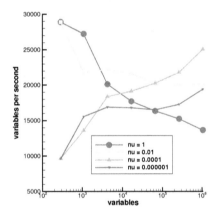

Figure 6.12: Calculation speed for the 2D problem

Furthermore, the AMG solver only exhibits its superior convergence rates over GMRES with decreasing $h$. This is first of all due to the setup costs, which are relatively high compared to the iteration time for small matrices. On the other hand, the convergence rate of Krylov methods often depend on the condition of the matrix, which is higher, the smaller $h$ is.

In Figure 6.12 we see the AMG computation speed for the 2D problem for each diffusion parameter $\nu$ shown in 4 different curves. For the mesh widths $h = 1/16, \ldots, 1/1024$ the *number of variables* relative to the *overall solution time* is displayed on the y-axis. The overall solution time includes the AMG-setup time as well as the iteration time for the V-cycles. We observe, that the efficiency of the method even increases for small $\nu$ and $h$.

## 6.2.2 A 3D example

We would like to test the AMG performance also in a three dimensional setting. We examine a 3D rotation flow, which is described by the following problem:

Find $u(x, y, z) : \mathbb{R}^3 \to \mathbb{R}$, such that

$$-\nu \Delta u + \mathbf{b} \cdot \nabla u = f \quad \text{in } \Omega \in \mathbb{R}^3, \tag{6.8}$$

with $\nu \in \{1, 10^{-2}, 10^{-4}, 10^{-6}\}$,

$$\mathbf{b}(x, y, z) := \begin{pmatrix} -y \\ x \\ 0 \end{pmatrix}, \tag{6.9}$$

and $f(x, y, z) := 0$. For the domain $\Omega$ we use the unit cube $\Omega = (0, 1) \times (0, 1) \times (0, 1)$. We prescribe the following mixed boundary conditions:

$$\vec{n} \cdot \nabla u = 0 \quad \text{for} \quad x = 0 \qquad \text{(Neumann)}$$

$$u = \begin{cases} 1 & \text{for} \quad y = 0 \wedge 0.3 \le x \le 0.7 \wedge 0.3 \le z \le 0.7 \\ 0 & \text{else.} \end{cases} \qquad \text{(Dirichlet)}$$

This problem is discretized on a structured 3D grid (tetrahedrons) using linear elements und GLS stabilization.

For all problems with $\nu \in \{1, 10^{-2}, 10^{-4}, 10^{-6}\}$, the stabilization parameter $\delta_{T_i}$ was chosen as in formula (4.15) in Chapter 4.

The vector field $\mathbf{b}$ (see Figure 6.14) induces a circular convection around the $z$-axis. This convection drags the solution profile of the inflow boundary (Figure 6.13) at $y = 0$ through the whole domain and transports it to the outflow boundary at $x = 0$. Slice plots of the three-dimensional solution are shown in the next four subsections.

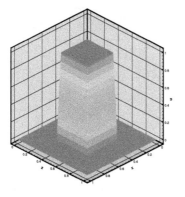

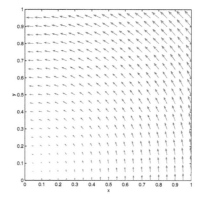

Figure 6.13: 3D convection diffusion, solution profile at the inflow border

Figure 6.14: Convection field viewed from above ($z \equiv const$)

| $h$ | 1/4 | 1/8 | 1/16 | 1/32 | 1/64 | 1/129 |
|---|---|---|---|---|---|---|
| inner points (= matrix dimension) | 36 | 392 | 3600 | 30752 | 254016 | 2064512 |
| nonzero entries | 290 | 4174 | 42662 | 382294 | 3230390 | 26547574 |

Table 6.8: Mesh widths and matrix properties for the 3D convection diffusion problem

In Table 6.8 we see the properties of the stiffness matrices resulting from a $P_1$ discretization on a structured mesh in $\mathcal{PNS}$.

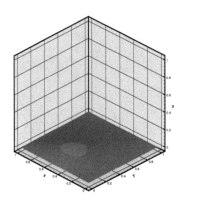

Figure 6.15: 3D convection diffusion, solution profile at the outflow border, $\nu = 1$     Figure 6.16: 3D convection diffusion, solution profile at $z = 0.5$, $\nu = 1$

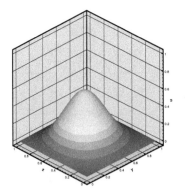
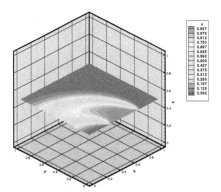

Figure 6.17: 3D convection diffusion, solution profile at the outflow border, $\nu = 10^{-2}$     Figure 6.18: 3D convection diffusion, solution profile at $z = 0.5$, $\nu = 10^{-2}$

The profile at the outflow boundary is determined by the amount of diffusion controlled by the viscosity parameter $\nu$. For $\nu = 1$ the diffusion dominates over the convection, the information stemming from the inflow boundary is transported slowly in every space dimension (nearly) uniformly (Figure 6.16). The convection is comparably weak, such that the solution at the outflow boundary is nearly zero (Figure 6.15). At $\nu = 10^{-2}$, more of the input profile is transported into the direction of the outflow boundary, however blurred by the diffusion (Figures 6.17 and 6.18).

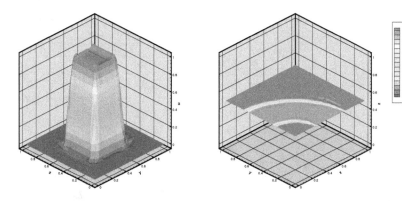

Figure 6.19: 3D convection diffusion, solution profile at the outflow border, $\nu = 10^{-4}$

Figure 6.20: 3D convection diffusion, solution profile at $z = 0.5$, $\nu = 10^{-4}$

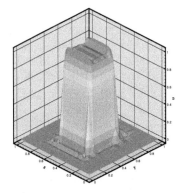
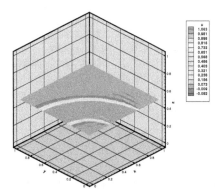

Figure 6.21: 3D convection diffusion, solution profile at the outflow border, $\nu = 10^{-6}$

Figure 6.22: 3D convection diffusion, solution profile at $z = 0.5$, $\nu = 10^{-6}$

With diminishing diffusion, at $\nu = 10^{-4}$ and $\nu = 10^{-6}$, we see that the sharp input profile is transported through the whole domain (Figures 6.20 and 6.22) to the output boundary (Figures 6.19 and 6.21) nearly without any losses.

**The effect of the strong coupling parameter $\theta$ on the coarsening process**

Again we would like to look on the way the strong coupling determinates the generated levels. The coarsening parameter $\theta$ is again chosen out of the set $\Theta$ from (6.4). The according setup times are shown in Tables 6.9 to 6.12. Using the legend from Figure 6.5 we display the data of the generated levels in the Figures 6.23 to 6.26 for the four values of $\nu$, exemplarily for mesh width $h = 1/65$. The upper curves again show the nonzeros of the matrices, the lower curves indicate their dimension.

As we can see in Tables 6.9 to 6.12, the time factor from a mesh size $h$ to $\frac{h}{2}$ is at best about 9 to 10. This is somewhat bigger than the factor 8 that the problem sizes differ (cf. Table 6.8). However, since the number of generated levels is in all cases restricted to five, the SuperLU inverter has to treat a relatively large matrix on the coarsest level.

| $\theta$ | $h = \frac{1}{8}$ | $h = \frac{1}{16}$ | $h = \frac{1}{32}$ | $h = \frac{1}{64}$ |
|---|---|---|---|---|
| 0.2 | 0.02 | 0.31 | 3.31 | 34.22 |
| 0.3 | 0.02 | 0.21 | 2.09 | 18.82 |
| 0.4 | 0.02 | 0.21 | 2.08 | 18.89 |
| 0.5 | 0.02 | 0.23 | 2.18 | 19.36 |
| 0.6 | 0.02 | 0.24 | 2.29 | 20.44 |
| 0.7 | 0.02 | 0.22 | 2.36 | 23.4 |
| 0.8 | 0.02 | 0.24 | 2.26 | 21.86 |

Table 6.9: AMG setup times [s] for the 3D problem, $\nu = 1$

| $\theta$ | $h = \frac{1}{8}$ | $h = \frac{1}{16}$ | $h = \frac{1}{32}$ | $h = \frac{1}{64}$ |
|---|---|---|---|---|
| 0.2 | 0.02 | 0.17 | 1.68 | 17.1 |
| 0.3 | 0.02 | 0.17 | 1.7 | 15.53 |
| 0.4 | 0.01 | 0.18 | 1.55 | 13.43 |
| 0.5 | 0.02 | 0.16 | 1.34 | 13.92 |
| 0.6 | 0.01 | 0.14 | 1.63 | 17.5 |
| 0.7 | 0.02 | 0.15 | 1.65 | 19.58 |
| 0.8 | 0.01 | 0.14 | 1.5 | 21.49 |

Table 6.10: AMG setup times [s] for the 3D problem, $\nu = 10^{-2}$

| $\theta$ | $h = \frac{1}{8}$ | $h = \frac{1}{16}$ | $h = \frac{1}{32}$ | $h = \frac{1}{64}$ |
|---|---|---|---|---|
| 0.2 | 0.02 | 0.23 | 2.53 | 23.39 |
| 0.3 | 0.02 | 0.21 | 2.14 | 20.86 |
| 0.4 | 0.01 | 0.2 | 2.02 | 19.74 |
| 0.5 | 0.02 | 0.18 | 1.75 | 16.76 |
| 0.6 | 0.01 | 0.17 | 1.62 | 16.09 |
| 0.7 | 0.02 | 0.14 | 1.33 | 13.59 |
| 0.8 | 0.01 | 0.13 | 1.24 | 12.69 |

Table 6.11: AMG setup times [s] for the 3D problem, $\nu = 10^{-4}$

| $\theta$ | $h = \frac{1}{8}$ | $h = \frac{1}{16}$ | $h = \frac{1}{32}$ | $h = \frac{1}{64}$ |
|---|---|---|---|---|
| 0.2 | 0.02 | 0.23 | 2.71 | 25.11 |
| 0.3 | 0.02 | 0.21 | 2.1 | 20.32 |
| 0.4 | 0.02 | 0.21 | 2.1 | 20.14 |
| 0.5 | 0.02 | 0.17 | 1.74 | 16.71 |
| 0.6 | 0.02 | 0.17 | 1.6 | 16.12 |
| 0.7 | 0.01 | 0.14 | 1.39 | 13.32 |
| 0.8 | 0.02 | 0.12 | 1.22 | 11.74 |

Table 6.12: AMG setup times [s] for the 3D problem, $\nu = 10^{-6}$

For the diffusion dominated problems, we see that values between 0.3 and 0.5 for $\theta$ are optimal because they not only reduce the C variables, but also the nonzero entries. This is the same effect as mentioned in the 2D context, at first the levels doesn't differ much, lower values for $\theta$ introduce more nonzeros in the coarse level matrix, but this increased neighbourhood is likely to be coarsened drastically in the next step.

For convection dominated problems, values between 0.5 and 0.8 seem to be more appropriate, since they result in a stronger reduction of the nonzero entries. Again, as in the two-dimensional setting, bigger values for $\theta$ decrease the elements in the set of interpolation variables $\mathcal{P}_i$, therefore yielding prolongation and coarse level matrices with a smaller number of nonzero entries. This is also supported by the setup times listed in the Tables below. However, this effect is not so evident as for the 2D problem.

In the three dimensional setting, as for the two dimension case, we observe, that the number of variables from level to level is about halved in each step, independent of the space dimension. Since

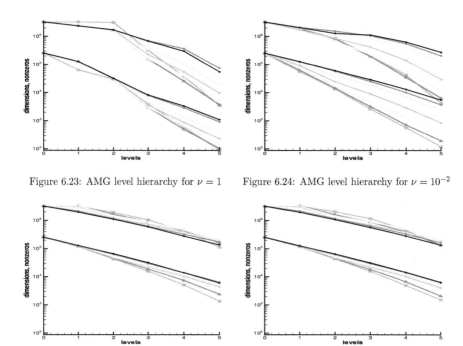

Figure 6.23: AMG level hierarchy for $\nu = 1$     Figure 6.24: AMG level hierarchy for $\nu = 10^{-2}$

Figure 6.25: AMG level hierarchy for $\nu = 10^{-4}$    Figure 6.26: AMG level hierarchy for $\nu = 10^{-6}$

it takes into account also the direction of the stream, this type of coarsening is also referred to as *directional coarsening* or *semi-coarsening*. In the AMG context, this is simply a byproduct of the strong neighbourhood relationship and the $C/F$-splitting.

For geometric multigrid, the factor from a fine level to a coarse level dimension is normally $1/4$ in 2D and $1/8$ in 3D, which results in a lesser computational complexity. However, for anisotropic grids or strong convection, the semi-coarsening approach often has superior convergence properties (cf. [Mul89]).

Nevertheless, in 3D, semi-coarsening has the drawback, that the overall complexity is not reduced strong enough, the AMG setup phase takes significantly longer than in the 2D case. A remedy can be to apply *agressive coarsening* as introduced in [Stü99], where not only direct connections, but also indirect connections (i.e. neighbours of neighbours) are considered.

### The effect of relaxation on the solution process

For the 3D problem, we seek the optimal relaxation parameter(s). Again, $\omega$ is taken from (6.6). As we see in the Tables 6.13 and 6.14, the algorithm converges over a wide range of values for diffusion dominated problem.

However, the smaller $\nu$ is, the more important becomes the underrelaxation of the smoother. In fact, many AMG level hierarchies (for different $\theta$) didn't yield convergence in the convection dominated case for $\omega \geq 1$. This sustains the fact that underrelaxation is inevitable for these types of problem.

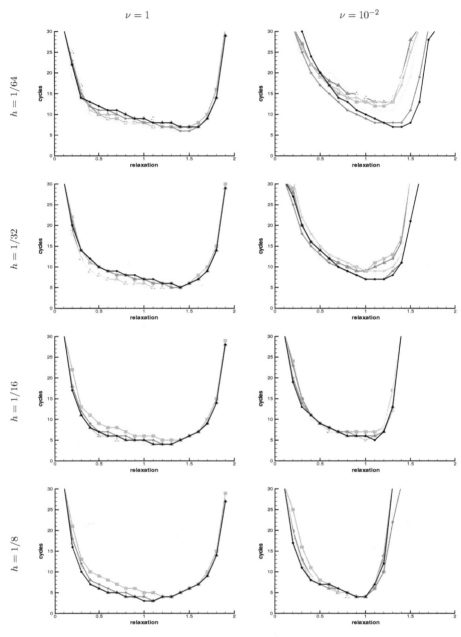

Table 6.13: SSOR smoothing for $\nu = 1, 10^{-2}$, $h = \frac{1}{8}, \ldots, \frac{1}{64}$

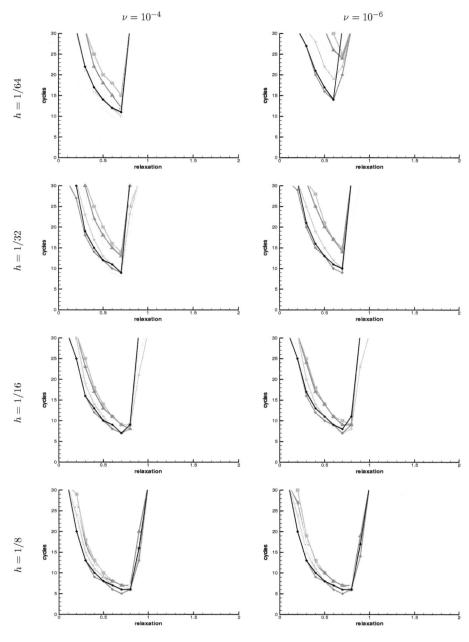

Table 6.14: SSOR smoothing for $\nu = 10^{-4}, 10^{-6}$, $h = \frac{1}{8}, \ldots, \frac{1}{64}$

## Convergence speed of the AMG method

Again, we compare the AMG method with a GMRES($m$) Krylov solver, using a restart length of $m = 20$, in combination with a SSOR preconditioner (with the optimal relaxation parameter $\omega = 0.7$).

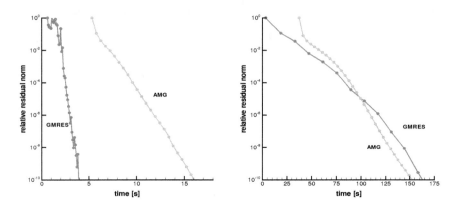

Figure 6.27: Convergence of GMRES vs. AMG for $h = \frac{1}{64}$    Figure 6.28: Convergence of GMRES vs. AMG for $h = \frac{1}{128}$

In Figures 6.27 and 6.28 we exemplarily see the convergence of the residual in the $L^2$-norm (6.7) for the strongly convection-dominated problem with $\nu = 10^{-6}$ at $h = \frac{1}{64}$ and $h = \frac{1}{128}$, the two finest mesh-widths, that were possible in 3D on a single workstation with 4GB of memory.

In order to shorten the setup time for the AMG solver, we increase the number of levels generated to 7 for $h = \frac{1}{64}$ and 8 for $h = \frac{1}{128}$. Since we have hardly any setup cost for the GMRES solver and the SSOR preconditioner, the Krylov solver has a headstart (red curves). The AMG setup time is much higher, roughly 5 sec. for $h = \frac{1}{64}$ and 38 sec. at $h = \frac{1}{128}$.

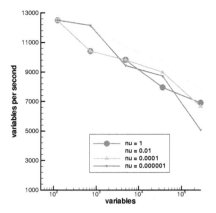

Figure 6.29: Calculation speed for the 3D problem

We can see, that the GMRES solver is clearly superior on the coarser mesh-width. At this problem size, the stiffness matrix' condition number is small enough to allow the Krylov solver to converge quickly. Also, the convection field and the boundary conditions are comparatively simple, and thus doesn't cause the problems with boundary layers as in the 2D example.

Only at the finer mesh-width, the AMG solver shows a more typical multigrid behaviour, it can compete with (and even outperform) the Krylov solver. Although the convergence curves doesn't differ much, we see that the scaling of AMG between the problem sizes is very much better (150 sec. to 16 sec. versus 160 sec to 4 sec.).

The diagram in Figure 6.29 finally shows the calculation speeds on the different problem sizes. Here the optimal parameters from the previous empirical studiess were used. In contrast to the 2D case, however, we observe a degradation of the speed for small $h$. The computational effort due to the increased densitity of the matrices slows down the setup (cf. Proposition 5.3.9) as well as the multigrid iteration.

# Part III

# AMG for mixed problems

# Chapter 7

# Mixed problems in computational fluid dynamics

The physical discipline of *fluid dynamics* is the study of fluids (that is liquids and gases) in motion. Its fundamental mathematical model, that describes continuous flows, is given by the *Navier-Stokes equations*[1]. Since a general solution can't be derived in closed form, one is dependent upon numerical approximations that the scientific area of *computational fluid dynamics* (CFD) is trying to give.

In this Chapter, we shortly describe the the (incompressible) Navier-Stokes problem, its linearization, the finite element discretization and the Oseen equation which emerges in this connection. Finally, we introduce the stabilization methods that needs to be applied for a successful computation.

## 7.1 The Navier-Stokes equations

We start with the definition of the main CFD problem, which is the background and reason for our research on numerical methods.

**Definition 7.1.1** (Navier-Stokes problem). *One of the most important and difficult problems in computational fluid dynamics consists of the evolutionary incompressible Navier-Stokes equations, which describes the flow and the pressure of a fluid in motion. More exactly, we are interested in the distribution of the pressure $p(t, x)$ and the velocity $\mathbf{u}(t, x) = (u_1, \ldots, u_d)^T(t, x)$ in the time-space cylinder $Q_T := (0, T) \times \Omega$ with respect to a given source-term $\mathbf{f}(t, x) = (f_1, \ldots, f_d)^T(t, x)$:*

$$\frac{\partial u}{\partial t} - \nu \Delta \mathbf{u} + (\mathbf{u} \cdot \nabla) \mathbf{u} + \nabla p = \mathbf{f} \quad in \ Q_T, \tag{7.1}$$

$$\nabla \cdot \mathbf{u} = 0 \quad in \ Q_T, \tag{7.2}$$

*with inital and boundary conditions*

$$\mathbf{u}(0, x) = \mathbf{u}^0(x), \tag{7.3}$$

$$\mathbf{u} = 0 \quad on \ (0, T) \times \partial \Omega \tag{7.4}$$

*where $0 < \nu \leq 1$, $(t, x) \in Q_T$, and $\Omega \subset \mathbb{R}^d$, $d \in \{1, 2, 3\}$. The scalar $\nu > 0$ is the viscosity parameter while equation (7.2) is the incompressibility constraint.*

A main obstacle in solving these equations is the nonlinearity, which prevents us from giving an analytical solution in the classical sense for arbitrary space dimension $d$. Leray ([Ler34]) in 1934 showed, that weak solutions exist under certain conditions. However, even if a weak solution exists,

---

[1]Named after *Claude-Louis Navier* (1785–1836), French engineer and physicist, and *George Gabriel Stokes* (1819–1903), Irish mathematician and physicist.

its uniqueness can not be guaranteed, especially in the three-dimensional case and for arbitrary large time-intervals $(0, T)$. Therefore, one is interested in computing a discrete numerical approximation in order to be able to simulate practical industrial applications.

This is usually achieved by the discretization in time and space, leading to systems of linear equations with a relatively high dimension number. Solving these linear systems, most Navier-Stokes solvers spend the biggest amount of time during the whole computing process. Here, efficient algorithms and a thorough implementation have to be applied.

Consequently, each component of the CFD software has to be chosen with care. An important topic, beside the mesh generation, is the discretization in time and space.

- The spatial (semi-) discretization on the domain $\Omega$ is usually done by using finite element (or finite difference or finite volume) methods.

- For the discretization of the time interval $(0, T)$ we normally use a time-stepping method like a single-step $\theta$-scheme.

We will apply the time discretization before the space discretization, resulting in an outer time loop, which seems to be a quite natural approach to an instationary problem, however other methods are also common. In each time step a stationary Navier-Stokes type of equation in the form of a (discrete) nonlinear and indefinite saddle point problem has to be solved.

A closer look at the corresponding discretization methods will be taken in the Subsections 7.1.1 and 7.1.2.

Now to solve the arising nonlinear problems, we have basically two alternatives:

- First treat the nonlinearity by a linearization technique for the whole problem like Newton or a fixed point iteration which leads to linear subproblems. These can be solved by using a fully coupled or a decoupled approach.

- Another possibility is to first split the problem into equations for the velocity and the pressure components, which then in turn can be treated with a linearization method for nonlinear problems.

We will focus on the first approach, using a fully coupled AMG solver for the linear problems (see Chapter 9). Decoupling methods, such as *Schur complement methods*, will shortly be discussed in Chapter 8.

In any case, our CFD-software is forced to calculate a solution to a linear system with a large-dimensional sparse matrix in the end. Mainly two variants of solver algorithms are eligible for this task:

- Krylov subspace methods like GMRES, BiCGSTAB, etc. are usually reliable methods. Though they need an appropriate preconditioning.

- Multigrid methods, especially when adapted to the concrete problem, promise even better performance.

Geometric multigrid however, is not trivial to implement, especially the interpolation for abitrary unstructured, anisotropic meshes. Also, for decreasing $\nu$ these methods often show degraded convergence rates. Instead, the focus of this work will lie on the implementation and application of algebraic multigrid methods for saddle point problems, to which Chapter 9 is dedicated.

### 7.1.1   Time discretization

For treating the time interval $(0, T)$ numerically, we need a time-stepping method, partitioning it into time levels $t_n$, $n = 0, \ldots, N$, and computing the solution at time $t_n$, using the results from the previous time level(s).

The single-step $\theta$-schemes are widely and successively used methods, they will be the methods of our choice. If applied to the problem in (7.1) – (7.2), using the partition $0 = t_0 < t_1 < \cdots < t_M = T$ with the time step size $\tau_n := t_{n+1} - t_n$, the parameter $\theta \in [0, 1]$ ,and the notation

$$p_\theta^{n+1} := \theta p^{n+1} + (1 - \theta)p^n, \quad p^n := p(t_n)$$
$$\mathbf{f}_\theta^{n+1} := \theta \mathbf{f}^{n+1} + (1 - \theta)\mathbf{f}^n, \quad \mathbf{f}^n := \mathbf{f}(t_n)$$

it delivers the following problem:

$$\frac{\mathbf{u}^{n+1} - \mathbf{u}^n}{\tau_n} + \theta(-\nu\Delta\mathbf{u}^{n+1} + (\mathbf{u}^{n+1} \cdot \nabla)\mathbf{u}^{n+1}) + \nabla p_\theta^{n+1} = g^{n+1}, \tag{7.5}$$

$$\nabla \cdot \mathbf{u}^{n+1} = 0 \tag{7.6}$$

with the right hand side

$$g^{n+1} = \mathbf{f}_\theta^{n+1} - (1 - \theta)(-\nu\Delta\mathbf{u}^n + (\mathbf{u}^n \cdot \nabla)\mathbf{u}^n). \tag{7.7}$$

### The implicit Euler method

For $\theta = 1$ we get the *implicit* or *backward Euler scheme*, and formula (7.5) simplifies to the following:

**Definition 7.1.2** (Implicit Euler). *For every time step $\tau_n$, solve*

$$\frac{\mathbf{u}^{n+1}}{\tau_n} + (-\nu\Delta\mathbf{u}^{n+1} + (\mathbf{u}^{n+1} \cdot \nabla)\mathbf{u}^{n+1}) + \nabla p^{n+1} = \mathbf{f}^{n+1} + \frac{\mathbf{u}^n}{\tau_n}, \tag{7.8}$$

$$\nabla \cdot \mathbf{u}^{n+1} = 0 \tag{7.9}$$

*where the right hand side $\mathbf{f}^{n+1} + \frac{\mathbf{u}^n}{\tau_n}$ is known by the previous step.*

In order to solve the nonlinear equation (7.8), we could use a Newton method, or a linearization which approximates

$$(\mathbf{u}^{n+1} \cdot \nabla)\mathbf{u}^{n+1} \approx (\mathbf{u}^n \cdot \nabla)\mathbf{u}^{n+1}. \tag{7.10}$$

The convergence rate of the implicit Euler scheme is of first order, thus the error is bounded by $O(\tau)$. Furthermore, this is not changed by the linearization.

### The Crank-Nicholson method

Setting $\theta = \frac{1}{2}$ leads to the *Crank-Nicholson scheme*:

**Definition 7.1.3** (Crank-Nicholson). *For every time step $\tau_n$, solve*

$$\frac{\mathbf{u}^{n+1}}{\tau_n} + \frac{1}{2}(-\nu\Delta\mathbf{u}^{n+1} + (\mathbf{u}^{n+1} \cdot \nabla)\mathbf{u}^{n+1}) + \nabla p_{\frac{1}{2}}^{n+1} = \mathbf{f}^{n+1} + \frac{\mathbf{u}^n}{\tau_n} - \frac{1}{2}(-\nu\Delta\mathbf{u}^n + (\mathbf{u}^n \cdot \nabla)\mathbf{u}^n), \tag{7.11}$$

$$\nabla \cdot \mathbf{u}^{n+1} = 0. \tag{7.12}$$

*Again, the right hand side of (7.11) is known from the previous step.*

Since the convergence rate of this scheme is of second order (bounded by $O(\tau^2)$), an appropriate linearization should preserve this. The desired result is obtained by replacing

$$(\mathbf{u}^{n+1} \cdot \nabla)\mathbf{u}^{n+1} \quad \text{with} \quad \left(\frac{3}{2}\mathbf{u}^n - \frac{1}{2}\mathbf{u}^{n-1}\right) \cdot \nabla\mathbf{u}^{n+1},$$

see e.g. [SS97].

### 7.1.2   Weak formulation and spatial discretization

The problems which arise in each time step are now transformed into a variational formulation, using the spaces

$$\mathbf{H} := L^2(\Omega)^d,$$
$$\mathbf{V} := W_0^{1,2}(\Omega)^d \quad (\textit{velocity space}),$$
$$Q := L_0^2(\Omega) := \{q \in L^2(\Omega) : (q,1)_{L^2(\Omega)} = 0\} \quad (\textit{pressure space})$$

with the scalar products

$$(\mathbf{u},\mathbf{v})_\mathbf{H} := \sum_{i=1}^d \int_\Omega u_i v_i \, dx, \qquad (\nabla\mathbf{u},\nabla\mathbf{v}) := \sum_{i=1}^d (\nabla u_i, \nabla v_i)_\mathbf{H} = \sum_{i,j=1}^d \int_\Omega \frac{\partial u_i}{\partial x_j} \frac{\partial v_i}{\partial x_j} \, dx.$$

Exemplarily done for the implicit Euler method, linearized with (7.10), and setting $\mathbf{u} := \mathbf{u}^{n+1}$, $\mathbf{w} := \mathbf{u}^n$ and the new right hand side $\mathbf{f} := \mathbf{f}^{n+1} + \frac{\mathbf{u}^n}{\tau_n}$, one gets

**Definition 7.1.4** (Weak formulation of the linearized Navier-Stokes equations). *Find* $\mathbf{u} \in \mathbf{H}$, $p \in Q$ *such that*

$$\frac{1}{\tau_n}(\mathbf{u},\mathbf{v})_\mathbf{H} + (\mathbf{w}\cdot\nabla\mathbf{u},\mathbf{v})_\mathbf{H} + \nu(\nabla\mathbf{u},\nabla\mathbf{v}) - (p,\nabla\cdot\mathbf{v})_\mathbf{H} = (\mathbf{f},\mathbf{v})_\mathbf{H} \quad \forall\mathbf{v} \in \mathbf{V} \tag{7.13}$$

$$(\nabla\cdot\mathbf{u},q)_\mathbf{H} = 0, \quad \forall q \in Q. \tag{7.14}$$

This linearization method is also referred to as the *Picard iteration*.

## 7.2   The Oseen equations

The last formula, in turn, with $c = \tau_n^{-1}$, $\mathbf{b} = \mathbf{w}$, is equivalent to the weak formulation of the generalized stationary *Oseen equations*[2], which reads

**Definition 7.2.1** (Oseen problem). *Find* $\mathbf{u} : \mathbb{R}^d \to \mathbb{R}^d$, *and* $p : \mathbb{R}^d \to \mathbb{R}$ *such that*

$$-\nu\Delta\mathbf{u} + (\mathbf{b}\cdot\nabla)\mathbf{u} + \nabla p + c\mathbf{u} = \mathbf{f} \quad \textit{in } \Omega \tag{7.15}$$
$$\nabla\cdot\mathbf{u} = g \quad \textit{in } \Omega, \tag{7.16}$$
$$u = 0 \quad \textit{on } \partial\Omega, \tag{7.17}$$

*with the data* $c \in L^\infty(\Omega)$, $c \geq 0$, $b \in W_0^{1,2}(\Omega)^d$, $f \in L^2(\Omega)^d$, $g \in L^2(\Omega)$.

In fact, the Oseen equations are a problem, that probably exclusively arises as a linearization of the Navier-Stokes equations. It is a steady state model of a flow $\mathbf{u}$ and the pressure $p$ of a fluid under the force $\mathbf{b}$, with according boundary conditions on $\partial\Omega$. In contrast the latter, it is a linear problem for which already a great amount of analysis and a series of discretization methods exists.

An even more basic problem are the Stokes equations, that in contrast to the former have no convection term. It is a model of highly viscous flow, where the convection can be neglected. Since it is the simplest mixed problem, but also exhibits the typical difficulties of saddle point problems, it is worthwhile to study.

**Definition 7.2.2** (Stokes problem). *Let* $f \in L^2(\Omega)^d$, $g \in L^2(\Omega)$. *Find* $\mathbf{u} : \mathbb{R}^d \to \mathbb{R}^d$, *and* $p : \mathbb{R}^d \to \mathbb{R}$ *such that*

$$-\Delta\mathbf{u} + \nabla p = \mathbf{f} \quad \textit{in } \Omega \tag{7.18}$$
$$\nabla\cdot\mathbf{u} = g \quad \textit{in } \Omega, \tag{7.19}$$
$$u = 0 \quad \textit{on } \partial\Omega. \tag{7.20}$$

---

[2]This equation was suggested in [Ose10] by the Swedish theoretical physicist *Carl Wilhelm Oseen* (1879–1944), in order to overcome certain paradoxes of the Stokes equations.

For the discrete approximation, we choose a finite element method. At this point, other methods like finite difference (FDM, on a staggered grid) and the finite volume methods (FVM) may also be applied instead. However, we are interested in a special ordering of the discrete linear system, which can be delivered by our FEM code $\mathcal{PNS}$. We choose a triangulation $\mathcal{T}_h = \{T_1, \ldots, T_M\}$ of the domain as in the scalar case and define the basis functions of our discrete subspaces only on these triangles (tetrahedrons).

Defining now the bilinear forms

$$\begin{aligned}
a(\cdot,\cdot) : \mathbf{V} \times \mathbf{V} \longrightarrow \mathbb{R} : \quad & a(\mathbf{u},\mathbf{v}) := c(\mathbf{u},\mathbf{v})_{\mathbf{H}} + ((\mathbf{b} \cdot \nabla)\mathbf{u},\mathbf{v})_{\mathbf{H}} + \nu(\nabla\mathbf{u},\nabla\mathbf{v}) \\
b(\cdot,\cdot) : \mathbf{V} \times Q \longrightarrow \mathbb{R} : \quad & b(\mathbf{u},q) := -(\nabla \cdot \mathbf{u},q)_{\mathbf{H}}
\end{aligned} \tag{7.21}$$

and the linear forms

$$\begin{aligned}
f(\cdot) : \mathbf{V} \longrightarrow \mathbb{R} : \quad & f(\mathbf{v}) := (\mathbf{f},\mathbf{v})_{\mathbf{H}} \\
g(\cdot) : Q \longrightarrow \mathbb{R} : \quad & g(q) := (g,q)_{L^2(\Omega)},
\end{aligned} \tag{7.22}$$

and then

$$\begin{aligned}
A(\cdot,\cdot) : \mathbf{W} \times \mathbf{W} \longrightarrow \mathbb{R} : \quad & A(U,V) := a(\mathbf{u},\mathbf{v}) + b(\mathbf{v},p) - b(\mathbf{u},q) \\
F(\cdot) : \mathbf{W} \longrightarrow \mathbb{R} : \quad & F(V) := f(\mathbf{v}) + g(q)
\end{aligned}$$

with $\mathbf{W} := \mathbf{V} \times Q$ and $U = \{\mathbf{u},p\} \in \mathbf{W}$, $V = \{\mathbf{v},q\} \in \mathbf{W}$, the discrete problem can be formulated:

**Definition 7.2.3** (Standard Galerkin discrete approximation). *For the discrete approximation of (7.15) – (7.16), we choose finite-dimensional subspaces $\mathbf{V}_h \subset \mathbf{V}$ and $Q_h \subset Q$ and search for $U_h = \{\mathbf{u}_h, p_h\} \in \mathbf{V}_h \times Q_h$ such that*

$$A(U_h, V_h) = F(V_h) \quad \forall V_h = \{\mathbf{v}_h, q_h\} \in \mathbf{V}_h \times Q_h. \tag{7.23}$$

The stiffness matrix is computed by inserting the basis functions $\{\Phi_i\}_{i=1,\ldots,N}$ and $\{\Psi_j\}_{j=1,\ldots,M}$ of $\mathbf{V}_h$ and $Q_h$ into the bilinear forms:

$$A := (a_{ij})_{i,j=1}^{N} \in \mathbb{R}^{N \times N}, \quad a_{ij} := a(\Phi_j, \Phi_i), \tag{7.24}$$

$$B := (b_{ij})_{i,j=1}^{N,M} \in \mathbb{R}^{M \times N}, \quad b_{ij} := b(\Phi_i, \Psi_j), \tag{7.25}$$

whereas the right hand side is assembled as

$$\mathbf{f} := (\mathbf{f}_i)_{i=1}^{N} \in \mathbb{R}^{N}, \quad \mathbf{f}_i := f(\Phi_i), \tag{7.26}$$

$$\mathbf{g} := (\mathbf{g}_j)_{j=1}^{M} \in \mathbb{R}^{M}, \quad \mathbf{g}_j := g(\Psi_j), \tag{7.27}$$

leading to a linear system of the form

$$\begin{pmatrix} A & B^T \\ B & 0 \end{pmatrix} \begin{pmatrix} \mathbf{u} \\ \mathbf{p} \end{pmatrix} = \begin{pmatrix} \mathbf{f} \\ \mathbf{g} \end{pmatrix}. \tag{7.28}$$

One immediately verifies that the above matrix is indefinite if the matrix $A$ is positive definite, which is why this type of problem is referrred to as a saddle point problem.

### 7.2.1 Relationship with the convection-diffusion equation

The Oseen equation is closely related with the weak formulation of the convection-diffusion-reaction problem from Section 4.1. For the Oseen problem, we have $\mathbf{u} = (u_1, \ldots, u_d)^T$ and test functions $\mathbf{v} = (v_1, \ldots, v_d)^T$. Defining now $\mathbf{u}_i = (0, \ldots, 0, u_i, 0, \ldots, 0)^T$ and $\mathbf{v}_i$ respectively, we have

$$\mathbf{u} = \sum_{i=1}^{d} \mathbf{u}_i, \quad \mathbf{v} = \sum_{i=1}^{d} \mathbf{v}_i.$$

Hence, the bilinear form $a(\cdot, \cdot)$ from (7.21) can be written as

$$a(\mathbf{u}, \mathbf{v}) = \sum_{i=1}^{d} a(\mathbf{u}_i, \mathbf{v}_i).$$

Obviously now those parts of $a(\cdot, \cdot)$ which refer to $a(\mathbf{u}_i, \mathbf{v}_i)$ are of the type (4.3). Thus, the block matrices on the diagonal of the stiffness matrix of the discrete Oseen problem are nothing but discrete convection-diffusion-reaction problems. As a consequence of this, one has to be able to (somehow) invert such a kind of problem in order to provide a successful discrete Navier-Stokes/Oseen solver.

### 7.2.2   LBB stability

Concerning the solvability of equation (7.28), we need, beside the ellipticity of $a(\cdot, \cdot)$, that the discrete LBB condition holds for $b(\cdot, \cdot)$ :

**Definition 7.2.4** (LBB condition). *The finite element spaces* $\mathbf{V}_h \subset \mathbf{V}$ *and* $Q_h \subset Q$ *fullfill the* discrete Ladyshenskaja-Babuska-Brezzi[3] *(LBB) condition, if there exists a constant* $\beta > 0$, *such that*

$$\sup_{\mathbf{v}_h \in \mathbf{V}_h} \frac{b(\mathbf{v}_h, q_h)}{\|v_h\|_{\mathbf{H}}} \geq \beta \|q_h\|_Q. \tag{7.29}$$

Defining the space

$$\mathbf{V}_h(g) := \{v_h \in V_h : b(v_h, q_h) = (g, q_h)_{\mathbf{H}} \quad \forall\, q_h \in Q_h\},$$

we are able to state a result like the following, which can be found for example in [GR86] (Theorem II.1.1) or in [BF91]:

**Theorem 7.2.5.** *Assume that the following is true:*

1. *the bilinear form* $a(\cdot, \cdot)$ *is coercive, i.e. there exists a constant* $\alpha > 0$ *such that*

$$a(v_h, v_h) \geq \alpha \|v_h\|_{\mathbf{V}}^2 \quad \forall\, v_h \in \mathbf{V}_h(0),$$

2. *the bilinear form* $b(\cdot, \cdot)$ *satifies the LBB condition (7.29).*

*Then problem (7.23) has a unique solution* $U_h = \{u_h, p_h\} \in \mathbf{V}_h(g) \times Q_h$.

Note that in general, we have $\mathbf{V}_h(g) \not\subset \mathbf{V}_h$, which results in a non conformal approximation. The $P_{k+1}/P_k$ elements from the Taylor-Hood family, where the polynomial order of the velocity space is one degree higher than that of the pressure space, are the classical case of LBB-stable elements (i.e. finite elements, that fulfill the LBB condition). If the LBB condition is not satisfied (e.g. for equal-order elements), extra stabilization is needed, as we will see in the next section.

## 7.3   Stabilization techniques

It is known, that for large Reynolds numbers, the standard Galerkin approximation fails, if the grid isn't fine enough. As the viscosity coefficient $\nu$ goes to zero, the ellipticity of the bilinear form $a(\cdot, \cdot)$ can no longer be ensured and oscillations occur in the discrete solution, similar to the discrete convection-diffusion equation (see Section 4.3 in Part II).

Looking for a remedy for this problem, we have mainly two possibilities. One is the brute force attack by simply increasing the number of mesh points where it is necessary, in order to better approximate large gradients. However, this increases the problem size dramatically.

---

[3]The Russian mathematician Olga Ladyzhenskaya (1922 - 2004), the Czech mathematician Ivo Babuska and the Italian mathematician Franco Brezzi discovered this result independently from each other. It layed the foundations of a solvability theory for finite elements and especially for the discrete approximations of the Navier-Stokes equations.

The other, more practicable way, is to introduce a stabilization scheme like the *Streamline Upwind Petrov-Galerkin* (SUPG) method or the *Galerkin Least-Squares* (GLS) method.

Another issue is the requirement for the finite element spaces to fulfill the LBB condition (7.2.4). However, discrete spaces for velocity and pressure of equal polynomial degree, which are widely used, do not have this property. Using these spaces with the standard Galerkin FEM approach would result in a singular matrix. Instead, at least a grad-div stabilization scheme has to be applied.

### 7.3.1 Stabilization schemes for LBB-unstable elements

Assuming that the approximation is done on a triangulation $\mathcal{T}_h = \{T_1, \ldots, T_M\}$ of $\overline{\Omega}$, we use the local $L^2$ inner product of an element $T_i$ and denote it by $(\cdot, \cdot)_{T_i} := (\cdot, \cdot)_{L^2(T_i)}$, as well as the according local norm $\| \cdot \|_{0,T_i} := \| \cdot \|_{L^2(T_i)}$. It is assumed that the inverse inequalities

$$\|\Delta v_h\|_{0,T_i} \leq C_I^u h_{T_i}^{-1} \|\nabla v_h\|_{0,T_i}, \quad \|\nabla q_h\|_{0,T_i} \leq C_I^p h_{T_i}^{-1} \|q_h\|_{0,T_i}$$

hold for $v_h \in \mathbf{V}_h$, $q_h \in Q_h$, and all $i = 1, \ldots, M$, see e.g. [Cia91]. Furthermore, we define the differential operator $\mathcal{L}$ as

$$\mathcal{L}(U) := \nu \Delta \mathbf{u} + (\mathbf{b} \cdot \nabla)\mathbf{u} + \nabla p + c\mathbf{u},$$

which allows us to write the standard full stabilization scheme as

**Definition 7.3.1** (Full stabilization). *Find $U_h = \{\mathbf{u}_h, p_h\} \in \mathbf{W}_h = \mathbf{V}_h \times Q_h$ such that*

$$A_{stab}(U_h, V_h) = F_{stab}(V_h) \quad \forall V_h = \{\mathbf{v}_h, q_h\} \in \mathbf{W}_h \tag{7.30}$$

*with*

$$A_{stab}(U, V) := A(U, V) + \sum_{i=1}^{M} (\gamma_{T_i} \nabla \cdot \mathbf{u}, \nabla \cdot \mathbf{v})_{T_i} + \sum_{i=1}^{M} (\mathcal{L}(U), \delta_{T_i} \psi(V))_{T_i}, \tag{7.31}$$

$$F_{stab}(V) := F(V) + \sum_{i=1}^{M} (\gamma_{T_i} g, \nabla \cdot \mathbf{v})_{T_i} + (\mathbf{f}, \delta_{T_i} \psi(V))_{T_i} \tag{7.32}$$

*where $\gamma_{T_i}$ and $\delta_{T_i}$ are the stabilization parameters which can be chosen for each element $T_i \in \mathcal{T}_h$ accordingly.*

| $\psi(V)$ | method | references |
|---|---|---|
| $(\mathbf{b} \cdot \nabla)\mathbf{v} + \nabla q$ | SUPG/PSPG | [HFB86] [RST96], [LO02] |
| $\mathcal{L}(V)$ | GLS | [HF87] [Fra93] |
| $-\mathcal{L}^*(V)$ | algebraic subgrid scale | [Cod01] |

Table 7.1: Choices of operator $\psi$ for different stabilization methods

The operator $\psi : \mathbf{W} \longrightarrow \mathbf{W}$, has to be chosen accordingly to get the desired stabilization method. Table 7.1 gives an overview of the resulting methods. The adjoint operator of $\mathcal{L}$ is denoted with $\mathcal{L}^*$.

#### SUPG/PSPG stabilization

For example, the choice

$$\psi(V) = (\mathbf{b} \cdot \nabla)\mathbf{v} + \nabla q$$

leads to the *SUPG/PSPG* method. The following lemma ensures, that the resulting discrete bilinear form $A_{stab}$ fulfills an LBB condition, with respect to the norm $\| \cdot \|_{SUPG}$, defined as

$$\|V_h\|_{SUPG}^2 := \nu |\mathbf{v}_h|_{1,\Omega}^2 + \|\sqrt{c} \mathbf{v}_h\|_{0,\Omega}^2 + \sum_{i=1}^{M} \delta_{T_i} \|(\mathbf{b} \cdot \nabla)\mathbf{v}_h + \nabla q_h\|_{0,T_i}^2 + \sum_{i=1}^{M} \alpha_{T_i} \|\nabla \cdot \mathbf{v}_h\|_{0,T_i}^2,$$

with some constants $\alpha_{T_i} > 0$, $i = 1, \ldots, M$.

**Lemma 7.3.2** (Stability of the SUPG/PSPG method). *Let* $\psi(V) := (\mathbf{b} \cdot \nabla)\mathbf{v} + \nabla q$.

1. *The discrete bilinear form* $A_{stab}(\cdot, \cdot)$ *is coercive on* $\mathbf{W}_h = \mathbf{V}_h \times Q_h$ *with the norm* $\| \cdot \|_{SUPG}$, *i.e. for all* $V_h \in \mathbf{W}_h$ *the inequality*

$$A_{stab}(V_h, V_h) \geq \frac{1}{2}\|V_h\|^2_{SUPG}$$

   *holds.*

2. *If there are positive constants* $\mu_0$, $\delta$, $\alpha$ *and* $\alpha_0$ *such that*

$$0 < \mu_0 h^2_{T_i} \leq \delta_{T_i} \leq \delta \leq \min\left( \frac{h^2_{T_i}}{2\nu(C^u_I)^2}, \frac{1}{2c}, \frac{h^2_{T_i}\gamma^2_\Omega}{2(C^p_I)^2}, \frac{h^2_{T_i}}{2\nu(C^u_I)^2} \right), \qquad 0 \leq \alpha_{T_i} \leq \alpha \leq \alpha_0 \nu h^2_{T_i}$$

   *as well as*

$$C_I \sqrt{L}\left( \frac{1}{\sqrt{\mu_0}} + \frac{h_{T_i}\|\mathbf{b}\|_{\infty,T_i}}{\sqrt{\nu}} \right) \leq \frac{1}{2}C_S \left( \sqrt{\nu} + C_F\sqrt{c} + \frac{C_F\|\mathbf{b}\|_{\infty,\Omega}}{\sqrt{\nu}} \right),$$

   *then there exists a constant* $\beta_\Omega > 0$ *independent of* $h$ *and* $\nu$, *such that*

$$\inf_{U_h \in \mathbf{W}_h} \sup_{V_h \in \mathbf{W}_h} \frac{A_{stab}(U_h, V_h)}{\|\|U_h\|\|_{SUPG}\|\|V_h\|\|_{SUPG}} \geq \beta_\Omega,$$

   *with the norm* $\|\| \cdot \|\|_{SUPG}$ *being defined as*

$$\|\|V_h\|\|^2_{SUPG} := \|V_h\|^2_{SUPG} + \gamma^2_\Omega\|q_h\|^2_{0,\Omega}.$$

*Proof.* See [Mül01], Lemma 10.6. A further discussion on how to choose the constants can also be found there. □

In $\mathcal{PNS}$ we set the above parameters as

$$\delta_{T_i} := \frac{h^2_{T_i}}{2\nu}\left( 1 + (\frac{h_{T_i}\|\mathbf{b}\|_{\infty,T_i}}{\nu})^2 \right)$$

$$\gamma_{T_i} := h_{T_i}\|\mathbf{b}\|_{\infty,\Omega}.$$

Defining now the discrete bilinear forms

$$a_{stab}(\mathbf{u}_h, \mathbf{v}_h) := a(\mathbf{u}_h, \mathbf{v}_h) + \sum_{T_i} \gamma_{T_i}(\nabla \cdot \mathbf{u}_h, \nabla \cdot \mathbf{v}_h)_{T_i} \qquad (7.33)$$

$$+ \sum_{T_i} \delta_{T_i}(-\nu\Delta\mathbf{u}_h + (\mathbf{b}\cdot\nabla)\mathbf{u}_h + c\mathbf{u}_h, (\mathbf{b}\cdot\nabla)\mathbf{v}_h)_{T_i}, \qquad (7.34)$$

$$b(\mathbf{v}_h, p_h) := -(p_h, \nabla\cdot\mathbf{v}_h)_\mathbf{H},$$

$$k_{stab}(\mathbf{v}_h, p_h) := \sum_{T_i} \delta_{T_i}(\nabla p_h, (\mathbf{b}\cdot\nabla)\mathbf{v}_h)_{T_i},$$

$$l_{stab}(\mathbf{u}_h, q_h) := \sum_{T_i} \delta_{T_i}(-\nu\Delta\mathbf{u}_h + (\mathbf{b}\cdot\nabla)\mathbf{u}_h + c\mathbf{u}_h, \nabla q_h)_{T_i},$$

$$c_{stab}(p_h, q_h) := \sum_{T_i} \delta_{T_i}(\nabla p_h, \nabla q_h)_{T_i},$$

we can assemble the according matrices $A_{stab}, B, K_{stab}, L_{stab}, C_{stab}$ using the finite set of basis functions $\Phi_i \in \mathbf{V}_h$, $i = 1, \ldots, N$ and $\Psi_j \in Q_h$, $j = 1, \ldots, M$ as in (7.24) and (7.25) The linear forms

$$f_{stab}(\mathbf{v}_h) := f(\mathbf{v}_h) + \sum_{T_i} \gamma_{T_i}(g, \nabla \cdot \mathbf{v}_h)_{T_i} + \sum_{T_i} \delta_{T_i}(\mathbf{f}, (\mathbf{b} \cdot \nabla)\mathbf{v}_h)_{T_i},$$

$$g_{stab}(q_h) := g(q) + \sum_{T_i} \delta_{T_i}(\mathbf{f}, \nabla q_h)_{T_i}.$$

then lead to the according right hand side vectors $\mathbf{f}_{stab}$ and $\mathbf{g}_{stab}$. Thus the whole linear system has the form

$$\begin{pmatrix} A_{stab} & (B + K_{stab})^T \\ -B + L_{stab} & C_{stab} \end{pmatrix} \begin{pmatrix} \mathbf{u} \\ \mathbf{p} \end{pmatrix} = \begin{pmatrix} \mathbf{f}_{stab} \\ \mathbf{g}_{stab} \end{pmatrix}. \tag{7.35}$$

**GLS stabilization**

By choosing

$$\psi(V) = -\nu \Delta \mathbf{v}_h + (\mathbf{b} \cdot \nabla)\mathbf{v} + +c\mathbf{v}_h + \nabla q,$$

the Galerkin least-squares scheme adds even more terms to the bilinear form $A$ in (7.31). It leads to the discrete bilinear forms

$$a_{stab}(\mathbf{u}_h, \mathbf{v}_h) := a(\mathbf{u}_h, \mathbf{v}_h) + \sum_{T_i} \gamma_{T_i}(\nabla \cdot \mathbf{u}_h, \nabla \cdot \mathbf{v}_h)_{T_i} \tag{7.36}$$

$$+ \sum_{T_i} \delta_{T_i}(-\nu \Delta \mathbf{u}_h + (\mathbf{b} \cdot \nabla)\mathbf{u}_h + c\mathbf{u}_h, -\nu \Delta \mathbf{v}_h + (\mathbf{b} \cdot \nabla)\mathbf{v}_h + c\mathbf{v}_h)_{T_i}, \tag{7.37}$$

$$b(\mathbf{v}_h, p_h) := -(p_h, \nabla \cdot \mathbf{v}_h)_{\mathbf{H}},$$

$$k_{stab}(\mathbf{v}_h, p_h) := \sum_{T_i} \delta_{T_i}(\nabla p_h, -\nu \Delta \mathbf{v}_h + (\mathbf{b} \cdot \nabla)\mathbf{v}_h + c\mathbf{v}_h)_{T_i},$$

$$l_{stab}(\mathbf{u}_h, q_h) := \sum_{T_i} \delta_{T_i}(-\nu \Delta \mathbf{u}_h + (\mathbf{b} \cdot \nabla)\mathbf{u}_h + c\mathbf{u}_h, \nabla q_h)_{T_i},$$

$$c_{stab}(p_h, q_h) := \sum_{T_i} \delta_{T_i}(\nabla p_h, \nabla q_h)_{T_i},$$

and the linear forms

$$f_{stab}(\mathbf{v}_h) := f(\mathbf{v}_h) + \sum_{T_i} \gamma_{T_i}(g, \nabla \cdot \mathbf{v}_h)_{T_i} + \sum_{T_i} \delta_{T_i}(\mathbf{f}, -\nu \Delta \mathbf{v}_h + (\mathbf{b} \cdot \nabla)\mathbf{v}_h + c\mathbf{v}_h)_{T_i},$$

$$g_{stab}(q_h) := g(q) + \sum_{T_i} \delta_{T_i}(\mathbf{f}, \nabla q_h)_{T_i}.$$

defining now the linear system in (7.35). A stability result similar to Lemma 7.3.2 can be found in [Fra93]. Note that the GLS stabilization as introduced here doesn't preserve symmetry for symmetric problems like the Stokes equation. It is also referred to as the GLS− scheme, in contrast to the (original) variant GLS+, that leads to a symmetric matrix, however at the price of indefinitenes (see [BBGS04]). The GLS− scheme is also utilized in $\mathcal{PNS}$.

# Chapter 8

# Numerical linear algebra for saddle point problems

In this chapter, we will shortly describe the arising linear systems of the form

$$F\begin{pmatrix} u \\ p \end{pmatrix} := \begin{pmatrix} A & B_1^T \\ B_2 & C \end{pmatrix} \begin{pmatrix} u \\ p \end{pmatrix} = \begin{pmatrix} f \\ g \end{pmatrix}, \tag{8.1}$$

and give an overview of some usual iterative solution methods. Furthermore, the two different orderings of the unknowns are introduced, and the consequences for the solution methods, especially Krylov-methods and the preconditioning, are discussed. These are however only the preliminaries for the (algebraic) multi-level methods, which are described in the next chapter.

## 8.1 Unknown based ordering

The widely used *standard* (or *classical*) *ordering* of variables, consists of grouping together those degrees of freedom, which belong to one *unknown* of the original partial differential equation. Here, an unknown is a function, that is to be approximated, usually a physical quantity. For example for the 2D Oseen equation, the vector entries belonging to the $x$-direction of the velocity ($\mathbf{u}_1$) come first, then the components belonging to the $y$-direction ($\mathbf{u}_2$) , and then the vector entries belonging to the pressure ($p$).

The linear systems in (7.28) respectively (7.35) then have the form

$$\begin{pmatrix} A_{xx} & A_{xy} & B_{1,xp}^T \\ A_{yx} & A_{yy} & B_{1,yp}^T \\ B_{2,px} & B_{2,py} & C_{pp} \end{pmatrix} \begin{pmatrix} u_x \\ u_y \\ p \end{pmatrix} = \begin{pmatrix} f_x \\ f_y \\ g \end{pmatrix}, \tag{8.2}$$

with $A_{xx}, A_{xy}, A_{yx}, A_{yy} \in \mathbb{R}^{N/2 \times N/2}$, $B_{1,xp}, B_{1,yp}, B_{2,px}, B_{2,py} \in \mathbb{R}^{M \times N/2}$ and $C_{pp} \in \mathbb{R}^{M \times M}$ being sparse matrices.

The advantage of this ordering clearly is that it can be used with any combination of finite elements for the velocity and the pressure space, particularly for equal-order elements *as well as* for elements with different polynomial degrees (like the LBB-stable Taylor-Hood elements).

Basically two typical alternatives of numerical linear algebra methods are possible to solve this type of equation:

1. We can treat the whole *coupled* system as one with an iterative solver such as a Krylov subspace method (GMRES, BiCGStab, etc.) with an appropriate preconditioning.

2. The other variant, under the assumption, that $A^{-1}$ exists, is to use a pressure *Schur complement method* which decouples the velocity and the pressure component. These methods are based on

the block inverse of $F$ in (8.1):

$$F^{-1} = \begin{pmatrix} A^{-1} + A^{-1}B_1^T S^{-1} B_2 A^{-1} & -A^{-1}B_1^T S^{-1} \\ -S^{-1}B_2 A^{-1} & S^{-1} \end{pmatrix}, \tag{8.3}$$

with $S := C - B_2 A^{-1} B_1^T$ being the *Schur complement*. This leads to the *decoupled* system

$$Sp = g - B_2 A^{-1} f$$
$$Au = f - B_1^T p.$$

For this scheme, only $A$ and $S$ have to be inverted, where $A$ is a convection-diffusion-reaction type of matrix. Various update schemes for $u$ and $p$ lead to diverse methods, such as *pressure correction methods*, *Uzawa iterations* ([Uza72]) or *SIMPLE* ([PS72]). The Schur complement mostly can't be computed explicitly, especially for big problems, thus for inverting $S$, Krylov methods can be used, because they only require the *effect* of $S$ on a vector. This however has the drawback, that traditional preconditioners (like SSOR or ILU) cannot be applied. Therefore, another approach is to compute $S$ only approximately, using e.g. a preconditioner for $A$, instead of $A^{-1}$.

Often Krylov methods are combined with Schur complement methods as a preconditioner, since the usual standard methods like Jacobi, SOR, or ILU exhibit poor convergence behaviour when simply applied to the whole matrix $F$. A good overview on numerical methods for saddle point problems is given in the article of Benzi, Golub and Liesen, see [BGL05].

## 8.2   Point based ordering

The *node* (or *point*) *based* ordering is a variant that is only possible with equal-order elements, like $P_1$-$P_1$-stab, which is used in $\mathcal{PNS}$. Here, those variables that belong to the same degree of freedom (but different physical quantities) are grouped together. The new stiffness matrix $F^\pi$ can be derived from $F$ by applying an according permutation matrix $\Pi$:

$$F^\pi x = \Pi^T F \Pi \Pi^T \begin{pmatrix} u \\ p \end{pmatrix} = \Pi^T \begin{pmatrix} f \\ g \end{pmatrix} = b, \tag{8.4}$$

with $F^\pi = \Pi^T F \Pi \in \mathbb{R}^{K \times K}$, $K = 3M$. Looking at the example from above, the 2D Oseen problem would have the form:

$$\begin{pmatrix} F_{11} & \cdots & F_{1M} \\ \vdots & \ddots & \vdots \\ F_{M1} & \cdots & F_{MM} \end{pmatrix} \begin{pmatrix} x_1 \\ \vdots \\ x_M \end{pmatrix} = \begin{pmatrix} b_1 \\ \vdots \\ b_M \end{pmatrix}, \tag{8.5}$$

with

$$F_{ij} = \begin{pmatrix} (A_{xx})_{ij} & (A_{xy})_{ij} & (B_{1,xp}^T)_{ij} \\ (A_{yx})_{ij} & (A_{yy})_{ij} & (B_{1,yp}^T)_{ij} \\ (B_{2,px})_{ij} & (B_{2,py})_{ij} & (C_{pp})_{ij} \end{pmatrix} \in \mathbb{R}^{3 \times 3}, \qquad x_i = \begin{pmatrix} (u_x)_i \\ (u_y)_i \\ (p)_i \end{pmatrix} \in \mathbb{R}^3, \qquad b_i = \begin{pmatrix} (f_x)_i \\ (f_y)_i \\ (g)_i \end{pmatrix} \in \mathbb{R}^3.$$

Note that $(A_{yx})_{ij} = 0$ and $(A_{xy})_{ij} = 0$ for inner points of $\Omega$, if the bilinear form $a_{stab}$ is defined as in (7.34) or (7.37). This type of ordering is also referred to as *Vanka*-type of ordering. However, the original method in [Van86] consisted of an *element-wise* ordering, in contrast to the point-wise ordering used here.

Basically one has the possibility to solve the arising systems with iterative solvers such as Krylov methods, since the point based ordering obviously inhibits Schur complement methods. However, this type of ordering also has some advantages. For example, the data structure for the sparse matrix $F^\pi$ doesn't need to store the indices of all single scalar entries but only the indices[1] of each $3 \times 3$-block ($4 \times 4$-block in 3D).

Numerically, a Krylov method would lead to more or less the same result for (8.2) as well as for (8.5) – except for the permutation.

However, since the size of the blocks is known in advance, the matrix-vector multiplication can be better optimized and vectorized by the compiler (cf. Section 3.8). This has direct consequences for most Krylov subspace methods, which are strongly based on this operation. Thus, one and the same Krylov method for 8.2 and 8.5 would exhibit a greater execution speed for the latter (see also [DLH00]).

Furthermore, we are able to use specialized block versions of numerical algorithms, as we show in the following.

### 8.2.1 Simple iteration and preconditioning methods for the point based ordering

In order to increase the convergence speed of iterative methods, one is interested in a preconditioner $M \in \mathbb{R}^{K \times K}$ for $F^\pi$ (or $F$), such that $M^{-1}F^\pi \approx I$ or $F^\pi M^{-1} \approx I$. Generally, $M$ is some approximation to $F^\pi$. Traditional preconditioners arise from splitting methods, which split the matrix $F^\pi$ additively into $F^\pi = M - N$ where $M$ is easy to invert. Usual choices are

$$
\begin{aligned}
M &= D && \text{(Jacobi)}, \\
M &= \omega^{-1}D && \text{(damped Jacobi)}, \\
M &= L + D && \text{(Gauß-Seidel)}, \\
M &= \omega^{-1}(\omega L + D) && \text{(SOR)},
\end{aligned}
$$

where $L$ is the strict lower triagonal part $L$, $D$ is the diagonal part and $\omega \in (0, 2)$ some relaxation parameter. Because of their slow convergence rate, they are of course outdated as a pure solver when compared to e.g. Krylov methods, but still are important as a smoother for multigrid methods (cf. chapter 5).

For saddle point problems however, these traditional iteration schemes above show comparatively poor convergence rates, regardless of the ordering of the unknowns. This changes when exploiting the block structure of the matrix.

#### Generalized SOR

The relaxed Gauß-Seidel or SOR (*Successive Over-Relaxation*) algorithm can be formulated as a generalized version for block matrices of the following form. Let $A \in \mathbb{R}^{N \times N}$ be partitioned into $n \cdot n$ submatrices such that

$$
A = (A_{ij})_{i,j=1}^n, \quad A_{ij} \in \mathbb{R}^{n_i \times n_j}, \quad n_1, \ldots, n_n \in \mathbb{N}, \quad \sum_{i=1}^n n_i = N. \tag{8.6}
$$

Then we can formulate the generalized SOR method for block matrices like this:

Following the generic programming paradigm, Algorithm 5 is parameterized with invert, which shall depict an appropriate solution method, that determines or approximates $A_{ii}^{-1}y_i$. It might be chosen different types of solvers for different diagonal entries, for example exact solvers like an $LU$-decomposition if $A_{ii}$ is relatively small, or some iterative solver again, if $A_{ii}$ is relatively large and sparse, leading to a hybrid method. For $A_{ii} \in \mathbb{R}$ it is the simple inversion of a real number, leading to the standard SOR[2].

---

[1] see Section 2.5.2 in Chapter 2 about sparse storage formats

[2] Using SOR again for the inversion of the diagonal blocks would result in method that is mathematically equivalent to the standard SOR that simply is applied to the whole matrix $A$.

---

**Algorithm 5: Generalized SOR**

---

Input: Matrix $A \in \mathbb{R}^{n \times n}$, vector $b \in \mathbb{R}^n$, initial approximation $x^0 \in \mathbb{R}^n$
Output: An approximation $x^k$ to $A^{-1}b$
repeat

1     for $i = 1$ to $n$ do

2        $y_i \leftarrow b_i - \sum_{j=1}^{i-1} A_{ij} x_j^k - \sum_{j=1}^{i-1} A_{ij} x_j^{k-1}$
       $z_i \leftarrow \mathsf{invert}(A_{ii}, y_i)$
       $x_i^k \leftarrow \omega_i z_i (I_{n_i} - \omega_i) x_i^{k-1}$
    end

until convergence

---

For the point based ordering with $P_1$ elements for each unknown, we have $n_1 = \ldots = n_n = 3$ for a 2D problem (4 in 3D), in any case a small constant number, such that a direct solver can be employed. In BLANC and in our library MiLTON, we directly compute the inverses of all $A_{ii}$ in advance, since it obviously can be reused during the iteration. We will refer to this method also as *block SOR*.

The relaxation weights $\omega_i \in \mathbb{R}^{n_i \times n_i}$ are now matrices instead of scalars, however in BLANC, they are restricted to diagonal matrices. Numerical experiments show that it is important to be able to vary the relaxation parameters for different physical quantities, see [Mül01]. Experimental studies support that the choice of $\omega_{vel} \geq 1$ (overrelaxation of the velocity part) and $\omega_p \ll 1$ (underrelaxation of the pressure part), with the relaxation weight

$$\omega := \begin{pmatrix} \omega_{vel} & & \\ & \omega_{vel} & \\ & & \omega_p \end{pmatrix} \tag{8.7}$$

is beneficial for the 2D Oseen equation.

### Backward SOR, SSOR

In Algorithm 5, the components of $x^k$ are updated from $x_1^k$ to $x_n^k$. Therefore, the inner loop starting at line 1 it is also called a *forward* SOR step. If the directions of the outer loop in line 1 and of the summation in line 2 are reversed, such that the components of $x^k$ are updated from $x_n^k$ to $x_1^k$ it is called a *backward* SOR step.

Combing these two alternating steps together leads to the SSOR method, which exhibits greater stability for convection dominated problems in practical computations. It is used as a smoother for our algebraic multigrid methods throughout this thesis.

### Block ILU

Another class of methods that are widely used as preconditioners (and sometimes as multigrid smoothers) are the incomplete factorizations, the most famous being the ILU (*Incomplete LU*) decomposition. For matrices like (8.6) ILU and its variants can be formulated as block algorithms (often referred to as BILU) if $n_1 = \ldots = n_n$. Since the inverses of the diagonal entries have to be computed explicitly, the dimension of the submatrices cannot be arbitrarily high.

However, simple ILU(0) preconditioners often fail, especially when applied to indefinite systems as described in [Saa92]. Our own experience with ILU supports this observation, even when an ILU decomposition is feasible, it often shows a much worse convergence behaviour than e.g. an SSOR preconditioner. Variants of ILU, that allow fill-in (ILU($p$)), or that employ pivoting (ILUP), drop-tolerance (ILUT), or that add entries to the diagonal instead of dropping them (MILU), however seem to promise better convergence, see e.g. [CS97]. A short but comprehensive overview of these methods is given in [CvdV94].

# Chapter 9

# Algebraic multigrid for systems of equations

The methods introduced in Chapter 5 are well suited for scalar elliptic problems like the Poisson equation or the general (stabilized) advection diffusion reaction equation. However they become rather ineffective when applied to a matrix arising from a system of equations like a coupled Poisson, an Oseen or Navier-Stokes problem in two or three dimensions. Here, the classical AMG algorithm could find connectivity between physical quantities where there is none. Our own numerical computations support this – the standard AMG method from Section 5.2 applied to an Oseen problem may still converge (in simple cases) but the convergence rate heavily slows down[1]. A smoother may still work as a solver, but then the smooth error components (consisting of eigenvectors of $S_l$ that belong to large eigenvalues) are not well enough approximated on the next coarser level.

For saddle point problems like Oseen or Stokes, there is another difficulty: the incompressibility constraint (7.2) causes the indefiniteness of the system matrix for most of the standard discretizations. Only with according pressure stabilization schemes, a positive definite matrix can be gained.

So there is obviously a demand for adapted algebraic multigrid multigrid methods for saddle point problems. One of the first adaptions of algebraic multigrid ideas for the Navier-Stokes equations (for a finite volume discretization) was presented in [Raw95], where a Additive Correction Multigrid was used to construct the prologation and restriction operators. In [Web01] the smoothed and unsmoothed aggregation approaches where applied.

Furthermore there also exist hybrid methods, based on Schur complement iteration schemes, which use AMG only for inverting the Schur complement or the velocity part (see e.g. [EHST02] or [GNR98]).

In the following two sections, we present customized, fully coupled, algebraic multigrid methods for mixed problems. These methods basically differ in the ordering of the unknowns, that were introduced in the previous chapter. All of these methods however, are mainly based on the classical AMG approach presented by Ruge and Stüben in [RS87].

## 9.1 Algebraic multigrid for the unknown based ordering

An algebraic multigrid method for systems of equations that are assembled into a matrix using unknown based ordering as in (8.2) was already suggested in [RS87]. At least, it is recommended to prolongate and restrict the physical quantities separately, using a block-diagonal prolongation operator like

$$P^{var} = \begin{pmatrix} P_1 & & 0 \\ & \ddots & \\ 0 & & P_n \end{pmatrix}, \tag{9.1}$$

[1]This deterioration of convergence was e.g. also reported in [Oel01] for coupled Laplace equations.

137

with $n = 3$ for the two-dimensional Oseen problem ($n = 4$ in 3D). The prolongation matrices $P_1, \ldots, P_3$ are constructed like in the scalar case out of $A_{xx}, A_{yy}, C_{pp}$.

Problems then arise in the detail. Since equal-order elements are not LBB-stable, mixed problems are often discretized using $P_k - P_{k-1}$ (Taylor-Hood) elements. Different polynomial degrees however lead to different dimensions for $C_{pp}$ and the rest of the matrices on the diagonal. This leads to problems when no pressure stabilization matrix is assembled (how to construct $P_n$ in this case?). Even if $C_{pp} \neq 0$, and $P_n$ could be constructed out of it, it is not ensured, that $P_n$ coarsens away (geometrical) points of the underlying mesh, that $P_1, \ldots, P_{n-1}$ don't. This could lead to a situation, where the velocity variables on the coarse levels would live on totally different points than the pressure variables.

Another issue is the correct choice of the smoother. Standard SOR or SSOR smoothing has little effect on these equations. One suggestion is therefore to employ one step of a Schur complement method, such as the Braess-Sarazin smoother [BS97].

Various (successful) suggestions to overcome these problems are explored in [Wab03] for the Navier-Stokes, respectively the Oseen and Stokes equation. The method for $P_2$-$P_1$ elements introduced there however uses additional geometrical information to construct the coarser levels, therefore it is not purely algebraic.

## 9.2 Algebraic multigrid for the point based ordering

If we have the situation, that each equation of a problem like (7.1) – (7.2) or (7.15) – (7.16) is discretized on the same grid, we may reformulate the method by sorting all those variables together that depend on one point $p_i \in \Omega$, giving a linear system like in (8.5).

The AMG approach presented in this section will be referred to as *point-wise coupled AMG* or *point-wise block AMG*. Algebraic multigrid for point based orderings is not restricted to saddle point problems like the Oseen or Stokes problem, in fact, point-wise coupled AMG formally can be applied to many types of equations, given that all quantities/equations are discretized using the same finite elements on the same mesh. It was originally proposed already in [RS87] and was successfully applied to coupled Laplace/diffusion equations and linear elasticity problems in [Oel01]. So first we would like to formulate the general AMG approach for matrices arising from systems of equations and then later on describe the special treatment of saddle point problems.

In the following, we consider linear system $Ax = b$, where $A$ consists of small equally sized dense matrices and the whole system has the shape

$$Ax = \begin{pmatrix} A_{11} & \cdots & A_{1m} \\ \vdots & \ddots & \vdots \\ A_{m1} & \cdots & A_{mm} \end{pmatrix} \begin{pmatrix} x_1 \\ \vdots \\ x_m \end{pmatrix} = \begin{pmatrix} b_1 \\ \vdots \\ b_m \end{pmatrix} = b \qquad (9.2)$$

with $A_{ij} \in \mathbb{C}^{k \times k}$, $x_i, b_i \in \mathbb{C}^k$, $i, j = 1, \ldots, m$. The number of grid points is $m$, so that the total number of variables is $n = km$ and the local dimension $k$ would be for example equal to $d + 1$ for (7.1) – (7.2). The entries $A_{ij}$ in $A$ will be referred to as *blocks*.

In the following let $\underline{D}, \underline{L}$ and $\underline{U}$ denote the block diagonal, block lower and block upper part of $A$, such that $A = \underline{L} + \underline{D} + \underline{U}$:

$$\underline{D} = \begin{pmatrix} A_{11} & & 0 \\ & \ddots & \\ 0 & & A_{mm} \end{pmatrix}, \quad \underline{L} = \begin{pmatrix} 0 & A_{12} & \cdots & A_{1m} \\ & \ddots & \ddots & \vdots \\ & & \ddots & A_{m-1,m} \\ & & & 0 \end{pmatrix}, \quad \underline{U} = \begin{pmatrix} 0 & & & \\ A_{21} & \ddots & & \\ \vdots & \ddots & \ddots & \\ A_{m1} & \cdots & A_{m,m-1} & 0 \end{pmatrix}.$$

For $x \in \mathbb{C}^n$ and $A \in \mathbb{C}^{n \times n}$ the *adjoint* ($\hat{=}$ transposed and complex conjugated) vector respectively matrix will be denoted with

$$x^* := \bar{x}^T \quad \text{resp.} \quad A^* := \bar{A}^T.$$

Furthermore, if $\underline{D}$ is positive definite, we now additionally use the norms

$$\|x\|_{\underline{D}} := \sqrt{|x^*\underline{D}x|},$$
$$\||x\||_{\underline{A}} := \sqrt{|xA^*\underline{D}^{-1}Ax|}.$$

Note that $A$ is required to have full rank for the last one to be a norm, otherwise (or if $\underline{D}$ is not positive definite) it only defines a semi-norm.

We reformulate the approach from Section 5.2.1. Instead of coarsening the set of *variables*, we now speak of coarsening the set of *points*. The set of points are the grid points $\Omega = \{p_1, \ldots, p_m\}$ where on each point $p_i$ the $k$ variables $x_i^{(1)}, \ldots, x_i^{(k)}$ are defined.

**Definition 9.2.1** (Pointwise block AMG preprocess).
*Repeat for level $l = 0, \ldots, l_{max}$ until the linear system on level $l$ is small enough to use an exact solver:*

1. *Generate a $C/F$-Splitting : On a level $l$ with matrix $A_l \in \mathbb{C}^{km_l \times km_l}$ we separate coarse level points $C_l$ from those points $p_i \in \Omega_l := \{p_1, \ldots, p_{m_l}\}$ that can be interpolated by the coarser level points. The latter are gathered in a set $F_l := \Omega_l \setminus C_l$ and with $m_{l+1} = \#[C_l]$ the dimension of the next coarse level is $km_{l+1}$.*

2. *Define the* weighted interpolation $P^{node} = P_l \in \mathbb{C}^{km_{l+1} \times km_l}$ *as the prolongation operator in dependency of the block entries in $A_l$. Then the restriction will be set to*

$$R_l = (P_l)^*. \tag{9.3}$$

3. *Finally compute the next coarse level matrix with the* Galerkin product *:*

$$A_{l+1} := R_l A_l P_l. : \tag{9.4}$$

Of course, many results from Section 5.2.1 simply carry over to this approach, especially the Lemmas 5.2.2 and 5.2.3. We would just like to point out, that if the right stabilization (SUPG or GLS) is used, the matrix $A_0$ is positive definite, and therefore all following coarse level matrices $A_l$ are again positive definite.

### 9.2.1 Algebraic smoothness

The goal is to derive an AMG method in a point blockwise sense – all variables connected to one point $i$ are prolongated, relaxed and restricted together. Instead of conditions (5.27) to (5.30), we will use now

$$\|S_l e_l\|_{A_l}^2 \leq \|e_l\|_{A_l}^2 - \alpha_1 \||e_l\||_{\underline{A_l}}^2, \tag{9.5}$$
$$\|T_l e_l\|_{A_l}^2 \leq \beta_1 \||e_l\||_{\underline{A_l}}^2, \tag{9.6}$$

and

$$\|S_l e_l\|_{A_l}^2 \leq \|e_l\|_{A_l}^2 - \alpha_2 \||S_l e_l\||_{\underline{A_l}}^2, \tag{9.7}$$
$$\|T_l e_l\|_{A_l}^2 \leq \beta_2 \||e_l\||_{\underline{A_l}}^2, \tag{9.8}$$

with $\alpha_1, \alpha_2, \beta_1, \beta_2 > 0$, and which imply (5.22) and (5.23). If it is clear, which level is meant, we will leave out the index $l$.

Next we would like to show that the block SOR has the above smoothing properties (9.5) and (9.7). For this we need some axiliary results gathered in the following lemmas.

**Lemma 9.2.2.** *Let $A$ and $\underline{D}$ be Hermitian positive definite, and let $S \in \mathbb{C}^{n \times n}$ be of the form*

$$S = I - Q^{-1}A,$$

*with some nonsingular matrix $Q$, then the inequalities (9.5) and (9.7) are equivalent to*

$$\alpha_1 x^* Q^* \underline{D}^{-1} Q x \le x^*(Q + Q^* - A)x \quad \forall\, x \in \mathbb{C}^n$$

*and*

$$\alpha_2 x^*(A - Q^*)\underline{D}^{-1}(A - Q)x \le x^*(Q + Q^* - A)x \quad \forall\, x \in \mathbb{C}^n$$

*respectively.*

*Proof.* For the energy norm of $Se$, $e \in \mathbb{C}^n$ we have

$$\|Se\|_A^2 = \|(I - Q^{-1}A)e\|_A^2 = e^*Ae - [e^*A + e^*AQ^{-*}Q - e^*AQ^{-*}A]Q^{-1}Ae$$
$$= \|e\|_A^2 - e^*AQ^{-*}(Q + Q^* - A)Q^{-1}Ae.$$

Therefore, (9.5) is equivalent to

$$\alpha_1 \|e\|_A^2 \le e^*AQ^{-*}(Q + Q^* - A)Q^{-1}Ae,$$

which is equivalent to

$$\alpha_1 x^* Q^* \underline{D}^{-1} Q x \le x^*(Q + Q^* - A)x, \quad \text{with} \quad x := Q^{-1}Ae.$$

The inequality (9.7) is equivalent to

$$\alpha_2 \|Se\|_A^2 \le e^*AQ^{-*}(Q + Q^* - A)Q^{-1}Ae,$$

which is equivalent to

$$\alpha_2 x^*(Q^* - A)\underline{D}^{-1}(Q - A)x \le x^*(Q + Q^* - A)x, \quad \text{again with} \quad x := Q^{-1}Ae.$$

$\square$

**Lemma 9.2.3.** *Let $A \in \mathbb{C}^{n \times n}$ be an arbitrary matrix and $B \in \mathbb{C}^{n \times n}$ be Hermitian positive definite, furthermore let $\alpha > 0$ be some real number, then*

$$x^* A x \le \alpha x^* B x \quad \forall\, x \in \mathbb{C}^n \quad \Longleftrightarrow \quad \rho(B^{-1}A) \le \alpha. \tag{9.9}$$

*Proof.* $B$ is Hermitian positive definite $\Longleftrightarrow$ there exists a decomposition $B = P^*DP$ with unitary $P$ and a diagonal matrix $D$ consisting of the eigenvalues of $B$ and which, in turn, can be decomposed into root matrices $D = D^{\frac{1}{2}}D^{\frac{1}{2}}$. This means that the proposition (9.9), with $x = P^*D^{-\frac{1}{2}}w$ substituted, is equivalent to

$$\frac{w^* D^{-\frac{1}{2}} PAP^* D^{-\frac{1}{2}} w}{w^* w} \le \alpha \quad \forall\, w \in \mathbb{C}^n, w \ne 0.$$

Further, the above is equivalent to

$$\max_{\substack{w \in \mathbb{C}^n \\ w \ne 0}} \frac{w^* D^{-\frac{1}{2}} PAP^* D^{-\frac{1}{2}} w}{w^* w} = \rho(D^{-\frac{1}{2}} PAP^* D^{-\frac{1}{2}}) \le \alpha.$$

The proposition now follows from the observation that the matrices $D^{-\frac{1}{2}}PAP^*D^{-\frac{1}{2}}$, $D^{-1}PAP^*$ and $P^*D^{-1}PA = B^{-1}A$ have the same characteristic polynomial. $\square$

We are now able to verify the smoothing property of the block SOR method. For reasons of simplicity, we choose $\omega \in \mathbb{R}$ instead of $\mathbb{R}^{k \times k}$ as proposed in Section 8.2.1.

**Theorem 9.2.4** (Smoothing property of the block SOR). *Let $A$ and $\underline{D}$ be Hermitian positive definite, and for an arbitrary vector $w = (w_i)_{i=1}^m \in \mathbb{R}^m$ with $w_i > 0$, $i = 1, \ldots, m$ be*

$$\gamma_- = \max_{i=1,\ldots,m} \Big( \frac{1}{w_i} \sum_{j=1}^{i-1} w_j \|A_{ii}^{-1} A_{ij}\|_k \Big), \quad \gamma_+ = \max_{i=1,\ldots,m} \Big( \frac{1}{w_i} \sum_{j=i+1}^{m} w_j \|A_{ii}^{-1} A_{ij}\|_k \Big),$$

*with some matrix norm $\|\cdot\|_k$ in $\mathbb{C}^{k \times k}$. Then the block SOR method satisfies (9.5) and (9.7) with*

$$\alpha_1 \le \frac{2-\omega}{\omega(1+\gamma_-)(1+\gamma_+)}, \quad \alpha_2 \le \frac{2-\omega}{\omega(\frac{\omega-1}{\omega}+\gamma_-)(\frac{\omega-1}{\omega}+\gamma_+)}.$$

*Proof.* For the block SOR method we have $S = I - Q^{-1}A$ with $Q = Q(\omega) = \frac{1}{\omega}(\omega \underline{L} + \underline{D})$ and

$$Q + Q^* - A = (\frac{2}{\omega} - 1)\underline{D}.$$

Therefore, we are able to apply both Lemma 9.2.2 and then Lemma 9.2.3 to each of the inequalities (9.5) and (9.7). This leads to (9.5) being equivalent to

$$\alpha_1 x^* Q^* \underline{D}^{-1} Q x \le (\frac{2}{\omega} - 1)x^* \underline{D} x \quad \forall x \in \mathbb{C}^n,$$

$$\Longleftrightarrow$$

$$\rho(\underline{D}^{-1} Q^* \underline{D}^{-1} Q) \le \frac{2-\omega}{\alpha_1 \omega} \tag{9.10}$$

and (9.7) being equivalent to

$$\alpha_2 x^* (\underline{L} + (\frac{\omega-1}{\omega})\underline{D}) \underline{D}^{-1} (\underline{L}^* + (\frac{\omega-1}{\omega})\underline{D}) x \le (\frac{2}{\omega} - 1) x^* \underline{D} x \quad \forall x \in \mathbb{C}^n,$$

$$\Longleftrightarrow$$

$$\rho(\underline{D}^{-1}(\underline{L} + (\frac{\omega-1}{\omega})\underline{D}) \underline{D}^{-1} (\underline{L}^* + (\frac{\omega-1}{\omega})\underline{D})) \le \frac{2-\omega}{\alpha_2 \omega}. \tag{9.11}$$

For (9.10) and to (9.11) hold, it is sufficient that

$$\alpha_1 \le \frac{2-\omega}{\omega \|\underline{D}^{-1} Q^*\| \|\underline{D}^{-1} Q\|},$$

respectively

$$\alpha_2 \le \frac{2-\omega}{\omega \|\underline{D}^{-1}(\underline{L} + (\frac{\omega-1}{\omega})\underline{D})\| \|\underline{D}^{-1}(\underline{L}^* + (\frac{\omega-1}{\omega})\underline{D})\|}$$

with some matrix norm $\|\cdot\|$ in $\mathbb{C}^{n \times n}$. With the norm $\|\cdot\| = \|\cdot\|_w$,

$$\|A\|_w := \max_{i=1,\ldots,m} \Big( \frac{1}{w_i} \sum_{j=1}^{m} w_j \|A_{ij}\|_k \Big)$$

we get the above proposition. $\qquad \square$

The proof can easily be extended for relaxation weights $\omega \in \mathbb{R}^{k \times k}$, being diagonal matrices. A similar proof can be given for the backward SOR step with $\underline{L}$ being replaced with $\underline{R}$ and these results can be used to show an according property of the SSOR method. However, all these properties need the matrix $A$ to be Hermitian positive definite.

## 9.2.2   Smooth error in the block AMG variant

Similar to [RS87] and Section 5.2.5 we want to find a definition of strong connection – this time between points in the grid, identified with $k \times k$ block matrices.

First we observe a similar property of the norms $\|\cdot\|_{\underline{D}}$ and $\||x\||_{\underline{A}}$ as in Lemma 5.2.9.

**Lemma 9.2.5.** *Let $A \in \mathbb{C}^{mk \times mk}$. If $\underline{D}$ is Hermitian positive definite then*

$$\|e\|_A^2 \leq \|e\|_{\underline{D}} \||e\||_{\underline{A}}, \quad \forall e \in \mathbb{C}^n. \tag{9.12}$$

*Proof.* The proof is the same as that of Lemma 5.2.9, with $D$ being replaced by $\underline{D}$ (for which there is also a root matrix $\underline{D}^{\frac{1}{2}}$ if $\underline{D}$ is Hermitian positive definite). □

If $e \in \mathbb{C}^{mk}$ is a smooth error with $\|Se\|_A^2 \approx \|e\|_A^2$, the smoothing property (9.5) yields $0 \approx \|Se\|_A^2 - \|e\|_A^2 \leq -\alpha_1 \||e\||_{\underline{A}}^2 \implies \||e\||_{\underline{A}}^2 \approx 0$. For a still relatively large global error, we have then

$$\||e\||_{\underline{A}} \ll \|e\|_A \tag{9.13}$$

and the last lemma gives

$$\|e\|_A \ll \|e\|_{\underline{D}}. \tag{9.14}$$

**Definition 9.2.6** (Block transpose, block symmetric). *For a matrix $A \in \mathbb{C}^{mk \times mk}$ like in (9.2) let $\tilde{A}$ be defined as*

$$\tilde{A} = \begin{pmatrix} A_{11} & \cdots & A_{m1} \\ \vdots & \ddots & \vdots \\ A_{1m} & \cdots & A_{mm} \end{pmatrix}. \tag{9.15}$$

*$\tilde{A}$ will be called* block transpose *of $A$. If the equality*

$$A = \tilde{A} \tag{9.16}$$

*holds, then we will say that $A$ is* block symmetric.

**Definition 9.2.7** (Block M-matrix). *For a matrix $A \in \mathbb{C}^{mk \times mk}$ like in (9.2) let the diagonal entries $A_{ii}$ be positive definite, and the off-diagonal entries $A_{ij}$, $i \neq j$ be negative semi-definite. Then we will call this type of matrix a* block M-matrix.

Note that, if $A$ is a block M-matrix, $\tilde{A}$ is also.

**Lemma 9.2.8.** *For arbitrary $A \in \mathbb{C}^{mk \times mk}$ and its block transpose $\tilde{A}$ the following equality holds for every $e \in \mathbb{C}^{mk}$:*

$$\Re(e^* A e) + \Re(e^* \tilde{A} e) = -\sum_{i=1}^{m} \sum_{j=1}^{m} (e_i^* - e_j^*)(A_{ij} + A_{ij}^*)(e_i - e_j) + \Re\left( \sum_{i=1}^{m} e_i^* \left( \sum_{j=1}^{m} A_{ij} + A_{ij}^* \right) e_i \right), \tag{9.17}$$

*where $e_i \in \mathbb{C}^k$, $e^* = (e_1^*, \ldots, e_m^*)$.*

*Proof.* Let $e \in \mathbb{C}^{mk}$ be given, then one verifies easily:

$$
\begin{aligned}
\Re(e^* A e) + \Re(e^* \tilde{A} e) =& e^* \frac{1}{2}(A + A^*)e + e^* \frac{1}{2}(\tilde{A} + \tilde{A}^*)e \\
=& \frac{1}{2} \sum_{i=1}^{m} \sum_{j=1}^{m} e_i^* (A_{ij} + A_{ji}^* + A_{ji} + A_{ij}^*) e_j \\
=& \frac{1}{2} \sum_{i=1}^{m} \sum_{j=1}^{m} e_i^* (A_{ij} + A_{ij}^*) e_j + \frac{1}{2} \sum_{j=1}^{m} \sum_{i=1}^{m} e_j^* (A_{ij} + A_{ij}^*) e_i \\
=& -\frac{1}{2} \sum_{i=1}^{m} \sum_{j=1}^{m} e_i^* (A_{ij} + A_{ij}^*) e_i - e_i^* (A_{ij} + A_{ij}^*) e_j - e_j^* (A_{ij} + A_{ij}^*) e_i + e_j^* (A_{ij} + A_{ij}^*) e_j \\
& + \frac{1}{2} \sum_{i=1}^{m} \sum_{j=1}^{m} e_i^* (A_{ij} + A_{ij}^*) e_i + \frac{1}{2} \sum_{i=1}^{m} \sum_{j=1}^{m} e_j^* (A_{ij} + A_{ij}^*) e_j \\
=& -\frac{1}{2} \sum_{i=1}^{m} \sum_{j=1}^{m} (e_i^* - e_j^*)(A_{ij} + A_{ij}^*)(e_i - e_j) + \Re \left( \sum_{i=1}^{m} e_i^* \left( \sum_{j=1}^{m} A_{ij} + A_{ji} \right) e_i \right).
\end{aligned}
$$

$\square$

Let's now explore the real case, $A \in \mathbb{R}^{mk \times mk}$. Let $A$ and $\tilde{A}$ be positive definite with symmetric block diagonal $\underline{D}$. If (9.5) is fulfilled by $A$ with $\alpha_1$ and by $\tilde{A}$ with $\tilde{\alpha}_1{}^2$ we have, as a consequence of Lemma 9.2.5 for smooth error $e$:

$$
\|e\|_A + \|e\|_{\tilde{A}} \ll 2\|e\|_{\underline{D}}. \tag{9.18}
$$

Assume now again zero row and column sums (see also Equation (5.33) for the scalar case), or at least the positive semi-definiteness of the $i$-th row- and column-sum:

$$
e_i^T \left( \sum_{j=1}^{m} A_{ij} + A_{ji} \right) e_i \geq 0, \quad \forall\, e_i \in \mathbb{R}^k, \quad i = 1, \ldots, m, \tag{9.19}
$$

we get the estimate, using Lemma 9.2.8:

$$
\sum_{i=1}^{m} \sum_{\substack{j=1 \\ j \neq i}}^{m} -\frac{1}{2}(e_i^T - e_j^T)(A_{ij} + A_{ij}^T)(e_i - e_j) \ll 2 \sum_{i=1}^{m} e_i^T A_{ii} e_i. \tag{9.20}
$$

In the following, we assume $A$ to be a real block M-matrix. For $y \in \mathbb{R}^k$, we have $y^T A_{ij} y = y^T A_{ij}^T y$ and therefore

$$
y^T(-(A_{ij} + A_{ij}^T))y = \|y\|_{-(A_{ij} + A_{ij}^T)}^2 = 2\|y\|_{-A_{ij}}^2. \tag{9.21}
$$

Then $\|\cdot\|_{-A_{ij}}$ defines a semi-norm and in the left sum of (9.20) we only have summands that are greater or equal zero. The same heuristic averaging argument as in the scalar case (Section 5.2.3) leads to

$$
\sum_{\substack{j=1 \\ j \neq i}}^{m} \frac{1}{2} \|e_i - e_j\|_{-A_{ij}}^2 \ll \|e_i\|_{A_{ii}}^2. \tag{9.22}
$$

We interpret this inequality as follows: if $\|-A_{ij}\|$ is relatively large, the contribution of $\|e_i - e_j\|_{-A_{ij}}^2$ has to be rather small. In other words, the $i$-th component of the error varies only slightly in the

---

[2]Note that if $A = A^*$ e.g. the block SOR always also has the smoothing property with respect to the $\|\cdot\|_{\tilde{A}}$ and the $\|\|\cdot\|\|_{\tilde{A}}$ norm, since in this case, $\tilde{A}$ is also symmetric positive definite.

direction of the $j$-th component if $-A_{ij}$ is large in some sense, compared to the other entries in the $i$-th row. In general this would be the case if

$$-y^T A_{ij} y \geq -\theta y^T A_{ik} y, \quad \forall y \in \mathbb{R}^k, \, \forall k = 1, \ldots, m, \, k \neq i.$$

Again, $\theta \in (0, 1)$ is some threshold parameter. Because of Lemma 9.2.3 this is equivalent to

$$\max_{\substack{k=1,\ldots,m \\ k \neq i}} \rho(A_{ij}^{-1} A_{ik}) \leq \frac{1}{\theta}.$$

### 9.2.3   General block strong couplings

In order to build up a coarsening strategy as in the scalar case, we need a practical definition of strong couplings between these small blocks.

For a natural matrix norm $\|\cdot\|_k$ we have $\rho(A_{ij}^{-1} A_{ik}) \leq \|A_{ij}^{-1} A_{ik}\|_k \leq \|A_{ij}^{-1}\|_k \|A_{ik}\|_k$. So it would be sufficient to compare the norm of $A_{ij}^{-1}$ with the other matrix norms.

**Definition 9.2.9** (Block inverse norm strong coupling). *Two components $i$ and $j$ are strongly coupled in the block inverse norm sense, if*

$$\max_{\substack{k=1,\ldots,m \\ k \neq i}} \theta \|A_{ik}\|_k \leq \frac{1}{\|A_{ij}^{-1}\|_k}.$$

On the other hand, this criterion would result in the need of computing the inverse of each and every block matrix entry in the sparse block matrix, which is not only time consuming but also not always possible in the general case where we can have these entries to be nearly singular (at least sometimes very ill-conditioned). Thus, a faster, but less accurate method, would be to restrict ourselves to the norm of $A_{ij}$ instead of $A_{ij}^{-1}$.

**Definition 9.2.10** (Block strong coupling). *Two components $i$ and $j$ are strongly coupled in the block wise sense, if*

$$\max_{\substack{k=1,\ldots,m \\ k \neq i}} \theta \|A_{ik}\|_k \leq \|A_{ij}\|_k.$$

Another possibility is to restrict the coupling to the diagonal entries of $A_{ij}$, trusting that the diagonal is a good approximation of the spectrum.

**Definition 9.2.11** (Diagonal block strong coupling). *For $1 \leq i, j \leq n$, let $D_{ij} := \mathrm{diag}(A_{ij})$ be the diagonal of $A_{ij}$. Then two components $i$ and $j$ are strongly coupled in the diagonal block sense, if*

$$\max_{\substack{k=1,\ldots,m \\ k \neq i}} \theta \|D_{ik}\|_k \leq \|D_{ij}\|_k.$$

Considering only the diagonal elements has the advantage, that it reduces the computational effort. However it is mainly reasonable, if the coupling between the different equations/physical quantities is not too large.

In search of definitions that are easier to apply, one could also just inspect the single entries in each small block matrix and compare them one by one, taking the according maxima. This however is not further investigated in this context.

With these definitions the strong neighbourhood $\mathcal{S}_i$ can be defined exactly as in Definition 5.2.22 and the splitting process (algorithm 2) can be applied without a change.

### 9.2.4 Block strong couplings for stabilized saddle point problems

Since stiffness matrices arising from unstabilized saddle point problems are indefinite, they are unsuitable for a direct application of this AMG method. Instead we require a stabilization (Section 7.3), yielding a positive definite matrix. A direct consequence hereof is that all entries $A_{11}, \ldots, A_{mm}$ are positive definite.

**Lemma 9.2.12.** *Let $A \in \mathbb{R}^{mk \times mk}$ be a positive definite block matrix with a structure like in Equation (9.2). Then all its entries $A_{ii}$, $1 \leq i \leq m$ on the block-diagonal $\underline{D}$ are in turn positive definite $k \times k$-matrices.*

*Proof.* If $A$ is positive definite, it is

$$v^T A v > 0 \quad \forall \ v \in \mathbb{R}^{mk}, v \neq 0.$$

We conceive the vectors $v \in \mathbb{R}^{mk}$ as block vectors that have $m$ entries $v_1, \ldots, v_m$ with $v_j \in \mathbb{R}^k$, $1 \leq j \leq m$. Let now $i \in \{1, \ldots, m\}$, and $x \in \mathbb{R}^k$ be an arbitrary vector with $x \neq 0$. Then we define the block vector $v^{(i)}(x)$, which has all being entries zero, except for the $i$-th component:

$$v^{(i)}(x) := (v_j)_{j=1}^m \in \mathbb{R}^{mk}, \quad \text{with} \quad v_j := \begin{cases} 0 & \text{for } j \neq i \\ x & \text{for } j = i \end{cases}.$$

Then especially for this vector, the following inequality holds:

$$0 < v^{(i)}(x)^T A v^{(i)}(x) = x^T A_{ii} x.$$

Since $x$ was chosen arbitrarily from $\mathbb{R}^k$, $A_{ii}$ is positive definite. □

However, the straightforward application of Definition 9.2.10 or 9.2.11 didn't lead to satisfying results in our numerical tests. First of all, those definitions may lead to an unphysical coupling between the velocity and the pressure where there is none. Second, we have to ensure that on each level $l$ the according matrix $A_l \in \mathbb{R}^{km_l \times km_l}$ is invertable, which is true e.g., if each level fulfills the LBB-condition. In [Wab03] e.g. a property, which is a consequence of the LBB-condition, is shown for the variable based approach, however at the expense of a violation of the Galerkin equation (9.4), since the pressure block of a new level $A_{l+1}$ is scaled after the computation with the Galerkin product.

Looking back at Section 8.2, we see that the entries $A_{ij}$ have the form

$$A_{ij} = \begin{pmatrix} A_{ij}^{vv} & A_{ij}^{vp} \\ A_{ij}^{pv} & A_{ij}^{pp} \end{pmatrix}, \quad \text{with} A_{ij}^{vv} \in \mathbb{R}^{d \times d}, A_{ij}^{vp} \in \mathbb{R}^{d \times 1}, A_{ij}^{pv} \in \mathbb{R}^{1 \times d}, A_{ij}^{pp} \in \mathbb{R}. \tag{9.23}$$

We will call $A_{ij}^{vv}$ the *velocity block*, $A_{ij}^{vp}$ and $A_{ij}^{pv}$ *mixed block*, $A_{ij}^{pp}$ the *pressure part*.

Albeit an LBB condition couldn't be shown for each level, this isn't necessary either. It is sufficient if the inital level is LBB-stable and that the smoothing and the approximation property hold. At least, due to the Lemmas 9.2.12 and 5.2.2, we are able to state, that all the level's matrices and their block diagonal entries are positive definite again. However, we must pay attention, that the matrices don't degenerate to nearly positive *semi*-definiteness. We observed this case in numerical experiments where the pressure block nearly vanished. Looking back at how the SUPG/PSPG or GLS stabilization was defined in Section 7.3.1 we observe that the pressure part is of order $O(h^2)$, so if the AMG levels are the approximation of a geometrical setting, this entry should instead increase as the overall dimension $m_l$ decreases.

Another desirable property of an AMG method is the coarsening along the streamlines for convection dominated problems as we have learned in the scalar case (see e.g. Section 5.2.6). Thus we suggest the following definitions of the strong coupling, that only depend on the velocity blocks.

**Definition 9.2.13** (Velocity block strong coupling). *Two components $i$ and $j$ are strongly coupled in the velocity block sense, if*

$$\max_{\substack{k=1,\dots,m \\ k \neq i}} \theta \| A_{ik}^{vv} \|_{k-1} \leq \| A_{ij}^{vv} \|_{k-1}.$$

And equivalent to Definition 9.2.11, the diagonally restricted variant:

**Definition 9.2.14** (Diagonal velocity block strong coupling). *For $1 \leq i,j \leq n$, let $D_{ij}^{vv} := \mathrm{diag}(A_{ij}^{vv})$ be the diagonal of $A_{ij}^{vv}$. Then two components $i$ and $j$ are strongly coupled in the diagonal velocity block sense, if*

$$\max_{\substack{k=1,\dots,m \\ k \neq i}} \theta \| D_{ik}^{vv} \|_{k-1} \leq \| D_{ij}^{vv} \|_{k-1}.$$

For practical implementations, we consider the row-sum norm $\|\cdot\|_\infty$ or the column-sum norm $\|\cdot\|_1$ for $\|\cdot\|_{k-1}$, because of the ease of their implementation. Both norms worked well in this context for the Stokes and Oseen equation.

### 9.2.5  General block interpolation

The interpolation that was defined in the scalar case in Section 5.2.4 can now be adapted to the point-wise block AMG. This leads to the block direct interpolation.

If the splitting algorithm was applied successfully, we have two disjoint sets $C_l$ and $F_l$ and the dimension on the next level is $km_{l+1}$ with $m_{l+1} := \#[C_l]$. The prolongation matrix for the point based approach

$$P_l^{node} = P^{node} := (P_{ij})_{i,j=1}^{m_l, m_{l+1}} \in \mathbb{C}^{km_{l+1} \times km_l} \tag{9.24}$$

from level $l+1$ to level $l$ is defined as

$$P_{ij} := \begin{cases} W_{ij} & \text{if } i \in F_l \text{ and } \varphi^{-1}(k) \in \mathcal{P}_i^l \\ I_k & \text{if } i \in C_l \text{ and } \varphi^{-1}(k) = i \\ 0 & \text{else} \end{cases} \tag{9.25}$$

with $I_k$ being the $k$-dimensional unity matrix, the according interpolation weights $W_{ij} \in \mathbb{C}^{k \times k}$ and the interpolation variables $\mathcal{P}_i \subset C_l$, from which the variables at the $i$-th point are interpolated. The set $\mathcal{P}_i$ is chosen as $\mathcal{P}_i = C_l \cap \mathcal{S}_i$.

For algebraically smooth error $e$, remembering (9.13) and (9.14), the residual $r = Ae$ is relatively small compared to $e$, namely we have the relation $\|r\|_{D^{-1}} \ll e^T r \ll \|e\|_D$. Thus, especially for a point $i \in F$, we can assume the $i$-th component of the residual vector to be nearly zero:

$$r_i = A_{ii} e_i + \sum_{n \in \mathcal{N}_i} A_{in} e_n \approx 0. \tag{9.26}$$

Furthermore, if enough strong neighbours are included in $\mathcal{P}_i$, we can approximate:

$$\left( \sum_{j \in \mathcal{P}_i} A_{ij} \right)^{-1} \sum_{j \in \mathcal{P}_i} A_{ij} e_j \approx \left( \sum_{\in \mathcal{N}_i} A_{in} \right)^{-1} \sum_{\in \mathcal{N}_i} A_{in} e_n. \tag{9.27}$$

Inserting (9.27) into (9.26) now gives a method for determining the interpolation weights $W_{ij}$, that will be referred to as *direct interpolation* in accordance with [Oel01] and [Stü99].

**Definition 9.2.15** (Block direct interpolation). *The interpolation weights of the* block direct inter- *polation are defined as*

$$W_{ij} := -A_{ii}^{-1} \left( \sum_{n \in \mathcal{N}_i} A_{in} \right) \left( \sum_{n \in \mathcal{P}_i} A_{in} \right)^{-1} A_{ij} \tag{9.28}$$

In [Oel01], it was shown, that the above interpolation satifies an approximation property similar to (5.39) if $A$ is a symmetric positive definite block M-matrix, in which the block matrices in each row are pairwise commutating.

The according version for the diagonal block strong coupling consists of considering only the diagonals.

**Definition 9.2.16** (Diagonal block direct interpolation). *For $1 \leq i, j \leq n$, let $D_{ij} := \mathrm{diag}(A_{ij})$ be the diagonal of $A_{ij}$. The interpolation weights of the diagonal block direct interpolation are defined as*

$$W_{ij} := -D_{ii}^{-1}\Big(\sum_{n \in \mathcal{N}_i} D_{in}\Big)\Big(\sum_{n \in \mathcal{P}_i} D_{in}\Big)^{-1} D_{ij} \tag{9.29}$$

It should be mentioned that the diagonal block interpolation corresponds to the prolongation (9.1) that was proposed for the variable based AMG approach. It is mathematically the same as when we first apply the scalar direct interpolation to each of the diagonal blocks in (8.2), and then transform it with the permutation matrices $\Pi$ from Equation (8.4) in Section 8.2. More precisely, if $\Pi_l$ and $\Pi_{l+1}$ are the according permutation matrices on the consecutive levels $l$ and $l + 1$, the following relation holds:

$$A_{l+1}^{node} = \Pi_{l+1}^T A_{l+1}^{var} \Pi_{l+1} = \underbrace{\Pi_{l+1}^T (P_l^{var})^T \Pi_l}_{=(P_l^{node})^T} \underbrace{\Pi_l^T A_l^{var} \Pi_l}_{=A_l^{node}} \underbrace{\Pi_l^T P_l^{var} \Pi_{l+1}}_{=P_l^{node}}, \tag{9.30}$$

when we use the notation $A_0^{var} := F$, $A_0^{node} := F^\pi$ for the matrices from (8.4).

### 9.2.6 Block interpolation for stabilized saddle point problems

Because of the issues mentioned in Section 9.2.4 we also need to adapt the interpolation to the saddle point case. If we define the strong connection by only considering the velocity part, we need to decouple the pressure by choosing an appropriate shape of the interpolation weight.

For an interpolation weight $W_{ij} \in \mathbb{R}^{k \times k}$ with $k = d + 1$ we suggest the following form:

$$W_{ij} := \begin{pmatrix} W_{ij}^{vv} & 0 \\ 0 & c_p \end{pmatrix}, \quad \text{with} \quad W_{ij}^{vv} \in \mathbb{R}^{d \times d}, \tag{9.31}$$

and where $c_p \in \mathbb{R}$ is some constant $> 0$ that just uniformly transports the pressure from level to level, without a mixture with velocity components. Based on this special shape for saddle point problems, we adapt the two basic interpolations from the last Section.

**Definition 9.2.17** (Velocity block direct interpolation). *The interpolation weights of the velocity block direct interpolation are computed as*

$$W_{ij}^{vv} := -(A_{ii}^{vv})^{-1}\Big(\sum_{n \in \mathcal{N}_i} A_{in}^{vv}\Big)\Big(\sum_{n \in \mathcal{P}_i} A_{in}^{vv}\Big)^{-1} A_{ij}^{vv} \tag{9.32}$$

The according diagonal block version of the direct interpolation even decouples the velocity components.

**Definition 9.2.18** (Diagonal velocity block direct interpolation). *For $1 \leq i, j \leq n$, let $D_{ij} := \mathrm{diag}(A_{ij})$ be the diagonal of $A_{ij}$. The interpolation weights of the diagonal block direct interpolation are computed as*

$$W_{ij}^{vv} := -(D_{ii}^{vv})^{-1}\Big(\sum_{n \in \mathcal{N}_i} D_{in}^{vv}\Big)\Big(\sum_{n \in \mathcal{P}_i} D_{in}^{vv}\Big)^{-1} D_{ij}^{vv} \tag{9.33}$$

Note, that for Oseen problems, at the inner points, the off-diagonal entries of $A_{ij}^{vv}$ are zero anyway, thus the above diagonal velocity block version of the interpolation should be sufficient.

For diffusion dominated problems, we observed the entries in $W_{ij}^{vv}$ to differ enourmously, especially from the 2nd and 3rd level on. For fine mesh widths $h < 1/128$ this deteriorates the performance of the solver. Therefore, in this cases, we suggest an equilibration of the diagonal entries. More precisely, let 9.33 deliver a weight

$$W_{ij}^{vv} = \begin{pmatrix} w_1 & & \\ & \ddots & \\ & & w_d \end{pmatrix} \tag{9.34}$$

and let

$$w_{\min} := \min_{i=1,\dots,d} |w_i|, \qquad w_{\max} := \max_{i=1,\dots,d} |w_i|. \tag{9.35}$$

Then we adaptively replace $W_{ij}^{vv}$ with

$$\hat{W}_{ij}^{vv} = \begin{pmatrix} \hat{w}_1 & & \\ & \ddots & \\ & & \hat{w}_d \end{pmatrix}, \qquad \hat{w}_i := \begin{cases} \sum_{i=1}^{d} |w_i|/d & \text{if} \quad w_{\min}/w_{\max} < \zeta, \\ |w_i| & \text{else} \end{cases} \tag{9.36}$$

Although this averaging is only considered as a workaround, however, choosing $\zeta$ in the order of the viscosity parameter $\nu$ yields very proper results, as we will see in the next chapter.

# Chapter 10

# Numerical Results

## 10.1 The AMG method

In this chapter, we investigate the convergence behaviour of the point-wise AMG for saddle point systems, which was introduced in the last chapter. The solver is again implemented using the MiLTON matrix library, whereas the $\mathcal{PNS}$ finite element program system was used to generate the linear systems with the point based ordering approach.

For the practical implementation, we have used only the diagonal velocity block strong coupling from Definition 9.2.14 and the according interpolation from Definition 9.2.18. The preprocess follows the Definition 9.2.1 using the standard splitting algorithm 2. Again, as in the scalar case, the effect of varying the coarsening parameter $\theta$ will be investigated.

This coarsening process is now used to generate four coarse level matrices, giving a total of five levels, which in most cases yields a matrix on the coarsest level, that is small enough to be treated with a direct solver. At this place, we use the SuperLU ([DEG$^+$99]) decomposition method again, as for the scalar problems. Note that this involves time and memory consuming format conversions (from *block* and *row-wise* to *single value* and *column-wise*), which increases the setup-time.

The smoother for all our computations will be the block SSOR method (cf. Section 8.2.1), where we however increase the number of smoothing steps compared to the scalar case. We will apply between one and five pre- and post-smoothing steps, depending on the problem.

For the first problem, we work with default values for the relaxation weight $\omega$, which has the form (8.7). It turned out, that $\omega_{vel} = 1$ and $\omega_p = 0.2$ deliver sufficient convergence rates for many problems. However, this was not the case for the second Oseen problem, and since no theoretical work is available that investigates optimal relaxation parameters for these problems, it is considered under variation of the velocity and pressure relaxation, $\omega_{vel}$ and $\omega_p$.

We choose the vector

$$x_0 := \frac{1}{\sqrt{n}}(1, \ldots, 1)^T \in \mathbb{R}^n \tag{10.1}$$

as an initial solution to the problem on the finest level, where $n$ is the dimension of the first level. The iteration consists of standard V-cycles (W-cycles didn't improve the convergence, on the contrary), until the start residual $r_0 := Ax_0 - b$ is reduced by six orders of magnitude, $\|r_k\|_2/\|r_0\|_2 < 10^{-6}$, or if the count of 50 V-cycles is reached.

Finally, AMG for selected problems (with small $h$ and $\nu$) is compared with Krylov subspace methods from the BLANC library, in order to compare the $h$-dependency of the methods. Note, that the AMG solver is always used as a stand-alone solver, without the acceleration by a Krylov method.

## 10.2 A Stokes problem

As a first and simple type of saddle-point problems, we apply the point block AMG solver to a Stokes problem. More precisely, we consider

Find $\mathbf{u}(x) : \mathbb{R}^2 \to \mathbb{R}^2$, and $p(x) : \mathbb{R}^2 \to \mathbb{R}$ such that

$$-\Delta \mathbf{u} + \nabla p = \mathbf{f} \quad \text{in } \Omega \in \mathbb{R}^2, \tag{10.2}$$

$$\nabla \cdot \mathbf{u} = 0 \quad \text{in } \Omega \in \mathbb{R}^2, \tag{10.3}$$

with $\Omega = (0,1) \times (0,1)$ again being the unit square. The right hand side is set to $\mathbf{f} := (0,0)^T$, and the boundary $\partial\Omega$ is set to have the following Dirichlet conditions

$$\mathbf{u}(x,y) := \begin{pmatrix} \mathbf{u}_1(x,y) \\ \mathbf{u}_2(x,y) \end{pmatrix} := \begin{pmatrix} -y \\ x \end{pmatrix}, \quad \text{for} \quad (x,y)^T \in \partial\Omega.$$

The equation was discretized with the FEM code $\mathcal{PNS}$ (Parallel Navier Stokes, [AMOG99]) using $P_1$ elements for the velocity as well as for the pressure and SUPG/PSPG with grad-div stabilization (see Section 7.3.1). The boundary conditions are imposed strongly.

Within this software, the matrix entries that belong to one mesh point are grouped together. This means that if we have a two-dimensional problem like above, the entries of the stiffness matrix are in turn (dense) $3 \times 3$ matrices, because we have two components for the velocity and one for the pressure per grid point.

Table 10.1 shows the sizes of the generated matrices. Note that *overall nonzeros* counts all scalar entries (`double` values in C/C++) in the whole matrix. Since the $3 \times 3$ matrix blocks are stored in a dense format, we have some memory overhead in storing zero entries, which is however unavoidable in this approach.

| $h$ | 1/16 | 1/32 | 1/64 | 1/128 | 1/256 | 1/512 |
|---|---|---|---|---|---|---|
| mesh points | 289 | 1089 | 4225 | 16641 | 66049 | 263169 |
| matrix dimension | 867 | 3267 | 12675 | 49923 | 198147 | 789507 |
| overall nonzeros | 17001 | 66249 | 261513 | 1039113 | 4142601 | 16542729 |

Table 10.1: Mesh widths and matrix dimensions for the 2D Stokes and Oseen problems

For the AMG setup procedure, we chose the coarsening parameter $\theta = 0.5$, which led to reasonable setup times for all considered mesh sizes. In Table 10.2 the setup times are listed together with the average number of nonzero entries per row

$$r_{avg} := \frac{1}{l_{\max} + 1} \sum_{i=0}^{l_{\max}} \frac{nnz_i}{n_i}. \tag{10.4}$$

In contrast to (6.5) this value counts the number of nonzero $\mathbb{R}^{3 \times 3}$ matrices as entries. We can see that the AMG preprocess increases the relation of nonzero entries to the dimension of the coarse levels: the initial ratio of a FEM matrix originating from structured triangulation is $nnz_0/n_0 \approx 7$, however the average number for all levels is nearly twice as high. This is due to the diffusive nature of the Stokes equation: the part $A_{ij}^{vv}$ from (9.23) is essentially the same as for a Poisson equation plus stabilization terms.

| $h$ | 1/16 | 1/32 | 1/64 | 1/128 | 1/256 | 1/512 |
|---|---|---|---|---|---|---|
| AMG setup time [s] | 0.02 | 0.08 | 0.28 | 1.09 | 4.71 | 19.8 |
| $r_{avg}$ | 13.9 | 13.7 | 13.8 | 13.8 | 13.7 | 13.8 |
| SuperLU setup time [s] | 0.01 | 0.01 | 0.02 | 0.11 | 0.95 | 4.93 |

Table 10.2: AMG setup times and average row entries for the Stokes problem

The consequence is, that all off-diagonal entries are of nearly equal size, giving large sets $\mathcal{S}_i$ and $\mathcal{S}_i^T$ (and thus $\mathcal{P}_i^T$). Therefore, the according prolongation operators have many nonzero entries for $i \in F$, resulting in a denser coarse level matrix. We see, that the AMG setup times increase (as the problem size) by a factor of nearly 4. The SuperLU sparse LU decompostion, though, has an increasing portion of the overall setup time, because we have restricted the setup process to the generation of constantly four levels independent of $h$. For a more efficient method, one would adaptively choose $l_{\max}$ such that the coarsest matrix is so small, that its exact inversion is not too expensive. However here we must find a compromise between a small (and thus easy to invert) coarse level matrix, and the quality of the coarse level correction, that is of course the better, the bigger the coarse level matrix is.

| $h$ | 1/16 | 1/32 | 1/64 | 1/128 | 1/256 | 1/512 |
|---|---|---|---|---|---|---|
| AMG solver time [s] | 0.09 | 0.3 | 1.06 | 3.96 | 16.3 | 65.3 |
| BiCGStab solver time [s] | 0.02 | 0.07 | 0.52 | 3.23 | 19.11 | 255.69 |
| GMRES solver time [s] | 0.03 | 0.16 | 1.12 | 5.82 | 64.57 | >500 |

Table 10.3: Comparison of solver times for the Stokes problem

Table 10.3 now shows the overall solution times for different solvers. For the AMG solver, we used one SSOR pre- and postsmoothing step with the standard setting of $\omega_{vel} := 1.0$ for the velocity and an underrelaxation of $\omega_p := 0.2$ for the pressure, which led to satisfying convergence results. Both Krylov solvers are preconditioned with SSOR, however only extreme over-relaxation of $\omega_{vel} := 1.95$ for the velocity and $\omega_p := 0.05$ for the pressure yielded convergence for all mesh sizes $h$. For $h = 1/512$, the choice of $\omega_{vel} := 1.975$ and $\omega_p := 0.025$ reduces the BiCGStab time to 166 seconds, which is however still twice and a half as long as the AMG solver's time.

The block ILU(0) preconditioner couldn't improve the convergence of the BiCGStab nor the GM-RES solver, on the contrary, for $h = 1/256$ and $h = 1/512$ one could observe a stagnation of the residual reduction.

For small mesh sizes, the AMG method cannot compete with Krylov methods (but then exact sparse LU decomposition methods, such as SuperLU are even faster!). However, with decreasing $h$, AMG is ahead of these methods, and it is expected that this discrepancy is even more distinct for $h < 1/512$.

The iteration times of the AMG solver suggest that we have a nearly optimal method, with complexity in the order of $O(N)$, where $N \approx 1/h^2$. This is what one usually expects from a multigrid method: A convergence rate, that is independent of the mesh size. This behaviour also was observed for other right hand sides $\mathbf{f}$ and other boundary conditions.

## 10.3  Oseen problems

In this section we will take a closer look at two Oseen problems. These problems, although rather academic, still give an impression of the AMG solvers' capabilities.

### 10.3.1  Channel flow

We consider an idealized flow through a channel (here the unit square) where we have walls at $y = 0$ and $y = 1$ and a convection field, that is running parallel to these walls. This is modelled with the following equations:
Find a velocity $\mathbf{u}(x, y) : \mathbb{R}^2 \to \mathbb{R}^2$, and pressure $p(x, y) : \mathbb{R}^2 \to \mathbb{R}$ such that

$$-\nu \Delta \mathbf{u} + (\mathbf{b} \cdot \nabla)\mathbf{u} + c\mathbf{u} + \nabla p = \mathbf{f} \quad \text{in } \Omega \in \mathbb{R}^2, \tag{10.5}$$

$$\nabla \cdot \mathbf{u} = g \quad \text{in } \Omega \in \mathbb{R}^2, \tag{10.6}$$

with $\Omega := (0,1) \times (0,1)$. The reaction term is assumed to be a constant $c \in \mathbb{R}$ – in our numerical experiments we will consider the cases $c = 0$ and $c = 1$. The velocity field $\mathbf{b}$ ist set to

$$\mathbf{b}(x,y) = \begin{pmatrix} \mathbf{b}_1(x,y) \\ \mathbf{b}_2(x,y) \end{pmatrix} := \begin{pmatrix} 1 - e^{-\frac{y}{\sqrt{\nu}}} - e^{\frac{-(1-y)}{\sqrt{\nu}}} \\ 0 \end{pmatrix}, \tag{10.7}$$

which gives a flow parallel to the walls, with the largest amount of velocity in the middle between them. For decreasing viscosity, $\nu \ll 1$, the velocity is nearly zero at the walls. We will determine the right hand side $\mathbf{f}$ and the boundary by inserting the velocity $\mathbf{u} := \mathbf{b}$ and the pressure

$$p(x,y) := \sqrt{\nu} x (e^{-\frac{y}{\sqrt{\nu}}} + e^{\frac{-(1-y)}{\sqrt{\nu}}})$$

into the equation (10.5). Inserting $\mathbf{b}$ into (10.6) gives $g = 0$, an incompressible flow. For $(x,y)^T \in \partial\Omega$ the following Dirichlet boundary conditions are applied:

$$\mathbf{u}_1(x,y) := \begin{cases} -e^{\frac{1}{\sqrt{\nu}}} & \text{for} \quad y = 0 \lor y = 1, \\ 1 - e^{-\frac{y}{\sqrt{\nu}}} - e^{\frac{-(1-y)}{\sqrt{\nu}}} & \text{for} \quad x = 0 \lor x = 1 \end{cases},$$

$$\mathbf{u}_2(x,y) := 0.$$

Furthermore we will vary the viscosity parameter $\nu$ as we did for the scalar convection-diffusion equations:

$$\nu \in \{1, 10^{-2}, 10^{-4}, 10^{-6}\}.$$

Concerning the discretization, the same as was said for the Stokes equation in the last Section also applies to the Oseen problem. In the Tables 10.1 – 10.4 the first component of the exact solution $\mathbf{u} = (\mathbf{u}_1, \mathbf{u}_2)^T$ is plotted (since the second component is 0, it is not shown).

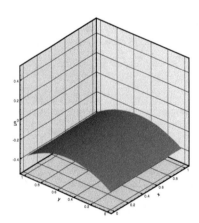
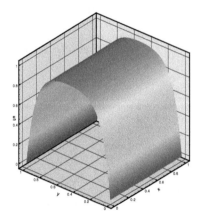

Figure 10.1: Oseen channel flow, exact solution for $\nu = 1$

Figure 10.2: Oseen channel flow, exact solution for $\nu = 10^{-2}$

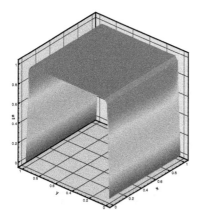
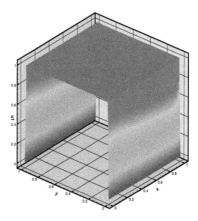

Figure 10.3: Oseen channel flow, exact solution for $\nu = 10^{-4}$

Figure 10.4: Oseen channel flow, exact solution for $\nu = 10^{-6}$

**The effect of velocity block strong coupling on the coarsening process**

First we take a closer look on the AMG setup process, and how the coarsening parameter $\theta$ influences the splitting. Since for the Oseen problems, we discovered, that the convergence of the method for convection dominated problems can only be ensured, if $\theta$ is close to one, we restricted the range of values $\Theta$ depending on $\nu$.

In Tables 10.4–10.11 we see the setup times (in seconds), as well as the average row numbers $r_{avg}$ for the different problems. Note that (6.5) now refers to the number of block matrices $\in \mathbb{R}^{3\times 3}$.

The diagrams in Figures 10.13 to 10.16 show the results of the coarsening preprocess: the lower curves represent the dimensions, the upper curves the nonzero entries of each level. The legend in Figure 10.5 – 10.7 indicates which colour is used to distinguish the curves for different $\theta$.

Figure 10.5: Legend: coupling parameter colouring for $\nu = 1$

theta=0.2    theta=0.3    theta=0.4    theta=0.5    theta=0.6    theta=0.7    theta=0.8

theta=0.3    theta=0.4    theta=0.5    theta=0.6    theta=0.7    theta=0.8    theta=0.9

Figure 10.6: Legend: coupling parameter colouring for $\nu = 10^{-2}$

Figure 10.7: Legend: coupling parameter colouring for $\nu = 10^{-4}$ and $10^{-6}$

We observe that the diffusion dominated case (Tables 10.4, 10.5, 10.8, and 10.9) profits from small to moderate values for theta, which resembles the scalar case very much (cf. Section 6.2). Since only the convection-diffusion part (cf. Section 7.2.1) is considered in the coarsening, the coarse level hierarchy is similar. In Figure (10.8) we see the structured criss cross mesh, that we have used in $\mathcal{PNS}$. Figure 10.9 shows the coarsening that has been generated for $\nu = 1$, $c = 0$ at $h = \frac{1}{32}$ using the coarsening parameter $\theta = 0.2$.

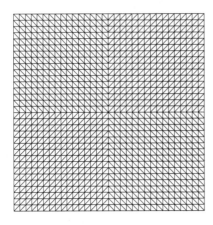

Figure 10.8: Criss-cross mesh, $h = \frac{1}{32}$

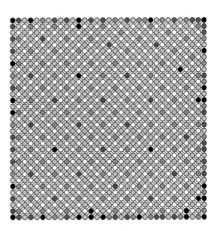

Figure 10.9: Oseen channel flow, coarsening structure, $\nu = 1$, $\theta = 0.2$

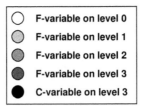

Figure 10.10: Legend: level colouring

The legend in Figure 10.10 specifies how to interprete the pictures, that show the coarse level hierarchy. The darker a point is, the later it is coarsened away by the $C/F$ splitting procedure. Figure 10.9 exhibits a coarsening in *all* space directions, exactly as we observed in the scalar case (cf. Figure 5.1 in Section 5.2.6) for diffusion dominated problems. Because the nature of diffusion is the information transport in all directions, this is the desired coarsening strategy, since no direction can be preferred over another.

Note that choosing a coarsening parameter $\theta$ bigger than 0.2 doesn't give a picture, that is much different from Figure 10.9. Only for $l \geq 3$ the coarse levels begin to differ significantly (see Figure 10.13), yielding smaller sets $F_l$, which is due to similar effects as described in Section 6.2.1: Since the average number of neighbours for $\nu = 1$ lies between 10 and 14 (which is up to twice the number of neighbours in the inital matrix on level $l = 0$) we have also bigger sets $\mathcal{S}_i$ and $\mathcal{S}_i^T$ for decreasing $\theta$. This means, that on subsequent levels, many neighbours (points) are coarsened away if $\theta$ is not too large.

Thus, for dominating diffusion, the reduction of points is rather strong, it is between $1/2$ and $1/4$ the size of the previous level, which more resembles the uniform coarsening known from geometric multigrid.

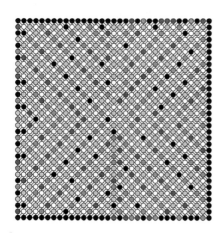

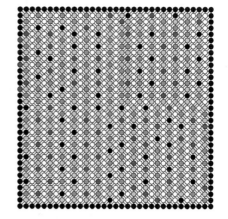

Figure 10.11: Oseen channel flow, coarsening structure, $\nu = 10^{-6}$, $\theta = 0.6$

Figure 10.12: Oseen channel flow, coarsening structure, $\nu = 10^{-6}$, $\theta = 0.95$

For the convection dominated case (Tables 10.6, 10.7, 10.10, and 10.11) the coarsening parameter plays a more important role. In the Figures 10.11 and 10.12 we see the difference in the coarsening structure for $\nu = 10^{-6}$, $c = 0$, once with $\theta = 0.6$ on the left and once with $\theta = 0.95$ on the right. The vector field $\mathbf{b}$ in (10.7) induces a convection only in $x$-direction and the greater value for $\theta$ yields a coarsening nearly only in the direction of this streamlines, whereas for smaller $\theta$, the algorithm cannot identify such a general coarsening direction.

The larger $\theta$ doesn't only reduce the setup time (20.9 sec. for $\theta = 0.95$ versus 88.6 sec. for $\theta = 0.6$ at the finest mesh width, $h = 1/512$), it leads to a restriction to those components, which can be smoothed better on the next level: the coarse level hierachy generated by $\theta = 0.95$ needs another 47 seconds to reduce the residual by 6 orders of magnitude, while the method with the coarse levels constructed with $\theta = 0.6$ didn't converge after 400 seconds.

Again, as we have seen in the scalar convection-diffusion examples for $\nu = 10^{-6}$ and $\nu = 10^{-4}$, the reduction rates from level to level are about $1/2$. Therefore, we can speak of a semi-coarsening property also for this type of AMG variant.

| | $h = 1/16$ | | $h = 1/32$ | | $h = 1/64$ | | $h = 1/128$ | | $h = 1/256$ | | $h = 1/512$ | |
|---|---|---|---|---|---|---|---|---|---|---|---|---|
| $\theta$ | $r_{avg}$ | time | $r_{avg}$ | time | $r_{avg}$ | time | $r_{avg}$ | time | $r_{avg}$ | time | $r_{avg}$ | time |
| 0.2 | 10.9 | 0.02 | 11.5 | 0.07 | 11.6 | 0.2 | 11.9 | 0.9 | 12.4 | 3.8 | 12.4 | 15.4 |
| 0.3 | 11.4 | 0.03 | 11.5 | 0.07 | 12.0 | 0.2 | 12.2 | 0.9 | 12.7 | 3.8 | 13.1 | 15.8 |
| 0.4 | 12.8 | 0.02 | 13.1 | 0.08 | 13.2 | 0.3 | 13.4 | 1.0 | 13.2 | 3.9 | 13.0 | 15.8 |
| 0.5 | 13.3 | 0.02 | 13.9 | 0.08 | 14.2 | 0.3 | 14.0 | 1.1 | 13.7 | 4.6 | 13.8 | 20.0 |
| 0.6 | 13.3 | 0.02 | 13.8 | 0.11 | 14.0 | 0.3 | 13.9 | 1.1 | 13.6 | 4.6 | 13.3 | 20.0 |
| 0.7 | 11.9 | 0.02 | 12.5 | 0.08 | 13.2 | 0.3 | 13.4 | 1.1 | 13.6 | 4.4 | 13.8 | 21.4 |
| 0.8 | 11.8 | 0.02 | 12.6 | 0.08 | 13.5 | 0.3 | 14.2 | 1.1 | 14.8 | 4.8 | 15.2 | 23.7 |

Table 10.4: AMG setup for the Oseen channel flow, $\nu = 1$, $c = 0$

| | $h = 1/16$ | | $h = 1/32$ | | $h = 1/64$ | | $h = 1/128$ | | $h = 1/256$ | | $h = 1/512$ | |
|---|---|---|---|---|---|---|---|---|---|---|---|---|
| $\theta$ | $r_{avg}$ | time | $r_{avg}$ | time | $r_{avg}$ | time | $r_{avg}$ | time | $r_{avg}$ | time | $r_{avg}$ | time |
| 0.3 | 9.8 | 0.01 | 11.9 | 0.06 | 12.3 | 0.2 | 12.4 | 0.9 | 12.7 | 3.9 | 12.8 | 15.7 |
| 0.4 | 10.3 | 0.02 | 11.6 | 0.07 | 13.1 | 0.2 | 12.9 | 1.0 | 13.1 | 4.0 | 13.5 | 16.9 |
| 0.5 | 9.7 | 0.01 | 11.1 | 0.07 | 12.5 | 0.2 | 12.9 | 1.0 | 13.4 | 4.2 | 13.5 | 17.2 |
| 0.6 | 9.0 | 0.01 | 11.4 | 0.08 | 12.2 | 0.3 | 13.4 | 1.1 | 13.3 | 4.4 | 13.2 | 17.7 |
| 0.7 | 7.8 | 0.01 | 10.0 | 0.05 | 12.4 | 0.2 | 12.8 | 1.1 | 13.2 | 4.3 | 14.7 | 21.9 |
| 0.8 | 6.9 | 0.01 | 7.5 | 0.06 | 11.9 | 0.2 | 13.6 | 1.1 | 13.3 | 4.4 | 13.6 | 19.6 |
| 0.9 | 6.0 | 0.01 | 6.7 | 0.05 | 8.0 | 0.2 | 11.5 | 1.0 | 13.5 | 5.0 | 13.3 | 24.3 |

Table 10.5: AMG setup for the Oseen channel flow, $\nu = 10^{-2}$, $c = 0$

| | $h = 1/16$ | | $h = 1/32$ | | $h = 1/64$ | | $h = 1/128$ | | $h = 1/256$ | | $h = 1/512$ | |
|---|---|---|---|---|---|---|---|---|---|---|---|---|
| $\theta$ | $r_{avg}$ | time | $r_{avg}$ | time | $r_{avg}$ | time | $r_{avg}$ | time | $r_{avg}$ | time | $r_{avg}$ | time |
| 0.6 | 8.7 | 0.02 | 10.2 | 0.06 | 12.2 | 0.2 | 14.0 | 1.3 | 15.1 | 8.6 | 12.6 | 27.1 |
| 0.7 | 7.3 | 0.01 | 9.0 | 0.05 | 10.6 | 0.2 | 12.1 | 1.1 | 13.0 | 9.2 | 13.4 | 109.8 |
| 0.8 | 7.0 | 0.01 | 8.1 | 0.06 | 9.7 | 0.2 | 10.6 | 0.9 | 13.0 | 9.0 | 13.1 | 98.3 |
| 0.9 | 6.2 | 0.01 | 6.5 | 0.04 | 6.7 | 0.1 | 7.0 | 0.6 | 7.2 | 2.8 | 7.3 | 18.3 |
| 0.95 | 6.0 | 0.01 | 6.4 | 0.03 | 6.6 | 0.1 | 6.8 | 0.6 | 6.9 | 2.5 | 7.0 | 13.2 |
| 0.975 | 6.0 | 0.01 | 6.4 | 0.04 | 6.6 | 0.1 | 6.8 | 0.6 | 6.8 | 2.6 | 6.9 | 13.9 |
| 0.9875 | 5.9 | 0.01 | 6.3 | 0.04 | 6.5 | 0.1 | 6.7 | 0.6 | 6.8 | 2.6 | 6.9 | 13.8 |

Table 10.6: AMG setup for the Oseen channel flow, $\nu = 10^{-4}$, $c = 0$

| | $h = 1/16$ | | $h = 1/32$ | | $h = 1/64$ | | $h = 1/128$ | | $h = 1/256$ | | $h = 1/512$ | |
|---|---|---|---|---|---|---|---|---|---|---|---|---|
| $\theta$ | $r_{avg}$ | time | $r_{avg}$ | time | $r_{avg}$ | time | $r_{avg}$ | time | $r_{avg}$ | time | $r_{avg}$ | time |
| 0.6 | 8.7 | 0.01 | 10.2 | 0.06 | 12.4 | 0.3 | 14.0 | 1.3 | 15.1 | 8.7 | 15.8 | 88.6 |
| 0.7 | 7.3 | 0.02 | 8.8 | 0.05 | 10.5 | 0.2 | 12.0 | 1.2 | 13.0 | 9.8 | 13.8 | 99.6 |
| 0.8 | 7.0 | 0.01 | 8.0 | 0.04 | 9.4 | 0.2 | 10.4 | 0.9 | 11.1 | 5.4 | 12.3 | 56.0 |
| 0.9 | 6.2 | 0.01 | 6.6 | 0.04 | 7.0 | 0.1 | 7.3 | 0.7 | 7.5 | 3.3 | 7.6 | 20.9 |
| 0.95 | 6.0 | 0.01 | 6.4 | 0.04 | 6.7 | 0.1 | 6.8 | 0.6 | 6.9 | 2.6 | 6.9 | 12.9 |
| 0.975 | 6.0 | 0.01 | 6.4 | 0.04 | 6.6 | 0.1 | 6.8 | 0.6 | 6.9 | 2.7 | 6.9 | 13.1 |
| 0.9875 | 5.9 | 0.01 | 6.3 | 0.04 | 6.5 | 0.1 | 6.7 | 0.6 | 6.8 | 2.6 | 6.9 | 13.7 |

Table 10.7: AMG setup for the Oseen channel flow, $\nu = 10^{-6}$, $c = 0$

| $\theta$ | $h = 1/16$ | | $h = 1/32$ | | $h = 1/64$ | | $h = 1/128$ | | $h = 1/256$ | | $h = 1/512$ | |
|---|---|---|---|---|---|---|---|---|---|---|---|---|
| | $r_{avg}$ | time | $r_{avg}$ | time | $r_{avg}$ | time | $r_{avg}$ | time | $r_{avg}$ | time | $r_{avg}$ | time |
| 0.2 | 10.9 | 0.02 | 11.5 | 0.07 | 11.6 | 0.2 | 11.9 | 0.9 | 12.4 | 3.8 | 12.4 | 15.4 |
| 0.3 | 11.3 | 0.02 | 11.5 | 0.06 | 12.0 | 0.2 | 12.2 | 0.9 | 12.7 | 3.8 | 13.1 | 15.8 |
| 0.4 | 12.8 | 0.02 | 13.1 | 0.08 | 13.2 | 0.3 | 13.4 | 1.0 | 13.2 | 4.0 | 13.0 | 15.7 |
| 0.5 | 13.3 | 0.03 | 13.9 | 0.09 | 14.2 | 0.3 | 14.0 | 1.1 | 13.7 | 4.6 | 13.8 | 20.0 |
| 0.6 | 13.3 | 0.02 | 13.8 | 0.08 | 14.0 | 0.3 | 13.9 | 1.1 | 13.6 | 4.5 | 13.3 | 19.8 |
| 0.7 | 11.9 | 0.02 | 12.6 | 0.08 | 13.1 | 0.3 | 13.4 | 1.1 | 13.6 | 4.4 | 13.8 | 21.4 |
| 0.8 | 11.8 | 0.02 | 12.6 | 0.09 | 13.5 | 0.3 | 14.2 | 1.1 | 14.8 | 4.8 | 15.2 | 23.7 |

Table 10.8: AMG setup for the Oseen channel flow, $\nu = 1$, $c = 1$

| $\theta$ | $h = 1/16$ | | $h = 1/32$ | | $h = 1/64$ | | $h = 1/128$ | | $h = 1/256$ | | $h = 1/512$ | |
|---|---|---|---|---|---|---|---|---|---|---|---|---|
| | $r_{avg}$ | time | $r_{avg}$ | time | $r_{avg}$ | time | $r_{avg}$ | time | $r_{avg}$ | time | $r_{avg}$ | time |
| 0.3 | 9.7 | 0.02 | 11.9 | 0.08 | 12.4 | 0.2 | 12.4 | 0.9 | 12.7 | 3.9 | 12.8 | 15.8 |
| 0.4 | 9.9 | 0.02 | 11.5 | 0.06 | 13.1 | 0.3 | 12.9 | 1.0 | 13.1 | 4.1 | 13.5 | 17.0 |
| 0.5 | 10.4 | 0.02 | 11.3 | 0.07 | 12.4 | 0.2 | 13.0 | 1.0 | 13.2 | 4.1 | 13.5 | 17.3 |
| 0.6 | 9.2 | 0.01 | 11.4 | 0.07 | 12.2 | 0.3 | 13.4 | 1.1 | 13.3 | 4.4 | 13.2 | 17.4 |
| 0.7 | 8.0 | 0.01 | 10.4 | 0.05 | 12.4 | 0.2 | 12.8 | 1.1 | 13.2 | 4.3 | 14.7 | 21.6 |
| 0.8 | 6.9 | 0.01 | 7.5 | 0.05 | 12.1 | 0.2 | 13.6 | 1.1 | 13.3 | 4.4 | 13.7 | 19.1 |
| 0.9 | 6.0 | 0.01 | 6.7 | 0.04 | 8.0 | 0.2 | 11.5 | 1.0 | 13.5 | 5.0 | 13.5 | 25.6 |

Table 10.9: AMG setup for the Oseen channel flow, $\nu = 10^{-2}$, $c = 1$

| $\theta$ | $h = 1/16$ | | $h = 1/32$ | | $h = 1/64$ | | $h = 1/128$ | | $h = 1/256$ | | $h = 1/512$ | |
|---|---|---|---|---|---|---|---|---|---|---|---|---|
| | $r_{avg}$ | time | $r_{avg}$ | time | $r_{avg}$ | time | $r_{avg}$ | time | $r_{avg}$ | time | $r_{avg}$ | time |
| 0.6 | 8.4 | 0.01 | 10.1 | 0.06 | 12.1 | 0.2 | 14.1 | 1.3 | 15.1 | 9.0 | 13.0 | 29.6 |
| 0.7 | 7.1 | 0.02 | 8.8 | 0.06 | 10.6 | 0.2 | 12.1 | 1.3 | 13.0 | 9.3 | 13.5 | 110.1 |
| 0.8 | 7.0 | 0.01 | 8.1 | 0.05 | 9.6 | 0.2 | 10.6 | 0.9 | 12.8 | 8.8 | 13.1 | 99.0 |
| 0.9 | 6.2 | 0.01 | 6.6 | 0.05 | 6.9 | 0.2 | 7.0 | 0.6 | 7.2 | 2.8 | 7.3 | 17.4 |
| 0.95 | 6.0 | 0.01 | 6.4 | 0.04 | 6.6 | 0.1 | 6.8 | 0.6 | 6.9 | 2.5 | 7.0 | 13.4 |
| 0.975 | 6.0 | 0.01 | 6.4 | 0.04 | 6.6 | 0.1 | 6.8 | 0.6 | 6.9 | 2.6 | 6.9 | 14.2 |
| 0.9875 | 6.0 | 0.01 | 6.3 | 0.05 | 6.6 | 0.2 | 6.7 | 0.6 | 6.8 | 2.7 | 6.9 | 14.0 |

Table 10.10: AMG setup for the Oseen channel flow, $\nu = 10^{-4}$, $c = 1$

| $\theta$ | $h = 1/16$ | | $h = 1/32$ | | $h = 1/64$ | | $h = 1/128$ | | $h = 1/256$ | | $h = 1/512$ | |
|---|---|---|---|---|---|---|---|---|---|---|---|---|
| | $r_{avg}$ | time | $r_{avg}$ | time | $r_{avg}$ | time | $r_{avg}$ | time | $r_{avg}$ | time | $r_{avg}$ | time |
| 0.6 | 8.4 | 0.02 | 10.2 | 0.06 | 12.4 | 0.3 | 14.0 | 1.3 | 15.2 | 8.5 | 15.8 | 88.1 |
| 0.7 | 7.1 | 0.01 | 8.6 | 0.06 | 10.4 | 0.2 | 11.8 | 1.3 | 12.7 | 10.2 | 13.8 | 101.4 |
| 0.8 | 7.0 | 0.01 | 8.1 | 0.05 | 9.3 | 0.2 | 10.1 | 0.9 | 10.9 | 5.1 | 12.3 | 57.6 |
| 0.9 | 6.2 | 0.01 | 6.6 | 0.04 | 6.9 | 0.1 | 7.3 | 0.7 | 7.5 | 3.2 | 7.6 | 22.0 |
| 0.95 | 6.0 | 0.01 | 6.4 | 0.04 | 6.6 | 0.2 | 6.8 | 0.6 | 6.9 | 2.6 | 6.9 | 13.2 |
| 0.975 | 6.0 | 0.02 | 6.3 | 0.04 | 6.6 | 0.1 | 6.8 | 0.6 | 6.9 | 2.6 | 6.9 | 13.0 |
| 0.9875 | 5.9 | 0.01 | 6.3 | 0.04 | 6.6 | 0.2 | 6.8 | 0.6 | 6.9 | 2.7 | 6.9 | 13.9 |

Table 10.11: AMG setup for the Oseen channel flow, $\nu = 10^{-6}$, $c = 1$

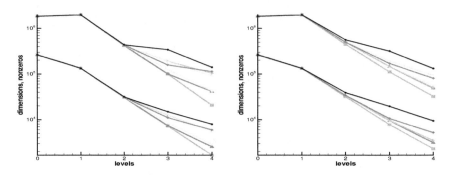

Figure 10.13: AMG level hierarchy for $\nu = 1$      Figure 10.14: AMG level hierarchy for $\nu = 10^{-2}$

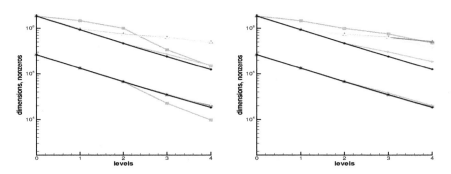

Figure 10.15: AMG level hierarchy for $\nu = 10^{-4}$    Figure 10.16: AMG level hierarchy for $\nu = 10^{-6}$

Note for the Oseen type of problem, we yet don't have a special method to treat the (Dirichlet) boundary points. For the scalar problems, we could eliminate them from the matrix, however this is impossible for the point based approach, since we have no boundary condition for the pressure. Because the according convection diffusion part is the unity matrix on the diagonal and zero otherwise:

$$A_{ii}^{vv} = I \qquad \text{and} \qquad A_{ij}^{vv} = 0, \quad \text{for} \quad i \neq j,$$

these points don't have any neighbours according to the splitting algorithm, and consequently, they stay $C$-points until the end. This is the reason for the boundary being darker than the inner region in the above pictures. Exceptions can occur, because a boundary point $i$ can be included in the set $S_j^T$ of an inner point $j$.

### Convergence speed of the AMG method

In the following diagrams, we can see the overall solution times of the AMG solver, plotted for the mesh widths

$$h \in \{1/64, 1/128, 1/256, 1/512\},$$

(from the bottom to the top) and the different viscosities

$$\nu \in \{1, 10^{-2}, 10^{-4}, 10^{-6}\},$$

(from left to right) for each of the two reaction coefficients $c = 0$ (Tables 10.12 and 10.13) and $c = 1$ (Tables 10.14 and 10.15). In each figure, the setup time is plotted in blue, while the actual iteration time (consisting of V-cycles) is plotted in green for several values of $\theta$.

For all these numerical computations, we have used the SSOR smoother with 2 pre- and 2 post smoothing steps. The relaxtion was used with the fixed values $\omega_{vel} = 1$ and $\omega_p = 0.2$ which led to a comparatively robust convergence, independently of the mesh size and the viscosity. We didn't investigate whether this is the optimum, but single numerical tests seem to promise, that the performance can be slightly improved, however not by an order of magnitude.

First of all, we can see that the diffusion dominated case $\nu = 1$ in the left half of Tables 10.12 and 10.14 causes the least problems regarding the dependency of the coarsening parameter, it converges over a wide range of values for $\theta$. However, in contrast to the Stokes problem, the solution times from $h$ to the finer $h/2$ increase more than the factor 4.

For the moderate convection dominant case, $\nu = 10^{-2}$, we observe a degradation of the solution times, being considerably higher than for $\nu = 1$. Furthermore, the $\theta$-dependency doesn't give a clear picture. The convergence behaviour is improved however, by a non-vanishing reaction term $c$, as we see in the right half of Table 10.14. This is a persistent effect, since a positive reaction term increases the diagonal dominance of the matrix, and thus improves the convergence behaviour of the SSOR smoother.

Looking finally at the convection-dominated cases for $\nu = 10^{-4}$ and $\nu = 10^{-6}$, in the figures in Table 10.13 and 10.15, we can see, that the choice of $\theta$ does play a more important role. Not only the setup times, but also the iteration times are reduced by choosing $\theta$ close to 1. Also, we can see, that the scaling factor between two consecutive mesh-widths $h$ and $h/2$ is nearly optimal (close to 4).

Finally, we would like to examplarily compare our AMG method with some Krylov subspace methods for this example. In the Figures 10.17 to 10.20, we see some convergence diagrams for the convection dominated case at $\nu = 10^{-6}$ on the two finest meshs considered: $h = 1/256$ and $h = 1/512$. We have used the BiCGStab and the GMRES($m$) solvers out of the BLANC library, in comparison with our AMG method.

For the GMRES solver, a restart length of $m = 40$ was used. Both methods have been preconditioned with the block SSOR, using the relaxation parameters $\omega_{vel} = \omega_p = 1$, which turned out to be a good choice.

For the AMG method, we used $\omega_{vel} = 1.1$ and $\omega_p = 0.3$ for the block SSOR smoother, two smothing steps, and a coarsening parameter of $\theta = 0.975$ for $h = 1/256$, and $\theta = 0.9875$ for $h = 1/512$. For the finer mesh width, 6 levels were generated, whereas for $h = 1/256$, only 4 levels were generated.

All start vectors for the initial solution were initialized according to (10.1), ensuring the same starting conditions for all methods. This time, the iteration was stopped, if the residual was reduced by 10 orders of magnitude.

We see that the AMG method converges in all cases better than the Krylov methods, especially for the fine grids. AMG exhibits a much better scaling between the two different $h$: approximately from 35 sec. to 170 sec. for $c = 0$ and from 30 sec. to 150 sec. for $c = 1$. This factor of about 5 is definitely more than an optimal method would have, however, the Krylov methods are even worse, with a factor of about 9 and higher.

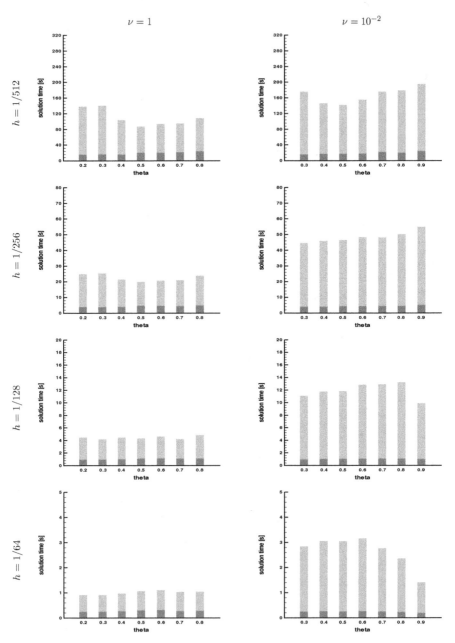

Table 10.12: AMG setup and solution times for $\nu = 1, 10^{-2}$, $c = 0$, $h = \frac{1}{64}, \ldots, \frac{1}{512}$

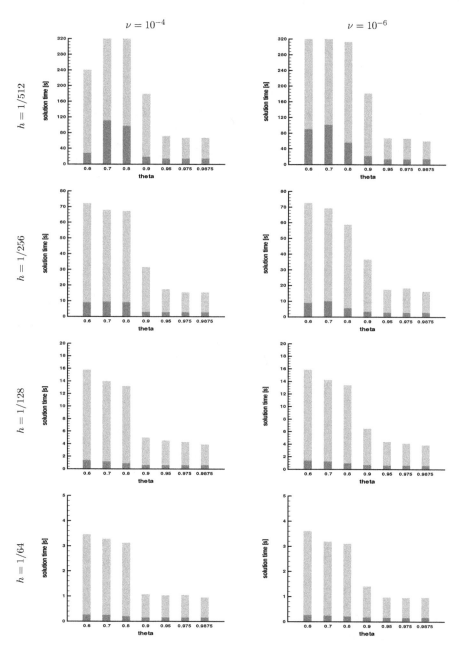

Table 10.13: AMG setup and solution times for $\nu = 10^{-4}, 10^{-6}$, $c = 0$, $h = \frac{1}{64}, \ldots, \frac{1}{512}$

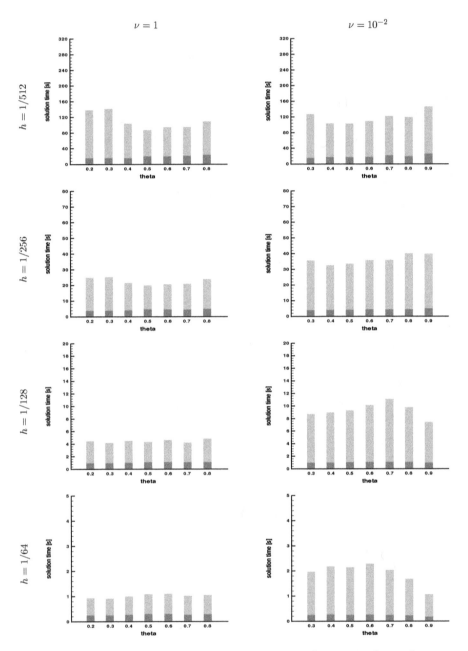

Table 10.14: AMG setup and solution times for $\nu = 1, 10^{-2}$, $c = 1$, $h = \frac{1}{64}, \ldots, \frac{1}{512}$

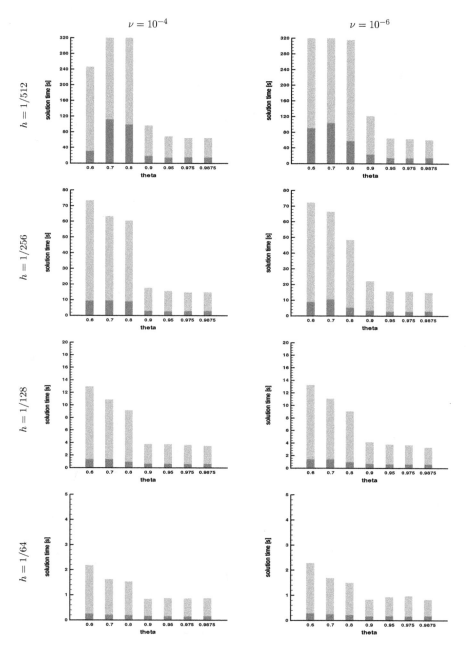

Table 10.15: AMG setup and solution times for $\nu = 10^{-4}, 10^{-6}$, $c = 1$, $h = \frac{1}{64}, \ldots, \frac{1}{512}$

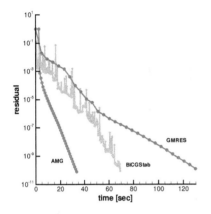

Figure 10.17: Convergence of AMG vs. Krylov methods for $\nu = 10^{-6}$, $c = 0$, $h = \frac{1}{256}$

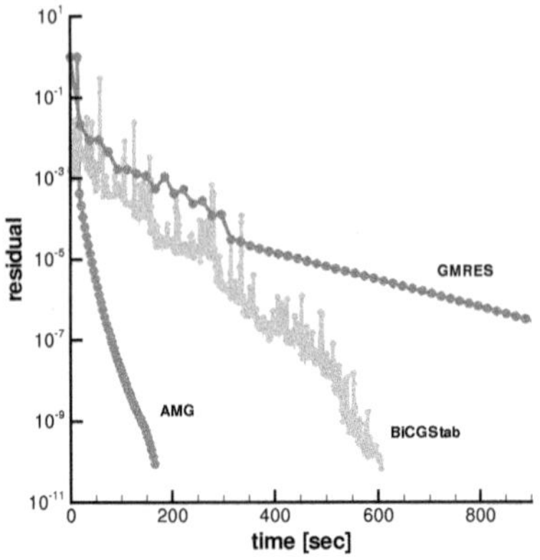

Figure 10.18: Convergence of AMG vs. Krylov methods for $\nu = 10^{-6}$, $c = 0$, $h = \frac{1}{512}$

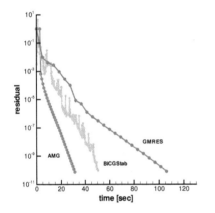
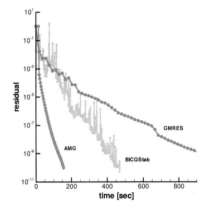

Figure 10.19: Convergence of AMG vs. Krylov methods for $\nu = 10^{-6}$, $c = 1$, $h = \frac{1}{256}$

Figure 10.20: Convergence of AMG vs. Krylov methods for $\nu = 10^{-6}$, $c = 1$, $h = \frac{1}{512}$

For $\nu = 10^{-4}$ one can even observe a scaling factor that is close to 4. However, it should be mentioned, that another choice of parameters may even improve the performance of the AMG as well as the Krylov methods, although, not by a large amount.

Concludingly, we should remark, that this example heavily profits from the special structure of the problem, that only has streamlines in one direction, which can be detected easily. The AMG coarsening then leads to a coarse level hierarchy, that is well-tailored for the smoother.

## 10.3.2 Polynomial drift

Here, we start with looking at the problem (cf. Definition 7.2.1):

Find $\mathbf{u}(x,y) : \mathbb{R}^2 \to \mathbb{R}^2$, and $p(x,y) : \mathbb{R}^2 \to \mathbb{R}$ such that

$$-\Delta \mathbf{u} + (\mathbf{b} \cdot \nabla)\mathbf{u} + c\mathbf{u} + \nabla p = \mathbf{f} \quad \text{in } \Omega \in \mathbb{R}^2, \tag{10.8}$$

$$\nabla \cdot \mathbf{u} = 0 \quad \text{in } \Omega \in \mathbb{R}^2, \tag{10.9}$$

with the domain $\Omega$ again being the unit square. The velocity field $\mathbf{b}$ ist set to

$$\mathbf{b} = \begin{pmatrix} \mathbf{b}_1(x,y) \\ \mathbf{b}_2(x,y) \end{pmatrix} := \begin{pmatrix} x^2 \\ -2xy \end{pmatrix}. \tag{10.10}$$

Again, we choose $c$ to be constant and study the cases $c = 0$ and $c = 1$. The right hand side $\mathbf{f}$ is chosen as

$$\mathbf{f} = \begin{pmatrix} \mathbf{f}_1(x,y) \\ \mathbf{f}_2(x,y) \end{pmatrix} := \begin{pmatrix} 2 + cx^2 + 2x^3 \\ 2x^2 y - 2cxy \end{pmatrix}.$$

We impose the following Dirichlet boundary conditions for $(x,y)^T \in \partial\Omega$:

$$\mathbf{u}_1(x,y) = \begin{cases} 0 & \text{for} \quad x = 0 \\ x^2 & \text{for} \quad y = 0 \\ 1 & \text{for} \quad x = 1 \\ x^2 & \text{for} \quad y = 1 \end{cases} \qquad \mathbf{u}_2(x,y) = \begin{cases} 0 & \text{for} \quad x = 0 \\ 0 & \text{for} \quad y = 0 \\ -y & \text{for} \quad x = 1 \\ -x & \text{for} \quad y = 1 \end{cases}$$

The vector field $\mathbf{b}$ depicts a kind of "drift" through the unit square, its streamlines are shown in Figure 10.21.

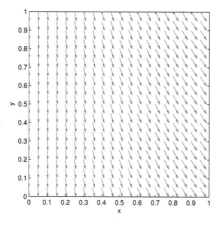

Figure 10.21: Oseen polynomial drift, streamlines of the convection field

**The effect of velocity block strong coupling on the coarsening process**

The $C/F$-splitting algorithm is of course always restricted to the underlying grid. It cannot detect a coarsening direction, when there is no edge into that direction in the according graph imposed by the matrix. Thus, for a vector field **b** from (10.10), Figure 10.21, where the convection changes its direction slightly from the left border to the right border, the coarse level hierarchy doesn't give such a clear picture as in the last example.

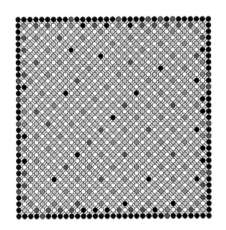
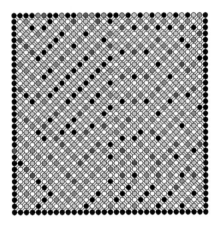

Figure 10.22: Oseen polynomial drift, coarsening structure, $\nu = 1$, $\theta = 0.6$

Figure 10.23: Oseen polynomial drift, coarsening structure, $\nu = 10^{-6}$, $\theta = 0.95$

This is especially true for the convection dominated problem in Figure 10.23. However, one could at least observe, that the coarse level structure changes its behaviour from the left to the right half of the domain. In the left half, the coarsening is more along the $y$-direction, and this is shifted a bit more to the $x$-direction in the right half.

Another difficulty of this flow is the fact, that the *amount* of convection changes over the domain, even if $\nu$ is small. For $\nu = 10^{-6}$ e.g., the local Reynolds number for elements close to $(0,0)^T$ is nearly zero, while at the top right corner, it is about $2 \cdot 10^6 \cdot h$. This means, that the problem varies from diffusion dominated to convection dominated over the whole domain, and thus a specific coarsening direction cannot be detected in every part of the domain.

For the diffusion dominated flow however, there is the usual coarsening in all directions, as we see in Figure 10.22, since in this case the convection doesn't play an important role.

Nevertheless, this problem again corroborates the observation, that rather large coarsening parameters $\theta$ (close to 1) are suited for convection dominated problems, while rather moderate values (between 0.5 and 0.7) are required for the diffusion dominated case.

Again, the coarse level properties are also plotted in Figures 10.25 to 10.28 using the legend from Figure 10.24 for $\nu = 1$ and $10^{-2}$ and Figure 10.7 for $\nu = 10^{-4}$ and $10^{-6}$.

Figure 10.24: Legend: coupling parameter colouring for $\nu = 1$ and $10^{-2}$

| $\theta$ | $h = 1/16$ | | $h = 1/32$ | | $h = 1/64$ | | $h = 1/128$ | | $h = 1/256$ | | $h = 1/512$ | |
|---|---|---|---|---|---|---|---|---|---|---|---|---|
| | $r_{avg}$ | time | $r_{avg}$ | time | $r_{avg}$ | time | $r_{avg}$ | time | $r_{avg}$ | time | $r_{avg}$ | time |
| 0.5 | 14.5 | 0.04 | 13.8 | 0.08 | 13.9 | 0.3 | 14.0 | 1.1 | 13.8 | 4.9 | 13.8 | 21.3 |
| 0.6 | 12.9 | 0.03 | 13.5 | 0.09 | 13.7 | 0.3 | 13.8 | 1.1 | 13.6 | 4.6 | 13.3 | 20.0 |
| 0.7 | 11.9 | 0.03 | 12.6 | 0.08 | 13.1 | 0.3 | 13.3 | 1.1 | 13.5 | 4.6 | 13.8 | 22.2 |
| 0.8 | 10.9 | 0.04 | 12.6 | 0.09 | 13.5 | 0.3 | 14.2 | 1.2 | 14.8 | 5.0 | 15.2 | 24.5 |
| 0.9 | 12.5 | 0.02 | 15.3 | 0.12 | 18.0 | 0.5 | 20.1 | 2.6 | 21.5 | 18.4 | 22.4 | 186.1 |
| 0.95 | 11.0 | 0.03 | 14.5 | 0.10 | 17.6 | 0.5 | 20.0 | 2.4 | 21.5 | 18.5 | 22.4 | 176.7 |

Table 10.16: AMG setup for the Oseen polynomial drift, $\nu = 1$, $c = 0$

| $\theta$ | $h = 1/16$ | | $h = 1/32$ | | $h = 1/64$ | | $h = 1/128$ | | $h = 1/256$ | | $h = 1/512$ | |
|---|---|---|---|---|---|---|---|---|---|---|---|---|
| | $r_{avg}$ | time | $r_{avg}$ | time | $r_{avg}$ | time | $r_{avg}$ | time | $r_{avg}$ | time | $r_{avg}$ | time |
| 0.5 | 12.3 | 0.03 | 13.3 | 0.08 | 13.2 | 0.3 | 13.6 | 1.1 | 12.9 | 4.4 | 12.7 | 19.5 |
| 0.6 | 12.0 | 0.02 | 15.0 | 0.09 | 13.9 | 0.3 | 13.2 | 1.1 | 13.1 | 4.3 | 13.2 | 17.4 |
| 0.7 | 11.4 | 0.02 | 14.0 | 0.08 | 16.6 | 0.4 | 13.5 | 1.1 | 13.2 | 4.3 | 13.1 | 17.7 |
| 0.8 | 10.3 | 0.01 | 12.3 | 0.07 | 15.1 | 0.3 | 14.3 | 1.2 | 13.5 | 4.4 | 13.5 | 19.5 |
| 0.9 | 7.7 | 0.01 | 9.8 | 0.06 | 11.4 | 0.3 | 14.6 | 1.4 | 13.9 | 5.3 | 14.0 | 22.2 |
| 0.95 | 6.7 | 0.02 | 8.0 | 0.06 | 9.3 | 0.2 | 11.1 | 1.0 | 14.2 | 6.9 | 13.7 | 39.6 |

Table 10.17: AMG setup for the Oseen polynomial drift, $\nu = 10^{-2}$, $c = 0$

| $\theta$ | $h = 1/16$ | | $h = 1/32$ | | $h = 1/64$ | | $h = 1/128$ | | $h = 1/256$ | | $h = 1/512$ | |
|---|---|---|---|---|---|---|---|---|---|---|---|---|
| | $r_{avg}$ | time | $r_{avg}$ | time | $r_{avg}$ | time | $r_{avg}$ | time | $r_{avg}$ | time | $r_{avg}$ | time |
| 0.7 | 9.9 | 0.01 | 11.3 | 0.07 | 13.2 | 0.3 | 15.5 | 1.8 | 18.3 | 15.8 | 20.7 | 183.7 |
| 0.8 | 8.5 | 0.01 | 10.1 | 0.06 | 11.5 | 0.3 | 13.5 | 1.4 | 15.8 | 11.8 | 17.1 | 107.7 |
| 0.9 | 8.3 | 0.03 | 8.5 | 0.06 | 9.8 | 0.2 | 11.2 | 1.3 | 12.7 | 10.6 | 12.8 | 76.1 |
| 0.95 | 7.1 | 0.02 | 7.8 | 0.05 | 8.6 | 0.2 | 9.8 | 1.1 | 10.5 | 6.9 | 10.8 | 47.6 |
| 0.975 | 6.3 | 0.01 | 7.1 | 0.04 | 7.8 | 0.2 | 8.5 | 0.9 | 9.0 | 4.4 | 9.4 | 30.8 |
| 0.9875 | 6.1 | 0.02 | 6.6 | 0.04 | 7.1 | 0.2 | 7.6 | 0.8 | 8.1 | 4.0 | 8.4 | 26.4 |

Table 10.18: AMG setup for the Oseen polynomial drift, $\nu = 10^{-4}$, $c = 0$

| $\theta$ | $h = 1/16$ | | $h = 1/32$ | | $h = 1/64$ | | $h = 1/128$ | | $h = 1/256$ | | $h = 1/512$ | |
|---|---|---|---|---|---|---|---|---|---|---|---|---|
| | $r_{avg}$ | time | $r_{avg}$ | time | $r_{avg}$ | time | $r_{avg}$ | time | $r_{avg}$ | time | $r_{avg}$ | time |
| 0.7 | 9.9 | 0.02 | 11.4 | 0.06 | 13.2 | 0.3 | 14.3 | 1.6 | 15.1 | 12.3 | 15.9 | 121.8 |
| 0.8 | 8.8 | 0.02 | 10.1 | 0.07 | 11.3 | 0.3 | 12.2 | 1.3 | 12.6 | 9.0 | 13.1 | 88.7 |
| 0.9 | 8.5 | 0.02 | 9.1 | 0.07 | 9.6 | 0.2 | 10.1 | 1.3 | 10.5 | 8.5 | 10.7 | 71.1 |
| 0.95 | 7.1 | 0.02 | 8.1 | 0.06 | 8.5 | 0.2 | 8.9 | 1.0 | 9.2 | 6.1 | 9.4 | 43.1 |
| 0.975 | 6.7 | 0.02 | 7.3 | 0.04 | 7.8 | 0.2 | 8.0 | 0.9 | 8.3 | 4.5 | 8.5 | 28.8 |
| 0.9875 | 6.1 | 0.02 | 6.8 | 0.04 | 7.3 | 0.2 | 7.5 | 0.8 | 7.7 | 4.0 | 7.8 | 22.0 |

Table 10.19: AMG setup for the Oseen polynomial drift, $\nu = 10^{-6}$, $c = 0$

| $\theta$ | $h = 1/16$ | | $h = 1/32$ | | $h = 1/64$ | | $h = 1/128$ | | $h = 1/256$ | | $h = 1/512$ | |
|---|---|---|---|---|---|---|---|---|---|---|---|---|
| | $r_{avg}$ | time | $r_{avg}$ | time | $r_{avg}$ | time | $r_{avg}$ | time | $r_{avg}$ | time | $r_{avg}$ | time |
| 0.5 | 14.5 | 0.03 | 13.8 | 0.09 | 13.9 | 0.3 | 14.0 | 1.1 | 13.8 | 4.9 | 13.8 | 21.3 |
| 0.6 | 13.1 | 0.02 | 13.5 | 0.09 | 13.7 | 0.3 | 13.8 | 1.1 | 13.6 | 4.6 | 13.3 | 19.8 |
| 0.7 | 12.0 | 0.03 | 12.6 | 0.08 | 13.1 | 0.3 | 13.4 | 1.1 | 13.6 | 4.7 | 13.8 | 22.0 |
| 0.8 | 10.5 | 0.03 | 12.6 | 0.08 | 13.5 | 0.3 | 14.2 | 1.2 | 14.8 | 5.0 | 15.2 | 24.5 |
| 0.9 | 12.5 | 0.03 | 15.3 | 0.11 | 18.0 | 0.5 | 20.1 | 2.6 | 21.5 | 18.3 | 22.4 | 185.0 |
| 0.95 | 11.0 | 0.03 | 14.5 | 0.10 | 17.6 | 0.5 | 20.0 | 2.4 | 21.5 | 18.2 | 22.4 | 176.5 |

Table 10.20: AMG setup for the Oseen polynomial drift, $\nu = 1$, $c = 1$

| $\theta$ | $h = 1/16$ | | $h = 1/32$ | | $h = 1/64$ | | $h = 1/128$ | | $h = 1/256$ | | $h = 1/512$ | |
|---|---|---|---|---|---|---|---|---|---|---|---|---|
| | $r_{avg}$ | time | $r_{avg}$ | time | $r_{avg}$ | time | $r_{avg}$ | time | $r_{avg}$ | time | $r_{avg}$ | time |
| 0.5 | 12.8 | 0.03 | 13.6 | 0.09 | 13.5 | 0.3 | 13.2 | 1.1 | 12.9 | 4.5 | 13.0 | 19.0 |
| 0.6 | 12.6 | 0.02 | 15.0 | 0.09 | 13.9 | 0.3 | 13.0 | 1.1 | 13.3 | 4.3 | 12.9 | 17.3 |
| 0.7 | 11.5 | 0.02 | 14.2 | 0.08 | 17.1 | 0.4 | 13.7 | 1.1 | 13.5 | 4.5 | 12.9 | 17.6 |
| 0.8 | 10.6 | 0.02 | 12.7 | 0.08 | 15.2 | 0.3 | 14.1 | 1.2 | 13.6 | 4.5 | 13.6 | 19.7 |
| 0.9 | 7.8 | 0.02 | 9.6 | 0.07 | 11.4 | 0.3 | 14.5 | 1.4 | 13.9 | 5.5 | 13.8 | 22.4 |
| 0.95 | 6.7 | 0.02 | 8.2 | 0.05 | 9.4 | 0.2 | 11.1 | 1.0 | 14.2 | 6.7 | 13.8 | 35.9 |

Table 10.21: AMG setup for the Oseen polynomial drift, $\nu = 10^{-2}$, $c = 1$

| $\theta$ | $h = 1/16$ | | $h = 1/32$ | | $h = 1/64$ | | $h = 1/128$ | | $h = 1/256$ | | $h = 1/512$ | |
|---|---|---|---|---|---|---|---|---|---|---|---|---|
| | $r_{avg}$ | time | $r_{avg}$ | time | $r_{avg}$ | time | $r_{avg}$ | time | $r_{avg}$ | time | $r_{avg}$ | time |
| 0.7 | 9.2 | 0.02 | 11.1 | 0.08 | 13.2 | 0.3 | 15.4 | 1.7 | 18.4 | 16.5 | 20.6 | 183.8 |
| 0.8 | 8.4 | 0.01 | 10.0 | 0.06 | 11.2 | 0.3 | 13.3 | 1.4 | 15.6 | 11.9 | 17.1 | 91.3 |
| 0.9 | 7.7 | 0.02 | 8.7 | 0.06 | 9.8 | 0.2 | 11.1 | 1.4 | 12.5 | 11.1 | 12.7 | 69.8 |
| 0.95 | 6.7 | 0.01 | 7.9 | 0.06 | 8.5 | 0.2 | 9.7 | 1.1 | 10.4 | 7.4 | 10.7 | 47.6 |
| 0.975 | 6.3 | 0.01 | 6.9 | 0.04 | 7.7 | 0.2 | 8.4 | 0.9 | 9.0 | 5.2 | 9.4 | 33.1 |
| 0.9875 | 6.1 | 0.01 | 6.7 | 0.04 | 7.1 | 0.2 | 7.6 | 0.7 | 8.1 | 3.9 | 8.4 | 23.2 |

Table 10.22: AMG setup for the Oseen polynomial drift, $\nu = 10^{-4}$, $c = 1$

| $\theta$ | $h = 1/16$ | | $h = 1/32$ | | $h = 1/64$ | | $h = 1/128$ | | $h = 1/256$ | | $h = 1/512$ | |
|---|---|---|---|---|---|---|---|---|---|---|---|---|
| | $r_{avg}$ | time | $r_{avg}$ | time | $r_{avg}$ | time | $r_{avg}$ | time | $r_{avg}$ | time | $r_{avg}$ | time |
| 0.7 | 8.8 | 0.02 | 10.8 | 0.07 | 12.8 | 0.3 | 14.1 | 1.6 | 14.9 | 11.8 | 16.0 | 121.8 |
| 0.8 | 8.1 | 0.02 | 9.9 | 0.06 | 10.9 | 0.3 | 12.0 | 1.2 | 12.5 | 8.2 | 13.1 | 80.2 |
| 0.9 | 7.6 | 0.02 | 8.6 | 0.06 | 9.3 | 0.2 | 10.0 | 1.2 | 10.6 | 8.1 | 10.8 | 64.0 |
| 0.95 | 6.7 | 0.02 | 7.5 | 0.06 | 8.3 | 0.2 | 8.7 | 1.0 | 9.2 | 6.0 | 9.4 | 47.6 |
| 0.975 | 6.3 | 0.02 | 6.8 | 0.04 | 7.5 | 0.2 | 7.9 | 0.8 | 8.1 | 4.3 | 8.5 | 28.6 |
| 0.9875 | 6.2 | 0.01 | 6.6 | 0.05 | 7.0 | 0.2 | 7.4 | 0.8 | 7.6 | 3.7 | 7.8 | 23.1 |

Table 10.23: AMG setup for the Oseen polynomial drift, $\nu = 10^{-6}$, $c = 1$

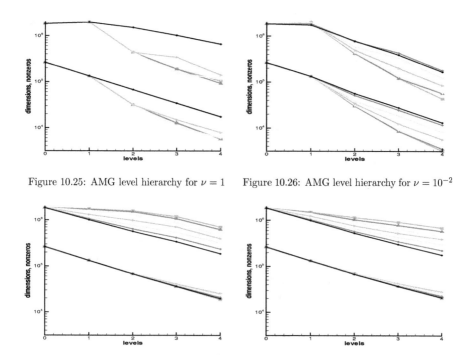

Figure 10.25: AMG level hierarchy for $\nu = 1$     Figure 10.26: AMG level hierarchy for $\nu = 10^{-2}$

Figure 10.27: AMG level hierarchy for $\nu = 10^{-4}$     Figure 10.28: AMG level hierarchy for $\nu = 10^{-6}$

### The effect of relaxation

For this Oseen example, we finally would like to examine how the variation of the relaxation parameter influences the convergence behaviour of the V-cycle iteration, as we did for the scalar case.

Thus, for problem (10.8), (10.9) we try out several values for $\omega_{vel}$ and $\omega_p$. Since we didn't to try every combination, we restricted the pressure relaxation to the set

$$\omega_p \in \{0.1, 0.2, 0.3\}, \tag{10.11}$$

since we observed, that in the majority of the cases, bigger values resulted in a fast divergence of the method. These values were combined with

$$\omega_{vel} \in \{0.1, 0.2, \ldots, 1.8, 1.9\} \tag{10.12}$$

for the velocity relaxation. Out of these combinations, those values $\omega_p$ that converged best with the set (10.12) are given in Table 10.28 and the according number of iterations are plotted in the figures in Tables 10.24 to 10.27.

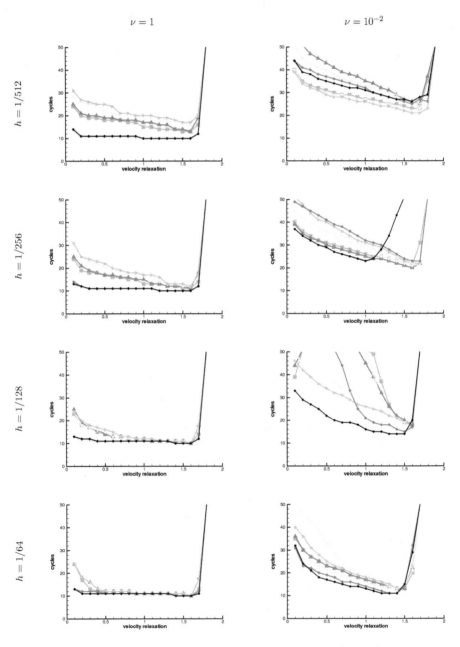

Table 10.24: SSOR smoothing for $\nu = 1, 10^{-2}$, $c = 0$, $h = \frac{1}{64}, \ldots, \frac{1}{512}$

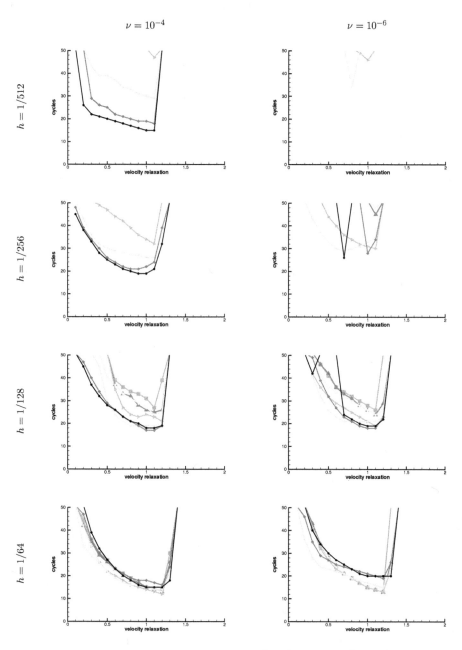

Table 10.25: SSOR smoothing for $\nu = 10^{-4}, 10^{-6}$, $c = 0$, $h = \frac{1}{64}, \ldots, \frac{1}{512}$

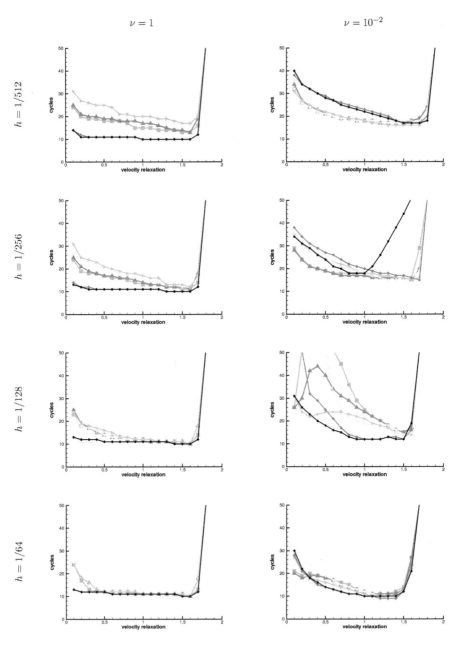

Table 10.26: SSOR smoothing for $\nu = 1, 10^{-2}$, $c = 1$, $h = \frac{1}{64}, \ldots, \frac{1}{512}$

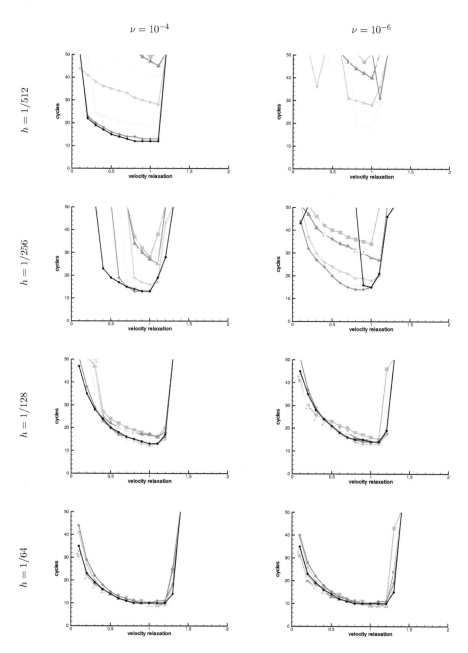

Table 10.27: SSOR smoothing for $\nu = 10^{-4}, 10^{-6}$, $c = 1$, $h = \frac{1}{64}, \ldots, \frac{1}{512}$

| $h$ | $\nu = 1$ | $\nu = 10^{-2}$ | $\nu = 10^{-4}$ | $\nu = 10^{-6}$ |
|------|------|------|------|------|
| 1/16 | 0.3 | 0.3 | 0.3 | 0.3 |
| 1/32 | 0.2 | 0.3 | 0.3 | 0.3 |
| 1/64 | 0.1 | 0.3 | 0.3 | 0.3 |
| 1/128 | 0.1 | 0.3 | 0.3 | 0.3 |
| 1/256 | 0.1 | 0.2 | 0.2 | 0.3 |
| 1/512 | 0.1 | 0.2 | 0.2 | 0.2 |

Table 10.28: Optimal pressure relaxation

First of all, we can state again, that the diffusive problems, i.e. $\nu = 1$ in the left columns of Table 10.24 and 10.26 doesn't cause bigger problems concerning the choice of $\omega_{vel}$. This is also true independent of the reaction term. Furthermore, the coarsening parameter doesn't have much influence on the convergence speed (however, it is crucial for the setup, as we have seen in the last section).

The moderate convection dominated case $\nu = 10^{-2}$ in the right columns of Table 10.24 and 10.26 benefits more from a distinct over-relaxation ($1.2 \leq \omega_{vel} \leq 1.8$). Also, this problem is more sensible to changes of $\theta$.

For the convection dominated cases in Tables 10.25 and 10.27 one can observe a stronger tendency towards under-relaxation. However, for $\nu = 10^{-6}$ and decreasing $h$, the smoothing deteriorates, and the convergence rates heavily slow down.

**Convergence speed of the AMG method**

In the Figures 10.29 to 10.32, we have exemplarily plotted the convergence histories for a convection-dominated problem at $\nu = 10^{-4}$, for the two finest mesh widths $h = 1/256$ and $h = 1/512$, with and without reaction term.

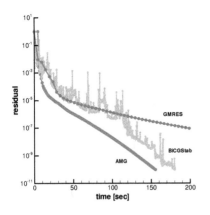
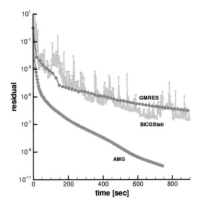

Figure 10.29: Convergence of AMG vs. Krylov methods for $\nu = 10^{-4}$, $c = 0$, $h = \frac{1}{256}$

Figure 10.30: Convergence of AMG vs. Krylov methods for $\nu = 10^{-4}$, $c = 0$, $h = \frac{1}{512}$

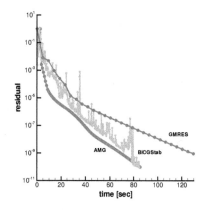
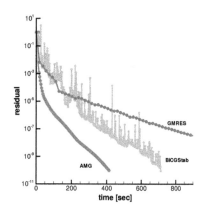

Figure 10.31: Convergence of AMG vs. Krylov methods for $\nu = 10^{-4}$, $c = 1$, $h = \frac{1}{256}$

Figure 10.32: Convergence of AMG vs. Krylov methods for $\nu = 10^{-4}$, $c = 1$, $h = \frac{1}{512}$

Concerning the parameters of the AMG method, we have used $\theta = 0.95$ for $h = 1/256$, $\theta = 0.975$ for $h = 1/513$, $c = 1$, and $\theta = 0.9875$ for $h = 1/513$, $c = 0$. In all cases, we have used the SSOR smoother with $\omega_{vel} = 1.1$, $\omega_{vel} = 0.2$, and two pre- and two post-smoothing steps.

For $h = 1/256$, five levels were generated, for $h = 1/513$ we found, that seven generated levels were an optimal compromise between setup-runtime and accuracy of the coarsest level. The Krylov solvers were used with the same parameters as in the last Oseen example.

Compared with the first Oseen problem, we see, that the convergence rates of both AMG and Krylov methods are deteriorated, which is basically due to the strongly varying local Reynolds number. This complicates the choice of the coarse levels.

Though, we observed, that the AMG coarse level correction still contributes to the error reduction, which is an indicator, that it is not the interpolation that fails. Obviously, in this context, the smoother is the weakest component in the AMG framework.

What we can however state again, is the better $h$-scaling of the AMG method. While $h$ is getting smaller, the condition number of the matrix increases, which directly degrades the convergence of the Krylov methods, but at the same time increases the gap to AMG.

## 10.4 Conclusion and Outlook

In the last two chapters, we have introduced and applied an algebraic multigrid method for discrete Stokes and Oseen problems under a specific point-wise ordering of the variables. For several examples, we could demonstrate the efficiency of the method. Especially, with decreasing $h$, we often observe an almost mesh independent convergence, in contrast to Krylov solvers.

Only for extremely small values of $\nu$ and strongly varying convection fields, we experienced a degradation of the method, if not optimal coarsening and relaxation parameters are chosen. As mentioned, this is to a large extent also a matter of smoothing, thus it seems to be necessary to apply and investigate other smoothers. Since the SOR and SSOR methods are known to be sensible to changes of the numbering of the unknowns, we suggest to use adapted methods, that changes the ordering of relaxation. This can be done either by applying a downwind numbering before the coarsening, or by first relaxing the C and then the F points (as it is suggested in [Stü99]). Also the point block versions of ILU and its several variants (cf. Section 8.2.1) can be employed as smoothers. Another possibility is to use a true Vanka smoother, that in contrast to the SOR, does an element-wise relaxation, instead of a point-wise.

Another issue in the finite element context are higher order elements. Although the point-wise AMG approach is not applicable to e.g. Taylor-Hood elements, it is – at least in principle – not restricted to $P_1$-$P_1$ elements, but could also be used for higher *equal order* elements.

Yet, for higher-order elements, other difficulties have to be overcome. Not only that the according matrices have much more nonzero entries, they are also ill-conditioned for usual equidistant grids and nodal bases. Recent research showed, that the type of basis functions, and the node locations play an important role, when applying AMG to higher order discretizations ([HMMO05]).

The application of the point-wise coupled AMG method to three-dimensional problems is straightforward. However, as for the scalar 3D problems in Section 6.2.2, we have to deal with the increased operator complexity, and therefore longer setup-times. Here, a stronger coarsening, that also considers the indirect connections (agressive coarsening) may lead to more sparse coarse level operators.

Generally, it has to be said, that the acceleration of the AMG with a Krylov method surely can improve the convergence compared to the stand-alone approach. Acceleration here simply means, that AMG serves as a preconditioner for the Krylov method. Especially since the residual reduction of AMG within the first few steps is immense, the combination of both methods seems to be promising.

Concerning the convergence theory, we admit, that a general convergence statement, especially for unsymmetric problems, is out of reach. However, at least, it should be possible, to transfer a proposition like Theorem 5.2.19 to the vector-valued context of the point-wise approach. A smoothing property of usual splitting methods, such as Gauss-Seidel and SSOR, however is still not verified for unsymmetric matrices.

Finally we would like to conclude with a few words about parallelization. Of course the sparse matrix-matrix multiplication required for the setup, and the matrix-vector multiplications for the multigrid cycles, can be easily split up into several parts, that can be executed by as many threads as there are CPU's in the system. Parallel versions of the according functions exist in MiLTON, utilizing the `PartitionLayer` and POSIX threads. Here, the crucial point however is indeed a parallel smoother. Classical smoothers, from Gauss-Seidel to SSOR, and nearly all ILU methods, however are highly recursive in nature. Jacobi methods can easily be parallelized, but have a lack of robustness. Instead, multi-colour SOR methods ([AO82]) or sparse approximate inverses (SPAI, [GH97]) are more likely to be used in a parallel environment.

# Part IV

# Appendix

# Appendix A

# Simple data structures

## A.1 Iterators

### Constant value iterators

This iterator template is mainly devised for the constant value sequences (Section A.2). The value of the constant is only known at run time. It is a random access iterator since `constant_tag` inherits from `std::random_access_iterator_tag`. Note that the default constructor can only be used, if `ValueType` has a default constructor.

```
──────────────── Constant value iterator ────────────────
template <class ValueType, class DifferenceType>
class constant_value_iterator
{
public:
  typedef ValueType value_type;
  typedef DifferenceType difference_type;
  typedef value_type& reference;
  typedef value_type* pointer;
  typedef constant_tag iterator_category;
private:
  value_type x;
  difference_type j;
public:
  constant_value_iterator(const DifferenceType j_=0) : j(j_)
  {}
  constant_value_iterator(const value_type& x_, const difference_type j_)
  : x(x_), j(j_)
  {}
  const value_type& operator*()
  {
    return x;
  }
  constant_value_iterator& operator++()
  {
    ++j;
    return *this;
  }
};
```

Here, only a few features of the class are displayed. The rest of the implementation is straightforward and can be viewed in the class text in the file "BaseIterators.hh".

### Fixed value iterators

The fixed value iterators are designed for sequences which store one value that is known at compile
time already (cf. Section A.2). The fixed value must be given as a template parameter. However,
the type of ValueType is restricted to integer types, because floating-point types are not yet allowed
by the C++ Standard ([Str97]). This may be only possible in the future, which is proposed in ([VJ03]).

```
――――――――――――――― fixed value iterator ――――――――――――――――
template <class ValueType, class DifferenceType, ValueType x>
class fixed_value_iterator
{
public:
  typedef fixed_tag iterator_category;
private:
  difference_type j;
public:
  static const value_type value=x;
public:
  fixed_value_iterator(const difference_type j_=0) : j(j_)
  {}
  fixed_value_iterator(const fixed_value_iterator& other) : j(other.j)
  {}
  const value_type operator*()
  {
    return x;
  }
};
```

### Function value iterators

The class template function_value_iterator implements the iterator belonging to the function value
sequence. It generates the value at position i using the according functor f.

```
――――――――――――――― Function value iterator ――――――――――――――――
template <class Functor>
class function_value_iterator
{
public:
  typedef typename Functor::result_type value_type;
  typedef typename Functor::argument_type difference_type;
  typedef value_type reference;
  typedef value_type* pointer;
  typedef functor_tag iterator_category;
private:
  Functor f;
  difference_type j;
public:
  function_value_iterator(const difference_type j_=0) : j(j_)
```

```
  {}
  function_value_iterator(const Functor& f_, const difference_type j_=0)
  : f(f_), j(j_)
  {}
  const value_type operator*()
  {
    return f(j);
  }
};
```

## A.2 Sequences

**Constant value sequence**

A sequence with run time constant value is implemented as follows (for the complete code we refer to the library source code):

```
──────────────────── Constant value sequence ────────────────────
template <class ValueType, class SizeType>
class ConstantValueSequence
{
public:
  typedef ValueType value_type;
  typedef SizeType size_type;
  typedef constant_value_iterator<ValueType,SizeType> iterator;
private:
  size_type dataSize;
  value_type x;
public:
  ConstantValueSequence(const size_type n, const value_type& x_)
  : dataSize(n), x(x_)
  {}
  size_type size() const
  {
    return dataSize;
  }
  iterator begin()
  {
    return iterator(x,0);
  }
  iterator end()
  {
    return iterator(x,dataSize);
  }
};
```

This of course is a quite simple piece of code, however we needed this in order to provide e.g. an according first row index sequence for the first targets layer (se the according item in Section 3.3.6). Since this type of container didn't exist we had to create it.

**Fixed value sequence**

We mainly present the differences to the constant value sequence:

```
───────────────── Fixed value sequence ─────────────
template <class ValueType, class DifferenceType, ValueType x>
class FixedValueSequence
{
public:
  typedef fixed_value_iterator<ValueType,DifferenceType,x> iterator;
public:
  FixedValueSequence() : dataSize(0)
  {}
  FixedValueSequence(const size_type n) : dataSize(n)
  {}
  iterator begin()
  {
    return iterator(0);
  }
  iterator end()
  {
    return iterator(dataSize);
  }
};
```

It is also possible to think of a version with a fixed length (known at compile time), since it is important for small data structures whether an additional integer variable has to be stored or not:

```
──────────── Fixed value sequence with fixed length ────────────
template <class ValueType, class DifferenceType,
          ValueType x, DifferenceType dataSize>
class FixedValueFixedLengthSequence
{
public:
  FixedValueFixedLengthSequence()
  {}
  static const size_type size()
  {
    return dataSize;
  }
  static iterator begin()
  {
    return iterator(0);
  }
  static iterator end()
  {
    return iterator(dataSize);
  }
};
```

**Function value sequence**

The function value sequence was originally intended for matrix types, where index information can be *computed* out of other information. For example, the column index of the first nonzero entry of row $i$ in a diagonal matrix is $f(i) = i$. The computation is done by an appropriate functor. Similar applications are e.g. band matrices.

But also the value of the matrix entries may be computable completely out of the indices, e.g. if we think of Hilbert matrices, where we have

$$H \in \mathbb{R}^{n \times n}, \quad H_{ij} := (i + j - 1)^{-1}, \quad i, j = 1, \ldots, n.$$

Since we intend to store the matrix entries in our data structures in one long sequence, we somehow need a mapping from the position in the edge sequence to the $(i, j)$ position. Let $e \in E(g)$ be the $k$-th edge of $g = \Phi^{-1}(H)$, we would have the indices

$$i(e) := \lfloor k/n \rfloor, \quad \text{and} \quad j(k) := k \mod n$$

for a (row wise ordered) full dense Hilbert matrix $H$. The according functor would be

$$f(e) := \Phi(i(e), j(e)) := (\lfloor k/n \rfloor + (k \mod n) - 1)^{-1}$$

for the entry value of $e$.

```
──────────────────────── Function value sequence ────────────────────────
template <class FunctionType>
class FunctionSequence
{
public:
  typedef typename FunctionType::argument_type size_type;
  typedef typename FunctionType::result_type value_type;
  typedef function_value_iterator<FunctionType> iterator;
private:
  FunctionType f;
public:
  FunctionSequence(const size_type n=0) : dataSize(n)
  {}
  FunctionSequence(const size_type n, const FunctionType& f_)
  : dataSize(n), f(f_)
  {}
  iterator begin()
  {
    return iterator(f,0);
  }
  iterator end()
  {
    return iterator(f,dataSize);
  }
};
```

**Arbitrary value sequence**

The arbitrary value sequence very much resembles the `std::vector` class. It is implemented in the `DataSequence` class template. The main difference to the vector class in the STL is one assignment operator, that allows to assign values from any other sequence. However it would be sufficient in many cases to simply use `std::vector`.

```
——————————————————————— Arbitrary value sequence ———————————————————————
template <class ValueType, class SizeType>
class DataSequence
{
public:
  typedef ValueType value_type;
  typedef SizeType size_type;
  typedef value_type* iterator;
  typedef value_type& reference;
private:
  size_type dataSize;
  value_type* dataStore;
public:
  DataSequence(const size_type n=0)
  : dataSize(n), dataStore(new value_type[n])
  {}
  DataSequence(const size_type n, const value_type& initvalue)
  : dataSize(n), dataStore(new value_type[n])
  {
    std::fill_n(dataStore,n,initvalue);
  }
  ~DataSequence()
  {
    delete[] dataStore;
  }
  template <class Sequence>
  DataSequence& operator=(Sequence& other)
  {
    delete[] dataStore;
    dataStore = new value_type[other.size()];
    copy(other.begin(), other.end(), dataStore);
    dataSize  = other.size();
    return *this;
  }
  iterator begin()
  {
    return dataStore;
  }
  iterator end()
  {
    return dataStore+dataSize;
  }
};
```

Of more importance (especially for small data structures) is the fixed length variant, since there is no appropriate class in the STL.

```
───────────── Arbitrary value sequence with fixed length ─────────────
template <class ValueType, class SizeType, SizeType dataSize>
class FixedLengthDataSequence
{
  //...
private:
  value_type dataStore[dataSize];
public:
  FixedLengthDataSequence() : dataStore()
  {}
  FixedLengthDataSequence(const value_type& initvalue)
  {
    std::fill_n(dataStore,dataSize,initvalue);
  }
  static const size_type size()
  {
    return dataSize;
  }
};
```

# Appendix B

# Test platform

All numerical experiments and benchmarks were carried out on the following hardware/software platforms:

- processor: Intel Pentium 4E 3.0 GHz

- main memory: between 2 GB and 4 GB on different machines

- level 1 cache: 16 KB

- level 2 cache: 1 MB

- operating system: SUSE Linux 9.3, kernel 2.6.11

- GNU compiler 3.4.1

# List of Figures

# List of Tables

# Bibliography

[ABDP81]   R. E. Alcouffe, A. Brandt, J. E. Dendy, and J. W. Painter. The Multigrid Method for the Diffusion Equation with Strongly Discontinuous Coefficients. *SIAM J. Sci. Stat. Comput.*, 2:430–454, 1981.

[AG04]   David Abrahams and Aleksey Gurtovoy. *C++ Template Metaprogramming Concepts, Tools, and Techniques from Boost and Beyond*. Addison Wesley Professional, 2004.

[AL98]   Owe Axelsson and Maxim Larin. An algebraic multilevel iteration method for finite element matrices. *Journal of Computational and Applied Mathematics*, 89(1):135–153, 1998.

[AMOG99]   Andreas Auge, Hannes Müller, Frank-Christian Otto, and Ralf Gritzki. *ParallelNS*. Institut für Numerische und Angewandte Mathematik, 1999.

[AO82]   Loyce M. Adams and J. M. Ortega. A Multi-Color SOR method for parallel computation. In *Proceedings of 1982 International Conference on Parallel Processing*, pages 53–58, 1982.

[Bak66]   Nikolai S. Bakhvalov. On the convergence of a relaxation method under natural constraints on an elliptic operator. *Z. Vycisl. Mat. i. Mat. Fiz.*, 6:861–883, 1966.

[BBGS04]   Teri Barth, Pavel Bochev, Max Gunzburger, and John Shadid. A Taxonomy of Consistently Stabilized Finite Element Methods for the Stokes Problem. *SIAM Journal on Scientific Computing*, 25(5):1585–1607, 2004.

[BC90]   Gilad Bracha and William Cook. Mixin-based inheritance. In *Proceedings of the European conference on object-oriented programming on Object-oriented programming systems, languages, and applications*, pages 303–311. ACM Press, 1990. Available from: http://www.bracha.org/oopsla90.ps.

[BD93]   Randolph E. Bank and Craig C. Douglas. Sparse matrix multiplication package (smmp). *Advances in Computational Mathematics*, 1(1):127–137, 1993. Available from: http://www.mgnet.org/~douglas/Preprints/pub34.pdf.

[Bec99]   Rudolf Beck. Graph-Based Algebraic Multigrid for Lagrange-Type Finite Elements on Simplicial Meshes. Technical report, Konrad-Zuse-Zentrum für Informationstechnik Berlin, Berlin, 1999. Available from: ftp://ftp.zib.de/pub/zib-publications/reports/SC-99-22.ps.Z.

[Ben86]   Jon Bentley. Programming pearls: little languages. *Commun. ACM*, 29(8):711–721, 1986.

[BF91]   Franco Brezzi and Michel Fortin. *Mixed and hybrid finite element methods*. Springer, New York, 1991.

[BGL05]   Michele Benzi, Gene H. Golub, and Jörg Liesen. Numerical solution of saddle point problems. *Acta Numerica*, 14:1–137, 2005. Available from: http://www.math.tu-berlin.de/~liesen/Publicat/BenGolLie05.pdf.

[BHZ54]    John W. Backus, Harlan Herrick, and Irving Ziller. Specifications for the IBM Mathematical FORmula TRANSlating System, FORTRAN. Preliminary report, Programming
Research Group, Applied Science Division, International Business Machines Corpora-
tion, New York, 1954. Available from: http://community.computerhistory.org/scc/
projects/FORTRAN/BackusEtAl-PreliminaryReport-1954.pdf.

[BMR84]    Achi Brandt, Stephen F. McCormick, and John W. Ruge. Algebraic multigrid (AMG) for
sparse matrix equations. In D. J. Evans, editor, *Sparsity and Its Applications*. Cambridge
University Press, Cambridge, 1984.

[Boo]      The Boost C++ libraries. Available from: http://www.boost.org.

[Bra73]    Achi Brandt. Multi–level adaptive technique (MLAT) for fast numerical solution to
boundary value problems. In H. Cabannes and R. Teman, editors, *Proceedings of the
Third International Conference on Numerical Methods in Fluid Mechanics*, volume 18 of
*Lecture Notes in Physics*, pages 82–89, Berlin, 1973. Springer.

[Bra86]    Achi Brandt. Algebraic multigrid theory: The symmetric case. *Appl. Math. Comput.*,
19:23–56, 1986.

[BS97]     Dietrich Braess and Regina Sarazin. An Efficient Smoother for the Stokes Problem.
*Applied Numerical Mathematics*, 23:3–20, 1997.

[BS99]     Randolph E. Bank and R. Kent Smith. The incomplete factorization multigraph algorithm. *SIAM Journal on Scientific Computing*, 20(4):1349–1364, 1999. Available from:
ftp://scicomp.ucsd.edu/pub/reb/reports/a77.ps.gz.

[BW95]     Jürgen Bey and Gabriel Wittum. Downwind numbering: A robust multigrid method
for convection diffusion problems on unstructured grids. Bericht 95/2, Institut für
Computeranwendungen der Universität Stuttgart, 1995. Available from: http://na.
uni-tuebingen.de/pub/bey/papers/kiel94.ps.Z.

[CCH+]     James A. Crotinger, Julian Cummings, Scott Haney, William Humphrey, Steve Karmesin,
John Reynders, Stephen Smith, and Timothy J. Williams. Generic Programming in
POOMA and PETE. Technical report, Los Alamos National Laboratory.

[CE00]     Krzysztof Czarnecki and Ulrich W. Eisenecker. *Generative Programming: Methods, Tools
and Applications*. Addison Wesley Longman, 2000.

[Cia91]    Philippe G. Ciarlet. Basic error estimates for elliptic problems. In Philippe G. Ciarlet and
Jacques-Louis Lions, editors, *Handbook of numerical analysis*, volume 2. North-Holland,
Amsterdam, 1991.

[CLRS01]   Thomas H. Cormen, Charles E. Leiserson, Ronald L. Rivest, and Clifford Stein. *Introduction to Algorithms*. The MIT Press, 2001.

[Cod01]    Ramon Codina. A stabilized finite element method for generalized stationary incompressible flows. *Computer Methods in Applied Mechanics and Engineering*, 190:2681–2706,
2001.

[CS97]     Edmond Chow and Youssef Saad. Experimental study of ILU preconditioners for indefinite
matrices. *Journal of Computational and Applied Mathematics*, 86(1):387–414, 1997.

[CvdV94]   Tony C. Chan and Henk A. van der Vorst. Approximate and Incomplete Factorizations.
Technical Report 871, University Utrecht, Department of Mathematics, 1994. Available
from: http://www.math.uu.nl/people/vorst/proc.ps.gz.

[Dav86]     David A. Moon. Object-oriented programming with flavors. In *Proceedings of the 1st ACM Conference on Object-Oriented Programming Languages and Applications (OOPSLA'86)*, volume 21 of *ACM SIGPLAN Notices*, pages 1–8, 1986.

[DD99]      Timothy A. Davis and Iain S. Duff. Combined unifrontal/multifrontal method for unsymmetric sparse matrices. *ACM Transactions on Mathematical Software*, 25(1):1–20, March 1999. Available from: http://doi.acm.org/10.1145/305658.287640.

[DEG+99]    James W. Demmel, Stanley C. Eisenstat, John R. Gilbert, Xiaoye S. Li, and Joseph W. H. Liu. A supernodal approach to sparse partial pivoting. *SIAM Journal on Matrix Analysis and Applications*, 20(3):720–755, 1999. Available from: http://crd.lbl.gov/~xiaoye/simax95.ps.gz.

[DLH00]     Laura C. Dutto, Claude Y. Lepage, and Wagdi G. Habashi. Effect of the storage format of sparse linear systems on parallel CFD computations. *Computer Methods in Applied Mechanics and Engineering*, 188:441–453, 2000.

[DLN+94]    Jack J. Dongarra, Andrew Lumsdaine, Xinhiu Niu, Roldan Pozo, and Karin Remington. A sparse matrix library in c++ for high performance architectures. In *Proceedings of the Second Object Oriented Numerics Conference*, pages 214–218, 1994. Available from: http://gams.nist.gov/pub/pozo/papers/sparse.ps.Z.

[DPW93]     Jack J. Dongarra, Roldan Pozo, and David W. Walker. Lapack++: A design overview of object-oriented extensions for high performance linear algebra. In *Proceedings of Supercomputing '93*, pages 162–171. IEEE Computer Society Press, 1993. Available from: http://math.nist.gov/lapack++/lapack++.ps.gz.

[dZ90]      Paulus Maria de Zeeuw. Matrix-dependent prolongations and restrictions in a black box multigrid solver. *J. Comput. Appl. Math.*, 33:1–27, 1990. Available from: http://www.cwi.nl/ftp/pauldz/Thesis/Chapter3.ps.Z.

[EBC00]     Ulrich W. Eisenecker, Frank Blinn, and Krzysztof Czarnecki. A solution to the constructor-problem of mixin-based programming in C++. In *First Workshop on C++ Template Programming, Erfurt, Germany*, October 10 2000. Available from: http://www.oonumerics.org/tmpw00/eisenecker.pdf.

[EHST02]    Howard Elman, V. E. Howle, John Shadid, and Ray Tuminaro. A parallel block multi-level preconditioner for the 3d incompressible navier-stokes equations. Technical report, Department of Computer Science and Institute for Advanced Computer Studies, University of Maryland, 2002.

[Fed61]     Radii P. Fedorenko. A relaxation method for solving elliptic difference equations. *Z. Vycisl. Mat. i. Mat. Fiz.*, 1:922–927, 1961. Also in U.S.S.R. Comput. Math. and Math. Phys., 1 (1962), pp. 1092–1096.

[Fef00]     Charles L. Fefferman. Existence & Smoothness of the Navier-Stokes Equation, Official Problem Description, Clay Mathematics Institute, 2000. Available from: http://www.claymath.org/millennium/Navier-Stokes_Equations/Official_Problem_Description.pdf.

[Fra93]     Leopoldo P. Franca. Convergence analyses of Galerkin least-squares methods for symmetric advective diffusive forms of the Stokes and incompressible Navier-Stokes equations. *Computer Methods in Applied Mechanics and Engineering*, 105:285–298, 1993.

[GH97]      Marcus J. Grote and Thomas Huckle. Parallel Preconditioning with Sparse Approximate Inverses. *SIAM Journal on Scientific Computing*, 18(3):838–853, 1997.

[GHJV94]    Erich Gamma, Richard Helm, Ralph Johnson, and John Vlissides. *Design Patterns: Elements of Reusable Object-Oriented Software.* Addison Wesley Longman, 1994.

[GNR98]     Michael Griebel, Tilman Neunhoeffer, and Hans Regler. Algebraic muligrid methods for the solution of the navier-stokes equations in complicated geometries. *International Journal for Numerical Methods in Fluids*, 26:281–301, 1998. also as SFB Bericht 342/1/96A, Institut für Informatik, TU München, 1996. Available from: http://wissrech.iam.uni-bonn.de/research/pub/griebel/TUM-I9601.ps.gz.

[GR86]      Viviette Girault and Pierre-Arnaud Raviart. *Finite Element Methods for Navier-Stokes Equations.* Springer, 1986.

[Hac85]     Wolfgang Hackbusch. *Multigrid Methods and Applications*, volume 4 of *Computational Mathematics*. Springer–Verlag, Berlin, 1985.

[HB79]      Thomas J. R. Hughes and Alexander N. Brooks. A Multi-Dimensional Upwind Scheme with No Crosswind Diffusion. In T. J. R. Hughes, editor, *in Finite Element Methods for Convection Dominated Flows*, volume 34 of *ASME AMD*, pages 19–35, New York, 1979. ASME.

[HF87]      Thomas J. R. Hughes and Leopoldo P. Franca. A new finite element formulation for computational fluid dynamics: VII. The Stokes problem with various well-posed boundary conditions: symmetric formulations that converge for all velocity/pressure spaces. *Computer Methods in Applied Mechanics and Engineering*, 65:85–96, 1987.

[HFB86]     Thomas J. R. Hughes, Leopoldo P. Franca, and M. Balestra. A new finite element formulation for computational fluid dynamics: V. Circumventing the Babuska-Brezzi condition: a stable Petrov-Galerkin formulation of the Stokes problem accommodating equal-order interpolations. *Computer Methods in Applied Mechanics and Engineering*, 59:85–99, 1986.

[HFH89]     Thomas J. R. Hughes, Leopoldo P. Franca, and Gregory M. Hulbert. A new finite element formulation for computational fluid dynamics: VIII. The Galerkin/least-squares method for advective-diffusive equations. *Computer Methods in Applied Mechanics and Engineering*, 73:173–189, 1989.

[HMMO05]    Jeff Heys, Tom Manteuffel, Steve McCormick, and Luke Olson. Algebraic Multigrid (AMG) for Higher-Order Finite Elements. *Journal of Computational Physics*, 204:520–532, 2005.

[HP97]      Wolfgang Hackbusch and Thomas Probst. Downwind Gauss-Seidel Smoothing for Convection Dominated Problems. *Numerical Linear Algebra with Applications*, 4:85–102, 1997. Available from: http://citeseer.ist.psu.edu/hackbusch93downwind.html.

[IY01]      Eun-Jin Im and Katherine Yelick. Optimization of Sparse Matrix Kernels for Data Mining. In *Proceedings of the Text Mine Workshop*, 2001. Available from: http://http.cs.berkeley.edu/~yelick/ejim/icdm01.ps.

[Jac45]     Carl G. J. Jacobi. Über eine neue Auflösungsart der bei der Methode der kleinsten Quadrate vorkommenden linearen Gleichungen. *Astronomische Nachrichten*, 22:297–306, 1845.

[JV01]      Jim E. Jones and Panayot S. Vassilevski. AMGe based on element agglomeration. *SIAM Journal on Scientific Computing*, 23(1):109–133, 2001. Available from: http://epubs.siam.org/sam-bin/getfile/SISC/articles/36104.pdf.

[Kic98]    F. Kickinger. Algebraic multigrid for discrete elliptic second-order problems. In Hackbusch, W. and Wittum, G., editors, *Multigrid Methods V. Proceedings of the Fifth European Multigrid Conference held in Stuttgart, Germany, 1.-4. October , 1996*, volume 3, pages 157–172, Berlin, 1998. Springer. Available from: http://citeseer.nj.nec.com/kickinger97algebraic.html.

[Kra04]    Johanes K. Kraus. Algebraic multilevel preconditioning of finite element matrices based on element agglomeration. Technical report, Johann Radon Institute for Computational and Applied Mathematics,Austrian Academy of Sciences, Wien, 2004. Available from: http://www.ricam.oeaw.ac.at/publications/reports/04/rep04-01.pdf.

[Ler34]    Jean Leray. Sur le mouvement d'un fluide visqueux emplissant l'espace. *Acta Mathematica*, 63:193–248, 1934.

[LO02]    Gert Lube and Maxim Olshanskii. Stable finite element calculation of incompressible flows using the rotation form of convection. *IMA Journal of Numerical Analysis*, 22:437–461, 2002.

[LRKK79]    C. Lawson, R.Hanson, D. Kincaid, and F. Krogh. Basic linear algebra subprograms for fortran usage. *ACM Transaction on Mathematical Software*, 5(3):308–323, 1979. Available from: http://doi.acm.org/10.1145/355841.3558474.

[Man88]    Jan Mandel. Algebraic study of multigrid methods for symmetric, definite problems. *Appl. Math. Comput.*, 25:39–56, 1988.

[MS00]    Brian McNamara and Yannis Smaragdakis. Static interfaces in C++. In *First Workshop on C++ Template Programming, Erfurt, Germany*, 10 2000. Available from: http://oonumerics.org/tmpw00/mcnamara.pdf.

[Mul89]    Wim A. Mulder. A new multigrid approach to convection problems. *Journal of Computational Physics*, 83:303–323, 1989.

[Mül01]    Susann Müller. *Zur Vorkonditionierung ausgewählter Krylov-Unterraum-Methoden bei stabilisierten Finite-Elemente-Verfahren*. PhD thesis, Georg-August-Universität, Göttingen, 2001.

[NVDY04]    Rajesh Nishtala, Richard Vuduc, James Demmel, and Katherine Yelick. When cache blocking sparse matrix multiply works and why. In *Proceedings of the PARA'04 Workshop on State-of-the-art in Scientific Computing*, Lecture Notes in Computer Science. Springer, 2004. To appear. Available from: http://www.cs.berkeley.edu/~rajeshn/pubs/nishtala_cache_smvm.pdf.

[Oel01]    Daniel Oeltz. Algebraische Mehrgittermethoden für Systeme partieller Differentialgleichungen. Diplomarbeit, Rheinische Friedrich-Wilhelms-Universität, Bonn, 2001. Available from: http://wissrech.ins.uni-bonn.de/teaching/diplom/daniel_oeltz_diplomarbeit.ps.bz2.

[Old02]    Jeffrey D. Oldham. *POOMA – A C++ Toolkit for High-Performance Parallel Scientific Computing*. CodeSourcery, LLC, 2002. Available from: http://www.codesourcery.com/pooma/pooma_manual_folder/pooma.pdf.

[OR03]    Maxim A. Olshanskii and Arnold Reusken. Convergence analysis of a multigrid method for a convection-dominated model problem. Technical Report IGPM Report Nr. 231, RWTH Aachen, 2003. Available from: ftp://ftp.igpm.rwth-aachen.de/pub/reports/ps/IGPM231.ps.gz.

[Ose10]    Carl W. Oseen. Über die Stokes'sche Formel und über eine verwandte Aufgabe in der Hydrodynamik. *Arkiv för Matematik, Astronomi och Fysik*, 6(29):1–20, 1910.

[Pfl01]    Christoph Pflaum. Expression Templates for Partial Differential Equations. *Computing and Visualization in Science*, 4:1–8, 2001. Available from: `http://www10.informatik.uni-erlangen.de/~pflaum/pflaum/ALT/pre239.ps.gz`.

[Poz97]    Roldan Pozo. *MV++ Reference Guide*. National Institute of Standards and Technology, 1997. Available from: `http://math.nist.gov/mv++/main.pdf`.

[Poz02]    Roldan Pozo. *Template Numerical Toolkit*. National Institute of Standards and Technology, 2002. Available from: `http://math.nist.gov/tnt/documentation.html`.

[Pri96]    Andreas P. Priesnitz. Untersuchung iterativer Lösungsverfahren am Beispiel diskretisierter Konvektions-Diffusions-Reaktions-Gleichungen. Diplomarbeit, Georg August Universität, Göttingen, 1996. Available from: `ftp://ftp.num.math.uni-goettingen.de/pub/dipl/diplom-priesnitz.ps.gz`.

[PS72]     Suhas V. Patankar and D. Brian Spalding. A calculation procedure for heat, mass and momentum transfer in three-dimensional parabolic flows. *International Journal of Heat and Mass Transfer*, 15(10):1787–1806, 1972.

[PSM97]    Amit Patel, Vitaly Shmatikov, and John Mitchell. Paremeterized inheritance vs. multiple inheritance. Technical report, Department of Computer Science, 1997. Available from: `http://citeseer.ist.psu.edu/336924.html`.

[QV97]     Alfio Quarteroni and Alberto Valli. *Numerical Approximation of Partial Differential Equations*. Springer Series in Computational Mathematics. Springer, 1997.

[Raw95]    Michael J. Raw. A Coupled Algebraic Multigrid Method for the 3D Navier-Stokes Equations. In *in Fast Solvers for Flow Problems, Proceedings of the 10th GAMM-Seminar*, volume 49 of *Notes on Numerical Fluid Mechanics*, pages 204–215, Wiesbaden, Germany, 1995. Vieweg.

[Reu00]    Arnold Reusken. Convergence analysis of a multigrid method for convection-diffusion equations. Technical Report IGPM Report 190, RWTH Aachen, 2000. Available from: `ftp://ftp.igpm.rwth-aachen.de/pub/reusken/MG_for_Convection-Diffusion.ps.gz`.

[Rit75]    Dennis M. Ritchie. *C Reference Manual*. Computing Sciences Research Center, Bell Labs, Murray Hill, New Jersey, 1975. Available from: `http://cm.bell-labs.com/cm/cs/who/dmr/cman.pdf`.

[RP]       K. A. Remington and R. Pozo. *NIST Sparse BLAS User's Guide*. National Institute of Standards and Technology.

[RS87]     John W. Ruge and Klaus Stüben. Algebraic multigrid (AMG). In S. F. McCormick, editor, *Multigrid Methods*, volume 3 of *Frontiers in Applied Mathematics*, pages 73–130. SIAM, Philadelphia, PA, 1987.

[RST96]    Hans-Görg Roos, Martin Stynes, and Lutz Tobiska. *Numerical Methods for Singularly Perturbed Differential Equations. Convection-Diffusion and Flow Problems*. Springer, 1996.

[Saa90]    Youssef Saad. SPARSKIT: a basic tool kit for sparse matrix computations. Technical report, NASA Ames Research Center, 1990. Available from: `http://www-users.cs.umn.edu/~saad/software/SPARSKIT/paper.ps`.

[Saa92]     Youssef Saad. Preconditioning techniques for nonsymmetric indefinite linear systems. Technical report, University of Illinois at Urbana-Champaign, Center for Supercomputing Research and Development, Urbana, Illinois, 1992. Available from: `ftp://ftp.cs.umn.edu/dept/users/saad/reports/PDF/RIACS-ILQ-TR.pdf`.

[Saa03]     Yousef Saad. *Iteractive methods for sparse linear systems*. Society for Industrial and Applied Mathematics, Philadelphia, PA, 2003.

[SB98]      Yannis Smaragdakis and Don Batory. Implementing Layered Designs with Mixin Layers. In *Proceedings of the 12th European Conference on Object-Oriented Programming (ECOOP'98)*, pages 550–570, 1998. Available from: `http://www.cc.gatech.edu/~yannis/templates.pdf`.

[SB00]      Yannis Smaragdakis and Don Batory. Mixin-Based Programming in C++. In *Generative and Component-Based Software Engineering Symposium (GCSE)*, Lecture Notes in Computer Science. Springer, 2000.

[SB02]      Yannis Smaragdakis and Don Batory. Mixin layers: an object-oriented implementation technique for refinements and collaboration-based designs. *ACM Trans. Softw. Eng. Methodol.*, 11(2):215–255, 2002. Available from: `http://www.cc.gatech.edu/~yannis/tosem01.pdf`.

[Sed01]     Robert Sedgewick. *Algorithms in C*. Addison-Wesley Professional, 2001.

[Sie99]     Jeremy G. Siek. A Modern Framework for Portable High Performance Numerical Linear Algebra. Master's thesis, University of Notre Dame, Indiana, Department of Computer Science and Engineering, Notre Dame, Indiana, 1999. Available from: `http://www.osl.iu.edu/downloads/research/mtl/papers/thesis.pdf`.

[Sou35]     Richard V. Southwell. Stress calculation in frameworks by the method of systematic relaxation of constraints. In *Proceedings of the Royal Society of London*, volume 151 of *Series A: Mathematical and Physical Sciences*, pages 56–95, 1935.

[SS95]      Y. Saad and B. Suchomel. Towards algebraic multigrid for elliptic problems of second order. *Computing*, 55, 1995.

[SS97]      Antony Smith and David Silvester. Implicit algorithms and their linearization for the transient incompressible Navier-Stokes quations. *IMA Journal of Numerical Analysis*, 17:527–545, 1997.

[SS02]      Y. Saad and B. Suchomel. ARMS: An algebraic recursive multilevel solver for general sparse linear systems. *Numerical Linear Algebra with Applications*, 9, 2002.

[Str97]     Bjarne Stroustrup. *The C++-Programming Language, Third Edition*. Addison Wesley Longman, Reading, 1997.

[Stü99]     Klaus Stüben. Algebraic Multigrid (AMG): An Introduction with Applications. Technical report, GMD, Sankt Augustin, 1999. Available from: `http://www.gmd.de/publications/report/0070/Text.pdf`.

[Sv00]      Yousef Saad and Henk A. van der Vorst. Iterative solution of linear systems in the 20th century. *Journal of Computational and Applied Mathematics*, 123:1–33, 2000.

[uBL]       Boost uBLAS – Basic Linear Algebra library. Available from: `http://www.boost.org/libs/numeric/ublas/doc/index.htm`.

[Unr94]     Erwin Unruh. Prime number computation. 1994. Available from: `http://www.erwin-unruh.de/prim.html`.

[Uza72]    Hirofumi Uzawa. Iterative methods for concave programming. In Leonid Hurwicz Kenneth J.Arrow and and Hirofumi Uzawa, editors, *Studies in Linear and Nonlinear Programming*, pages 154–165. Stanford University Press, Stanford, California, 1972.

[Van86]    S. P. Vanka. Block-implicit multigrid solution of Navier-Stokes equations in primitive variables. *Journal of Computational Physics*, 65:138–158, 1986.

[Vel95]    Todd L. Veldhuizen. Expression templates. *C++ Report*, 7(5):26–31, June 1995. Reprinted in C++ Gems, ed. Stanley Lippman. Available from: http://extreme.indiana.edu/~tveldhui/papers/cppworld.ps.

[Vel98]    Todd L. Veldhuizen. Arrays in Blitz++. In *Proceedings of the 2nd International Scientific Computing in Object-Oriented Parallel Environments (ISCOPE'98)*, Lecture Notes in Computer Science. Springer, 1998. Available from: http://osl.iu.edu/~tveldhui/papers/iscope98.ps.

[Vel01]    Todd L. Veldhuizen. *Blitz++ User's Guide*. National Institute of Standards and Technology, 2001. Available from: http://www.oonumerics.org/blitz/manual/blitz.ps.

[Vel03]    Todd L. Veldhuizen. C++ templates are turing-complete. Unpublished manuscript, 2003. Available from: http://osl.iu.edu/~tveldhui/papers/2003/turing.pdf.

[VJ97]    Todd L. Veldhuizen and Marvin E. Jernigan. Will C++ be faster than Fortran? In *Proceedings of the 1st International Scientific Computing in Object-Oriented Parallel Environments (ISCOPE'97)*, Lecture Notes in Computer Science. Springer, 1997.

[VJ03]    David Vandevoorde and Nicolai M. Josuttis. *C++ Templates: The Complete Guide*. Addison Wesley Professional, Boston, 2003.

[VMB94]    Petr Vanek, Jan Mandel, and Marian Brezina. Algebraic Multigrid on Unstructured Meshes. Technical Report 34, University of Colorado at Denver, Center for Computational Mathematics, Denver, Colorado, 1994. Available from: http://www-math.cudenver.edu/ccmreports/rep34.ps.gz.

[VMB95]    Petr Vanek, Jan Mandel, and Marian Brezina. Algebraic Multigrid by Smoothed Aggregation for Second and Fourth Order Elliptic Problems. Technical Report 36, University of Colorado at Denver, Center for Computational Mathematics, Denver, Colorado, 1995. Available from: http://www-math.cudenver.edu/ccmreports/rep36.ps.gz.

[Wab03]    Markus Wabro. *Algebraic Multigrid Methods for the Numerical Solution of the Incompressible Navier-Stokes Equations*. PhD thesis, Johannes Kepler Universität, Linz, 2003.

[Web01]    R. Webster. Performance of algebraic multi-grid solvers based on unsmoothed and smoothed aggregation. *International Journal for Numerical Methods in Fluids*, 36:743–772, 2001.

# Glossary

**AMG**

*Algebraic MultiGrid*, originally AMG refers to the numerical method developed by John Ruge and Klaus Stüben. The main idea is based on constructing the coarse levels solely algebraically (by using linear algebra operations) out of the initial matrix, instead of exploiting geometrical information. Meanwhile, several variants have been developed (AMGe, smoothed aggregation).

**BLANC**

*Blockwise Linear Algebra and Numerical Computations in C* is a numerical library, written in C by Andreas Priesnitz in 1996 at the Institute for Numerical and Applied Mathematics in Göttingen, that offers vectors and (sparse) matrix data formats as well as a great number of iterative solvers for linear algebra equations. A special feature is the storage of and operation with block matrices for all algorithms (e.g. block-wise ILU and SSOR).

**CFD**

*Computational Fluid Dynamics*, is a subdiscipline of fluid dynamics, a scientific research area that investigates the physical and mathematical behaviour of motions in gases and liquids. Instead of building a model and testing it in a wind channel, the intention in CFD is to simulate these flows in the computer. Important issues are for example the prediction of turbulences and instabilities that can occur at the wings of an aeroplane, or climate models for the weather forecast.

**FEM**

*Finite Element Method*, a so-called Galerkin method that is intended to solve variational problems (which arise e.g. from differential or integral equations) by approximating continuous quantities as a set of quantities at discrete points.

**Generative Programming**

Generative Programming is a programming paradigm, that is based on assembling arbitrary complex data structures out of small parts. A generator is responsible for constructing and choosing the best data structure according to the user's request.

**Generic Programming**

Generic programming is a technique that enables the software developer to parameterize a class or an algorithm with another class. Along with polymorphism, and the iterator design pattern it is an important object-oriented technique that helps to decouple algorithms and data structures. Languages like C++ (through templates), EIFFEL and Ada supported it from the start, while Java only recently (since Version 1.5) offers so-called generics.

**MiLTON**

*Matrix Library of Templates for Object oriented Numerics* is a C++ temlate library developed for this dissertation that investigates several modern programming techniques. It offers a wide range of matrix data structures (sparse, dense, block, etc.), that can be constructed out of smaller parts (layers). Template metaprogramming is used for internal decision making and optimization of the data structures and algorithms at compile time. The AMG solvers for scalar and mixed problems described in this thesis are built on top of these data structures.

**PNS**

*Parallelized solution of Navier-Stokes equations* is a finite element research software developed in C by Andreas Auge, Hans Müller and Frank-Christian Otto (among others) at the Institute for Numerical and Applied Mathematics in Göttingen. It is capable of solving scalar problems like convection-diffusion problems as well as systems of PDE's, especially mixed problems such as the Navier-Stokes equation. Time-dependent and stationary problems can be treated, and various stabilization schemes be applied. Domain-decomposition methods and the *pvm* library are used to parallelize the computation.

**pvm**

*parallel virtual machine* is a free C library that realizes a message passing interface to enable cluster computing in heterogeneous networks. It is maintained by the Computer Science and Mathematics Division at the Oak Ridge National Laboratory.

**STL**

The *Standard Template Library* is a collection of template classes and functions, that offers various very useful data structures and algorithms. It provides solutions to many standard problems in computer science. Originally, it was implemented at Hewlett-Packard Research Labs by Alexander Stepanov and Meng Lee and included in the C++ standard in 1994. Although the methods and solutions encorporated in the STL were showing the way for modern library developers, there are many efforts to enhance or overcome it, the most promising of which is *boost*.

**SuperLU**

*SuperLU* is a C library written by Xiaoye Li, James Demmel, and John Gilbert, that performs a very fast sparse LU decomposition of arbitrary nonsymmetric matrices. It is maintained at the Computational Research Division of the Lawrence Berkeley National Laboratory.

**Template Metaprogramming**

Template Metaprogramming can be viewed as a meta language, that is executed by the compiler during the compilation. Erwin Unruh was one of the first to discover that C++ templates (originally intended for generic programming) have this ability. However generic programming capabilities doesn't automatically allow metaprogramming, as the examples of EIFFEL and Java show. The speciality of C++ is, that each template is compiled as an own class (or function).

# Index

# Acknowledgements

First of all, I would like to thank my advisor Prof. Dr. Gert Lube for his assistance and the possibility to conduct research in the area of algebraic multigrid and generic programming. To him and to the "Graduiertenkolleg für Strömungsinstabilitäten und Turbulenz" I am also indebted for the financial support.

Special thanks go to Dr. Andreas Priesnitz, who helped to inspire me by many fruitful discussions and by his inexhaustible creativity. Also, I am deeply grateful, that Dr. Gerd Rapin contributed in proofreading several parts of the thesis. Also, he was always available for mathematical discussions that deepened my insight into the area of finite elements.

Furthermore, I thank Stefanie Dahms for her never ceasing understanding and support. Last but not least, I would like to thank the members of the Institute of Numerical and Applied Mathematics, especially Dr. Gerhard Siebrasse and Rolf Waßmann for the technical support.

Moreover, I thank my parents, who made it possible for me to study and encouraged me, God, who never let me down, and Christian, Jan and Torsten, who have waited much too long for the next Doppelkopf round.